PRAISE FOR PREVIOUS EDITIONS OF

Rhode Island
Off the Beaten Path ®

"This travel guide is the perfect way to get your Ocean-State trekking started off on the right foot."

—*Narragansett* (R.I.) *Times*

"*Off the Beaten Path Rhode Island* facilitated our many decisions while on the road and pointed us in fascinating, unexpected directions."

—*Country Living*

"Curley's book could be the bible for tourists looking for a different sort of vacation in the Ocean State."

—*Cranston* (R.I.) *Herald*

Help Us Keep This Guide Up to Date

Every effort has been made by the author and editors to make this guide as accurate and useful as possible. However, many changes can occur after a guide is published—establishments close, phone numbers change, hiking trails are rerouted, facilities come under new management, etc.

We would love to hear from you concerning your experiences with this guide and how you feel it could be improved and be kept up to date. While we may not be able to respond to all comments and suggestions, we'll take them to heart, and we'll make certain to share them with the author. Please send your comments and suggestions to the following address:

The Globe Pequot Press
Reader Response/Editorial Department
P.O. Box 480
Guilford, CT 06437

Or you may e-mail us at: editorial@GlobePequot.com

Thanks for your input, and happy travels!

INSIDERS' GUIDE®

OFF THE BEATEN PATH® SERIES

Off the Beaten Path®

SIXTH EDITION

rhode island

A GUIDE TO UNIQUE PLACES

ROBERT PATRICK CURLEY

INSIDERS' GUIDE®

GUILFORD, CONNECTICUT
AN IMPRINT OF THE GLOBE PEQUOT PRESS

The prices, rates, and hours listed in this guidebook were confirmed at press time. We recommend, however, that you call establishments to obtain current information before traveling.

INSIDERS' GUIDE®

Text design by Linda R. Loiewski
Maps by Equator Graphics © Morris Book Publishing, LLC
Illustrations by Carole Drong
Spot photography throughout © Enigma/Alamy

ISSN 1539-3771
ISBN 978-0-7627-4428-2

Manufactured in the United States of America
Sixth Edition/First Printing

To my wife, Christine, who is always there for me,
especially during deadline; and to Christopher and Shannon,
for being the best children anyone could ever hope to have.

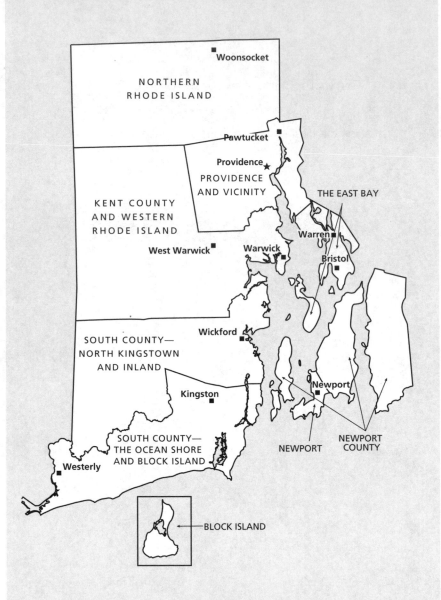

Woonsocket

NORTHERN
RHODE ISLAND

Pawtucket

Providence
PROVIDENCE
AND VICINITY

THE EAST BAY

KENT COUNTY
AND WESTERN
RHODE ISLAND

Warren

West Warwick   Warwick

Bristol

Wickford

SOUTH COUNTY—
NORTH KINGSTOWN
AND INLAND

Newport

Kingston

SOUTH COUNTY—
THE OCEAN SHORE
AND BLOCK ISLAND

NEWPORT

NEWPORT
COUNTY

Westerly

BLOCK ISLAND

Contents

Acknowledgments

Special thanks to the idea people: Frank Singer, Gary Enos, Melissa DeMeo, Mary Grady, Marie Kapsales, Cindy DeMaio, Karin Welt, Kerri Hicks, Jennifer Mooney, Bill Kanapaux, Eleyne Austen Sharp, Simone Joyaux, Lisa Starr, Loren Spears, Darlene Dame, Evan Smith, Maryellen Cicione, Dan Rocha, Bob Billington, Wendy Jencks, Heidi Clarke, Ann Marie McLaughlin, Susan Shea, Christopher Rondino, and Kerry Molloy. For their time and courteousness, thanks to all the people at all the sites in this book, and a special acknowledgment must go out to those who keep the fires of knowledge and history burning: the wonderful folks at Rhode Island's historical societies, libraries, visitor centers, and tourism agencies. Finally, thanks to Paula Bodah for thinking of me, to Mace Lewis for his blind faith in my ability to get this book done, and to Justine Rathbun, Christina Lester, Jan Cronan, Cary Hull, and Elizabeth Taylor for picking up the ball.

Introduction

Rhode Island may be the smallest state, but it has the biggest heart. And it definitely has the longest name.

Officially the State of Rhode Island and Providence Plantations, Rhode Island was founded on the principles that Americans hold most dear, such as freedom of speech, assembly, and religion—freedoms that were in short supply in the New World settlements of the seventeenth century. Sometimes known as "Rogue's Island" for its insider politics and past habit of harboring privateers and other free spirits, the colony (and later, state) of Rhode Island was more beloved as a haven for dissidents of every stripe. The state remains a place where self-expression is encouraged and strangers are welcomed—in short, the perfect place to spend a holiday.

With the exception of Newport, which unquestionably is one of the nation's most famous resort towns, it can be argued that all of Rhode Island is off the beaten path. Sure, prime-time television and Hollywood have thrust Providence into the spotlight, but many tourists, assuming that nothing so small can be very interesting, still know Rhode Island mostly as a speed bump on the interstate between New York and Boston. Closer examination, however, reveals a state of great contrasts, rich history, and quirks aplenty, as the following chapters will demonstrate.

A frequent problem when visiting an unfamiliar place is the nagging question of whether, amidst the tourist attractions, you are experiencing the real people and places—seeing what makes the area tick, not just the pretty face put on for visitors. So here are some suggestions if you want a taste of the real Rhode Island:

1. Stay off I–95. Instead, drive at a leisurely pace on the uncongested back roads that make the state a joy to explore. Route 102, for example, begins in South County's seaside town of Wickford and courses through the rural and wooded western part of the state, turning north for an enchanting drive that avoids all the big towns and cities, crosses over the beautiful Scituate Reservoir and through the quaint village of Chepachet, and doesn't end until it reaches the state's northern border near Woonsocket. A drive on Route 102 is a great way to spend a day.

2. Avoid fast food franchises. Rhode Island has some of the best seafood restaurants anywhere—try them! In places like East Providence and Bristol, fine Portuguese fare is on the menu. Providence's ethnic diversity is reflected in the city's wide array of eateries, from the Italian cuisine on Federal Hill to the Indian, vegetarian, and other offerings on Wickenden and Thayer Streets, to the fine continental dining featured downtown.

If you see a Del's lemonade stand—and the state is full of them—stop and order a cup. This mix of slush ice, sugar, and real lemon juice and lemon chunks is quite possibly the best drink ever invented for a hot summer day. If you are daring, try the little hot dogs served up at any store proclaiming the availability of NEW YORK SYSTEM WIENERS. Rhode Island legend has it that these spicy red wieners are best eaten after a night of revelry, and that the best purveyors are the places where the grillman lines the dogs up on his arm as he cooks.

Real Rhode Island jonnycakes—flint-corn pancakes spooned onto a hot grill—are found at many restaurants and also at traditional May breakfasts, sponsored each spring by local churches, Grange halls, and other civic groups. Instead of clam chowder, look for quahog chowder, made from Rhode Island's indigenous breed of bivalve.

3. Meet the people. Contrary to the caricature of the laconic, reserved Yankee, most Rhode Islanders you meet are friendly and fiercely proud of their home state—even if they do bad-mouth their politicians. Perhaps this easygoing nature is the result of living in a state where the total population is under one million people and everyone seems to know everyone else—and everyone else's business. Whatever the reason, Ocean State residents always seem happy to talk to visitors who show an interest in the state's great natural and historical heritage. This advice extends to those attractions in this book that are open by appointment only: Don't be afraid to call and ask for a showing—it's a great way to meet "real" Rhode Islanders.

So come along: "The Biggest Little State" is waiting to be explored.

(Rhode Island's only telephone area code is 401.)

Providence and Vicinity

Like all great cities, Providence draws its strength from its distinct, diverse neighborhoods, many of which center on a single, thriving street that serves as both business district and social center for the community.

Thayer Street is Providence's answer to Greenwich Village, an arty, multicultural pastiche that feeds on the energy of the students and faculty of nearby Brown University and the Rhode Island School of Design (RISD). Just a few blocks up College Hill from the historic homes lining Benefit Street, Thayer Street on the East Side of Providence moves to the beat of multiple *record stores, bookstores, and cafes* featuring Indian, Greek, and Southwestern cuisine. Shops peddling vintage clothing, New Age trinkets, and sportswear are a magnet for a young, hip crowd, as are the handful of bars that thrive here.

The *Avon Cinema* (260 Thayer Street, 421–3315; www.avoncinema.com) is the local art house, showing obscure foreign films and independent releases that the big theater chains won't touch. There are midnight screenings, animation festivals, and the occasional live performances, too.

The street comes alive at night—especially in the summer and on weekends when school is in session—when, between

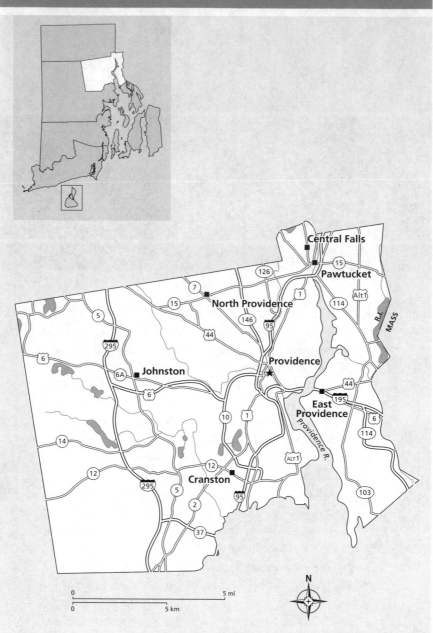

the sidewalk cafes, skateboarders, and throngs of strollers, Thayer Street resembles its New York counterpart even more closely.

In a college community where the choicest garments are often made of hemp, and the only thing cooler than being a vegetarian is to be a vegan, **Spike's Junkyard Dogs** (273 Thayer Street, 454–1459; www.spikesjunkyard dogs.com)—with its boast "100% Beef Dogs"—stands out. Nonetheless, this Providence-born franchise has thrived on Thayer Street by offering dozens of variations on the classic hot dog, as well as pizza and chicken sandwiches. Spike doesn't discriminate: A fat-free Veggie Dog is also on the menu, offered at the "same style and price as our beef dogs." Open Sunday to Wednesday 11:00 A.M. to 1:30 A.M. and Thursday to Saturday until 2:00 A.M.

Coffee-haters, rejoice: You, too, now have a place where you can relax in a comfy chair, chat with friends or read a favorite book, and sip an expensive caffeinated beverage. **Tealuxe** (231 Thayer Street, 453–4832; www.tealuxe.com) is a tea bar with a menu of literally dozens of blends to choose from, including six varieties of Captain Picard's favorite, "tea, Earl Grey, hot." There are classic teas, flavored teas, chai teas, herbal teas—even medicinal teas designed to soothe sore throats, fight the flu, prevent insomnia, and, bless them, cure a hangover.

If poring over that voluminous selection doesn't completely satisfy your voyeuristic tendencies, hop on one of the high window seats and watch the Thayer Street montage unfold outside. Open Monday to Thursday 9:00 A.M. to 10:00 P.M., Friday 8:00 A.M. to 11:00 P.M., Saturday 10:00 A.M. to 11:00 P.M., and Sunday 10:00 A.M. to 10:00 P.M.

Hidden on a side street off Thayer is the **Creperie** (82 Fones Alley, 751–5536), a tiny restaurant stuffed with local college kids that sells savory (entree) and sweet (dessert) crepes as well as Belgian waffles, salads, and wraps. For breakfast, try the Maria, a crepe filled with scrambled egg, bacon, and swiss cheese; the Nina, with fresh sliced apples and brie, makes a filling snack; while the Catherine, with chicken breast, cheddar, spinach, and olives is more of a meal. The Creperie also caters to Thayer Street's late-night denizens.

AUTHOR'S FAVORITES IN PROVIDENCE AND VICINITY

Federal Hill

Waterplace Park

Culinary Archives and Museum

Slater Mill

McCoy Stadium

Open Monday to Thursday 10:00 A.M. to midnight, Friday 10:00 A.M. to 2:00 A.M., Saturday 9:00 A.M. to 2:00 A.M., Sunday 9:00 A.M. to midnight.

Wickenden Street, located at the southern end of the East Side, is more sedate than Thayer Street but also offers an array of interesting places to shop and eat. Start your walk from the south end of the street. For hand-tossed, New York style thin-crust pizza served with a variety of imaginative toppings, **Fellini Pizzeria** (166 Wickenden Street, 751–6737; www.fellinipizzeria.com) is the place to go; open Sunday noon to midnight; Monday to Wednesday 11:00 A.M. to midnight, Thursday and Friday 11:00 A.M. to 2:00 A.M., and Saturday, noon to 2:00 A.M. Across the street at number 207 is the spiritual center of Wickenden Street, the **Coffee Exchange** (273–1198; www.coffeeexchange.com), which is so popular that it outgrew its former storefront location and now occupies a large house and outdoor deck. Stick around for a few weeks, and you might be able to sample their more than two dozen varieties of coffee, espresso, and cappuccino. For each pound of coffee sold, the Coffee Exchange donates 25 cents to help impoverished children working in coffee fields around the world. Open daily 6:30 A.M. to 11:00 P.M.

The **O-Cha Cafe** (221 Wickenden Street, 421–4699; www.ocharestaurant .com) serves up an adventurous mix of Thai and Japanese cuisine; they'll make your meal as spicy as you like. Open Sunday to Thursday noon to 10:00 P.M.,

The Armory District

Providence's Armory District is a diverse ethnic neighborhood centered on its namesake, a massive, turreted armory built in 1914 that is one of the city's great landmarks.

Until 1997, the armory was the home of the Rhode Island National Guard, but it's currently unoccupied. Film director and Rhode Island native Michael Corrente *(Federal Hill, American Buffalo)* toyed with the idea of transforming the armory—which has 165,000 square feet of floor space and a 90-foot ceiling in its drill hall—into a movie soundstage, but unfortunately that plan fell through. The Providence Preservation Society has placed the grand old castle on its endangered list, but the city of Providence made much-needed repairs to the armory's roof and may use the building to house the state archives.

The castellated, yellow-brick fortress also provides an attractive backdrop for West Side Wednesdays, a series of live performances held in July; and the neighborhood's annual September block party, a multicultural blend of Hispanic, African-American, and Asian food and music. For more information, contact the West Broadway Neighborhood Association (831–9344; www.wbna.org).

Friday and Saturday noon to 11:00 P.M. Duck down the alley at 234 Wickenden Street to find **Brickway Wickenden** (751–2477), the street's most relentlessly cheerful eatery. The bright, rainbow-painted walls are the perfect pick-me-up, complementing the Brickway's dozen three-egg omelets (including the create-your-own Frankenstein), griddle favorites, and Brickway Benedict (the classic cholesterol special perked up with slices of smoked salmon). Homemade soup by the cup or bowl, salads, flame-broiled burgers, and various wrap sandwiches round out the lunch menu. Open 7:00 A.M. to 3:00 P.M. Monday to Friday and 8:00 A.M. to 3:00 P.M. Saturday and Sunday.

For those who just can't live without an Elvis clock or a set of juice glasses from the 1964 World's Fair, the **This & That Shoppe** (236 Wickenden Street, 861–1394) has three solid floors of such, ahem, treasures. This antiques co-op features multiple dealers in a spectacular tribute to twentieth-century American kitsch and delightfully bad taste. Open Monday to Saturday 10:00 A.M. to 5:00 P.M. and Sunday noon to 5:00 P.M.

Steve Kotler is the music guru of **Round Again Records** (278 Wickenden Street, 351–6292), one of the few used-record stores that still sells actual LPs, not just CDs. Some of the coolest stuff, like a pair of 45s issued by Alabama Governor George Wallace featuring songs supporting Lieutenant Calley (of My Lai infamy) and decrying the evil of drug use, is for display purposes only. But among Steve's collection of albums from the past half century are one hundred copies of the Young Adults album; pick up yours today.

Round Again Records does have some used CDs for sale, as well, priced at $7.95 each. The store also features a selection of reconditioned turntables, meaning those old records in your closet don't have to gather dust, and you can once again torture friends and family with timeless tunes from the Strawberry Alarm Clock and the Electric Prunes. Open Monday to Friday 11:00 A.M. to 6:00 P.M. and 11:00 A.M. to 5:00 P.M. on Saturday.

On a street as eclectic as Wickenden, **Ristorante Romanza** (312 Wickenden Street, 421–5544) stands out for its sheer normality. The groundfloor rooms of an old colonial home have been converted into small, simple dining areas, and the liquor policy is strictly BYOB. But don't let any of that fool you: This Italian restaurant's menu is full of surprises, such as the tortellini katiuscia (stuffed with blue cheese and served in a pink vodka sauce) and the tortellini di zucca (filled with pumpkin, then topped with a pesto sauce suffused with diced tomatoes). Open Tuesday to Saturday 5:00 to 9:30 P.M.

Back when this was a much tougher neighborhood, 244 Wickenden was the address for Manny Almeida's Ringside Cafe, where the mealtime entertainment was provided by boxers swapping leather. Today the spot is occupied by the more sedate *Z Bar and Grille* (831–1566). It's open Monday to Friday 11:30 A.M. to 11:00 P.M. (bar till 1:00 A.M.), Friday and Saturday 11:30 A.M. to 11:00 P.M. (bar till 2:00 A.M.), and Sunday 11:30 A.M. to 10:00 P.M. For fascinating photographs of old Providence, framed prints, and old posters, check out the *Alaimo Gallery* at 301 Wickenden Street (421–5360). Open Monday to Saturday 9:30 A.M. to 5:00 P.M.

Near the top of the hill, where Wickenden Street ends at Governor Street, a cluster of antiques shops have sprung up, including Richard Kahan's *Red Bridge Antiques* (416 Wickenden Street, 453–3377), whose eclectic collection runs to twentieth-century design including pottery and glass. Open Monday to Saturday 11:00 A.M. to 5:00 P.M.; and *Antiques at India Point* (409 Wickenden Street, 273–5550), sellers of eighteenth-, nineteenth-, and twentieth-century furniture including American Empire and Neoclassical designs. Open Tuesday to Saturday 11:00 A.M. to 5:00 P.M.

OOP! (339 Ives Street, 800–281–4147; www.oopstuff.com) is a typically eclectic shop, where you can spend a few bucks or a few thousand on original works of art by more than one hundred local and national craftspeople. The collection of "fun stuff" includes dragonfly sculptures, blown glass, ceramics, and—a personal favorite—a chair shaped like a hand. Open Monday to Saturday 10:00 A.M. to 9:00 P.M., Sunday noon to 6:00 P.M.

Providence has long been a center for jewelry manufacturing, but at first blush there is nothing too entrancing about the city's *Jewelry District.* Amid the industrial sites and old warehouse buildings, though, a few gems shine. Part restaurant, part antiques store and gift shop, *CAV* (14 Imperial Place, 751–9164; www.cavrestaurant.com) is a Rhode Island original, much like owner Sylvia Moubayed. Located in an old factory building, CAV (the acronym stands for Coffee, Antiques, and Victuals) is consistent in its eclecticism. Beyond favorites like braised lamb shank in a red-wine raisin sauce, you'll find all sorts of interesting choices at CAV, in addition to a variety of vegetarian dishes. Dinner specials vary from day to day.

CAV's decor is a reflection of Sylvia's passion for collecting unusual antiques and artifacts from around the world, and the rambling, brick-walled restaurant is filled with African tribal masks, Finnish folk art dolls, and pre-Columbian artifacts. One corner of the building is used as a gift shop, selling unusual jewelry, scarves, and rugs. CAV also features live music, including blues and jazz artists, on Friday and Saturday nights. To get to CAV, take exit 2 off I–195 East, make a right at the end of the ramp onto Wickenden Street, and proceed half a mile to Hoppin Street and make another right. Pass the Harvard Pilgrim Health Care building and park in the large parking lot in front of Imperial Place. The door to CAV is located in the courtyard between the two brick buildings facing the lot. CAV is open Monday to Thursday 11:30 A.M. to 10:00 P.M., Friday and Saturday from 11:30 A.M. to 1:00 A.M., and Sunday 10:30 A.M. (for brunch) to 10:00 P.M.

Also worth a visit in the Jewelry District is **Snookers Pool Lounge** (145 Clifford Street, 351–7665), a huge billiards hall with sixteen pool tables; an outdoor patio complete with hammocks; a lounge with live music on weekends; and a bar that has numerous beers on tap. Snookers also serves food and runs eight-ball and nine-ball tournaments; expect to wait for a table on weekends. Snookers is open Monday to Thursday 4:00 P.M. to 1:00 A.M., Friday 4:00 P.M. to 2:00 A.M., Saturday 6:00 P.M. to 2:00 A.M., and Sunday noon to 1:00 A.M.

For cutting-edge live performances, the **Century Lounge** (150 Chestnut Street, 751–2255) has a stage in a cozy basement setting with open-beamed ceilings, oversized couches for lounging, and a copper-trimmed bar for imbibing.

The **Providence Children's Museum** (100 South Street, 273–5437; www .childrenmuseum.org) provides preteens with a hands-on, interactive experience that mixes play and learning. Whether your children like to brush a giant mouth full of teeth or sit at a computer, they'll have a great time here. Exhibits include Water Ways, where kids and parents can experiment with wave and bubble machines; a whole room devoted to teeth; and Littlewoods, an indoor forest designed for toddlers to explore. The museum is open Tuesday through Sunday 9:30 A.M. to 6:00 P.M.; Monday during the summer and on holidays. Admission is $6.50; free the third Friday of each month from September to May and every Friday in June, July, and August.

A big city is full of odors and fumes, not all of them pleasant. Come to the Jewelry District in the morning, however, and your nostrils will be suffused with the smell of freshly baked bread. This fantastic olfactory experience comes courtesy of **Olga's Cup and Saucer** (103 Point Street, 831–6666), a combination bakery and cafe that lures hungry office workers down from their towers on weekday mornings and lunch hours.

Olga's is the namesake of RISD grad Olga Bravo, so perhaps it's no surprise that the building and its surrounding gardens are so warmly designed, or that the products here are labeled "artisan breads." It's hard to argue with the latter: The staves and loaves of richly crusted *pane francese, pain de mie,* roasted garlic boule, and other varieties look almost too good to eat. On the other hand, it would be a shame to let such great bread go to waste, especially when it serves as the foundation for an ever-changing selection of sandwiches, pizzas, and calzones for sale in the cafe. Other options include salads and an assortment of fresh pasta and risotto dishes.

Many a local worker has come back late from lunch in the summer after lingering too long over an Olga's sandwich amid the flowering gardens. With luck, you'll have more time to relax and enjoy. Olga's is open Monday to Friday 7:00 A.M. to 4:00 P.M., and Saturday (for brunch) from 8:00 A.M. to 4:00 P.M.

The Jewelry District has a pool hall, bars, casual eateries, and a theater, but one thing it has always lacked is fine dining. Problem solved: **Restaurant Prov** (99 Chestnut Street, 621–8888; www.atomiccatering.com) beckons young, upscale diners with flickering candles in the windows, an array of semiprivate dining rooms, and a generous menu that features a one-pound New York strip steak, more than a half-dozen specialty pasta dishes, and a variety of wood-grilled pizzas—including one "scented" with truffles and topped with roasted peppers, herbs, portobello mushrooms, and fresh mozzarella.

Restaurant Prov's flexible space (dining rooms are separated by copious brown curtains and French doors) permits the transition to a nightclub after 11:00 P.M. on weekends, when a hidden dance floor opens in back and a DJ spins R&B, Top 40, house, techno, and hip-hop until the bars close at 2:00 A.M. The restaurant is open 5:00 to 10:30 P.M. Friday and Saturday.

Former Providence Mayor Buddy Cianci once held court in a booth at the Tribeca Supper Club; the booth is still there (lit by a crystal chandelier), but the club has been transformed into the **Art Bar** (171 Chestnut Street, 272–0177), an "over-25" dance club catering to a well-heeled crowd. The decor runs to black curtains, sofas, and high-top tables, with a smattering of framed paintings to justify the name over the door. Expect the music to be loud and a mix of '70s, '80s, and '90s dance tunes. Open Thursday 8:00 P.M. to 1:00 A.M., Friday and Saturday 9:00 P.M. to 2:00 A.M., and Sunday 7:00 P.M. to 1:00 A.M.

Federal Hill is Providence's Little Italy, and it has the food to prove it. At one time most of the New England Mafia operated out of a storefront on the Hill, but these days the area is known more for its cannoli and calzones than its crime figures.

To get to Federal Hill from downtown Providence, pick up Atwells Avenue from where it intersects with Broadway just west of the Dunkin' Donuts Center. Take Atwells Avenue across I–95, and you'll be greeted by a greenish **arch** (pronounced locally as "the Aahch") hung with an Italian pinecone—a traditional symbol of welcome much like the pineapples decorating stores and homes elsewhere in the state.

The Old World feel of Federal Hill is evident everywhere, from the umbrella-covered cafe tables surrounding the fountain in **Depasquale Square** to the chickens hanging in the window of the local poultry shop and the bread stacked high in bakery display cases.

From the simplest pizza joint to the most elegant dining room, Federal Hill is the place to go in Providence for Italian food. For sandwiches made with

Depasquale Square

imported Italian ingredients, exquisite desserts including tiramisu and delicate sorbets, and great coffee and cappuccino taken alfresco, pull up a chair at *Cafe Dolce Vita* (59 Depasquale Avenue, 331–8240). It is open Monday to Thursday 8:00 A.M. to 1:00 A.M., Friday and Saturday 8:00 A.M. to 2:00 A.M., and Sunday 8:00 A.M. to 1:00 A.M.

In fact, most of the restaurants on Depasquale Square have outside seating, but one you'll want to go inside for—if only to marvel at the bright, elegant decor—is *Walter's Restaurant* (286 Atwells Avenue, second floor, 273–2652; www.chefwalter.com), where fine Italian dishes are prepared using an ancient Etruscan method of terra-cotta cooking. Walter's also has chairs and tables outside in a private courtyard. Open Tuesday to Saturday 5:00 to 9:00 P.M. For a quick, inexpensive meal served in a lively, noisy communal setting, *Angelo's Civita Farnese* (141 Atwells Avenue, 621–8171; www.angelosonthehill.com) is your destination. Open Monday to Thursday 11:00 A.M. to 9:00 P.M., Friday and Saturday 11:00 A.M. to 10:00 P.M., and Sunday from noon to 9:00 P.M. A trio of upscale, black-tie restaurants vie for the attention of diners looking for a romantic, elegant meal with a good bottle of wine: the *Blue Grotto* (210 Atwells Avenue, 272–9030; www.bluegrottorestaurant.com), the *Old Canteen* (120 Atwells Avenue, 751–5544), and *Camille's* (71 Bradford Street, 751–4812; www .camillesonthehill.com).

One short block north of Atwells Avenue is Spruce Street, home of *Caserta's* (121 Spruce Street, 272–3618, 621–3618, or 621–9190), acclaimed as the best pizza place in the state. Don't leave Providence without trying one of its huge, square, cheesy pizzas. *Casa Christine* (145 Spruce Street, 453–6255) is a small, quiet Italian restaurant where you can bring your own wine. Open

The Federal Hill Stroll

The only problem with Federal Hill's restaurants is there are too many good ones: After living in Rhode Island for more than a decade, there are still places on the Hill that I haven't yet eaten, despite the recommendations of friends and colleagues. But to get at least a taste of what some of these great eateries are all about, I make a point of taking the Federal Hill Stroll.

The stroll, sponsored by the Providence Warwick Convention and Visitors Bureau, is a walking, tasting tour of more than twenty Federal Hill restaurants (a number of retail shops and boutiques also participate). Buying a stroll button for $25 allows you to check out restaurants up and down the Hill, sampling dishes from the area's abundance of Italian, Indian, Mexican, and other restaurants. Among those taking part are Caserta's, the Blue Grotto, and Scialo Brothers Bakery.

The stroll lasts about three hours, and the price includes a pair of drink tickets; it usually sells out, so plan ahead. For event dates and other information, check out the CVB Web site at www.goprovidence.com or call 274–1636.

Tuesday to Friday 11:30 A.M. to 1:45 P.M. for lunch and 5:00 to 7:30 P.M. for dinner; open Saturday 3:45 to 7:30 P.M.

If you really want to step back into the Old World, drop in at **Scialo Brothers Bakery** (257 Atwells Avenue, 421–0986; www.scialobakery.com) and indulge in some fresh Italian baked goods and delicacies. Opened in 1916, Scialo Brothers retains its traditional charms, with rounded candy bins and antique display cases; and the biscotti, amaretti, cannoli, and tiramisu are as delicious as ever. A free cup of coffee makes everything taste that much sweeter. Open Monday to Thursday 8:00 A.M. to 7:00 P.M., Friday 8:00 A.M. to 8:00 P.M., Saturday 8:00 A.M. to 7:00 P.M., and Sunday 7:30 A.M. to 5:00 P.M.

Diva's Palace (299 Atwells Avenue, 831–0148; www.divaspalace.com) owner Michael Turner has dressed up this vintage clothing and costume jewelry store as a magical world of mannequins and gaily painted chairs and settees, where everything from the floors to the walls to the columns supporting the ceiling has been beautified to create the illusion of luxury. In addition to gilded pins, lockets, picture frames, and sequined and feathered hats, Turner and his staff bring plain wool and velvet jackets back to life by adding artistic trim and jewels.

Diva's Palace is open Monday to Wednesday 11:00 A.M. TO 5:00 P.M., Thursday to Saturday 11:00 A.M. to 7:00 P.M., and Sunday noon to 5:00 P.M.

Finally, for a change of pace, a bit farther west on Atwells Avenue are **Mexico** (948 Atwells Avenue, 331–4985), a tiny restaurant that has won high praise for its authentic south-of-the-border cuisine, and **Mi Guatemala** (1049 Atwells Avenue, 621–9147), which starts you off with homemade nacho chips with three kinds of sauces for dipping and then serves up huge portions of grilled pork steak—the Central American nation's national dish—on fresh, hot corn tortillas. For an appetizer try the Tostados Chapinas, black beans on a flat tortilla garnished with onions and stewed tomatoes. You can wash it all down with a Mexican beer or choose from a selection of specialty juices, such as tamarind or cashew. Open Monday to Thursday 9:30 A.M. to 10:00 P.M., Friday to Sunday 8:00 A.M. to 11:00 P.M.

Tina's Jamaican Restaurant (223 Atwells Avenue, 490–4625; www.tinas jamaican.faithweb.com) serves authentic Jamaican dishes, from the familiar jerk chicken to curried goat (a tender personal favorite) and fried plantains. Owner Tina Rowe and her staff use only fresh ingredients, right down to grating coconut to make the coconut milk found in so many Caribbean dishes. The $8.00 lunch specials are an inexpensive way to be introduced to Jamaican cuisine if you haven't tried it before. Open daily 10:00 A.M. to 10:00 P.M.

Don't miss Federal Hill's raucous *Feast of Saint Joseph* celebration if you're in town in May; there's a red, white, and green stripe painted down the middle of Atwells Avenue to remind you of this annual party celebrating the patron saint of Italy.

Providence once had a place in the record books as home to the world's widest bridge, but the distinction was dubious: The bridge was part of an ill-conceived plan to enclose the polluted rivers that flowed through the city's downtown. In the 1990s, however, the rivers were cleaned up, and the city embarked on an ambitious plan to revitalize the waterways and the whole downtown area. The plan has been a huge success, and no more so than with the construction of *Waterplace Park* and the *Providence Riverwalk.*

Where once railroad tracks ran along a weedy right-of-way, a beautiful riverwalk today allows pedestrians to stroll both sides of the Woonasquatucket River. A round basin features a fountain and a small amphitheater for live outdoor performances. Near a tunnel that allows access from the riverwalk to *Kennedy Plaza*—the heart of downtown Providence—is a plaque describing the history of this area and its transformation from a natural cove to a place of landfill and concrete and back to an oasis of beauty.

From many spots on the riverwalk you can look up to admire the brilliant white marble dome of the *State House* (222–2357), just a short walk away and worth a visit to check out its architectural grandeur and an original painting of George Washington by native son Gilbert Stuart. Open free of charge Monday through Friday 8:30 A.M. to 3:00 P.M., with guided tours at 9:00, 10:00, and 11:00 A.M., noon and 1:00 p.m. Two weeks' notice required for guided group tours; call 222–3983 for information. A self-guided tour booklet can be downloaded at the Rhode Island Secretary of State's Web site, www.state.ri.us.

bigchangesfor downtown providence

The revival of downtown Providence has come a long way, but it's still a work in progress. Future plans include the creation of an arts and entertainment district in the Downcity area, which has seen a recent boom in residential redevelopment. The riverwalk has been extended south toward Narragansett Bay, and a major project is underway to push Interstate 195 out of downtown and a distance into Narragansett Bay, reconnecting the city to its historic waterfront.

But perhaps the most significant change to the downtown landscape is the Providence Place Mall, built on a former parking lot across the street from the Westin Hotel. The 150-store upscale mall spans the Woonasquatucket River with a graceful glass atrium bridge and is connected to the Westin and the Rhode Island Convention Center by a pedestrian skyway. Stores include Nordstrom, Filene's, and Lord & Taylor, and the mall features a state-of-the-art, twenty-screen cinema. Strollers have direct access from the mall to the riverwalk, as well as a series of outside restaurants and entertainment venues.

Abutting the riverwalk is Citizens' Plaza, home of the popular *Cafe Nuovo* (1 Citizens' Plaza, 421–2525; www.cafe nuovo.com), which has outdoor seating along the river and serves nouvelle cuisine with a multicultural twist, along with some spectacular desserts. Open Monday to Friday 11:30 A.M. to 3:00 P.M. for lunch and 5:00 to 10:30 P.M. for dinner Monday to Thursday; Friday and Saturday 5:00 to 11:00 P.M.

From Citizens' Plaza, which sits at the confluence of the Woonasquatucket, Moshassuck, and Providence Rivers, you can see the series of elegant arched bridges linking downtown Providence to the East Side, home of Brown University.

Perhaps the most unusual watercraft in New England can be found on the rivers of Providence: a pair of authentic Italian gondolas. From May to October, gondoliers Marco and Marcello push *La Gondola* (421–8877; www .gondolori.com) along on a sedate, thirty-minute ride down the length of the riverwalk to Waterplace Park. The gondola can accommodate groups of up to six people (although it's much more romantic with just two!). As you glide through the quiet city, you'll be serenaded by Italian love songs, and guests are welcome to bring a bottle of their favorite wine aboard. Gondola charters are available May through October evenings from 5:00 to 11:00 P.M.; the cost is $79 per couple, plus $15 for each additional passenger (added charges for WaterFire nights).

If you cross any of the bridges spanning the river to the East Side and walk 1 block, you'll come to *South Main Street,* popular with the local lunchtime crowd but not well known to out-of-town visitors. A stroll south along this broad thoroughfare will take you past the historic buildings housing the Rhode Island Supreme Court and Superior Court to an area where old warehouses and office buildings have been converted to retail space, and storefronts now are home to trendy restaurants and art galleries. Along the way, be sure to pause at **Gardiner-Jackson Park** between Westminster and Pine Streets, the latest addition to the riverwalk. At the center of the park is a 75-foot-tall World War I monument, topped by a statue of the Greek goddess Athena. The statue once stood at the focal point of a horrendous downtown traffic rotary known locally as "Suicide Circle"; it seems much more at home here.

On the river side of the park is South Water Street, which runs along a new section of the Providence Riverwalk. Plans call for the riverwalk to eventually reach Narragansett Bay; meanwhile, the new section allows pedestrians to take a scenic walk from downtown all the way to the foot of Wickenden Street.

The sleek modern building housing **Hemenway's** (121 South Main Street, 351–8570; www.hemenwaysrestaurant.com) may clash with the nineteenth-century buildings across South Main Street, but the floor-to-ceiling windows provide a great view from any seat in this atrium restaurant. Founded by local culinary legend Ned Grace, Hemenway's is renowned for its fresh seafood and raw bar; come for lunch or dinner. Open Monday to Thursday 11:30 A.M. to 10:00 P.M., Friday and Saturday 11:30 A.M. to 11:00 P.M., and Sunday noon to 9:00 P.M. After dinner you can stroll down to **L'Elizabeth** (285 South Main Street, 861–1974; www.1-elizabeth.com) to order dessert, coffee, or a drink at the bar; indulge while relaxing on a couch or easy chair. Open Sunday to Tuesday 3:00 P.M. to midnight, Wednesday to Saturday 3:00 P.M. to 1:00 A.M.

WaterFire Stokes the Senses

On special nights throughout the year, Providence plays host to an amazing fusion of fire, water, and music known as WaterFire. The work of RISD artist Barnaby Evans, the WaterFire display acts simultaneously on a variety of senses. A dozen cauldrons filled with firewood and perched above the Providence River are set ablaze to the strains of classical music. Watch the flames reflected off the dark water and casting shadowy forms on the stones of the Providence Riverwalk while the smell of burning wood tickles your nose and the music echoes hauntingly off the quiet buildings of downtown.

Evans says that the close proximity of the fire and water symbolizes the fragility of life—either is capable of destroying the other, yet they exist, at least for a time, in harmony. We say that WaterFire is an experience worth harmonizing your schedule for. For information on upcoming performances, call 272–3111, or visit www.waterfire.org.

If you've had dinner and dessert and still are looking for something to do, see what's playing at the **Cable Car Cinema** (204 South Main Street, 272–3970; www.cablecarcinema.com), where you and that special someone can curl up together on a couch (again!) and take in a movie. At night the theater plays off-beat, arty films; during the week, the Cable Car operates primarily as a cafe, with indoor and outdoor seating. Elliott Shorter's live, pre-show blues and jazz has become a Cable Car tradition. Open Monday to Friday 7:30 A.M. to 11:00 P.M. and Saturday and Sunday 9:00 A.M. to 11:00 P.M.

If you catch an early movie at the Cable Car, lay off the popcorn and save room for the pad thai at **Pakarang** (303 South Main Street, 453–3660; www .pakarangrestaurant.com), Providence's best Thai restaurant. It's open for lunch Monday to Friday 11:00 A.M. to 3:00 P.M. and noon to 3:00 P.M. on Saturday; and for dinner Sunday to Thursday 5:00 to 10:00 P.M., Friday and Saturday 5:00 to 10:30 P.M. Closed Monday.

For a late-night drink with a view of the river, check out the **Riverfront Loft at Barnsider's Mile and a Quarter** restaurant (375 South Main Street, 351–7300; www.barnsiderrestaurant.com). But get there early during events like WaterFire: Just four half-oval tables by the windows offer prime viewing spots. Friday and Saturday are murder mystery nights (www.murderonus.com); the show starts at 7:30 P.M. and costs $39.95, including dinner. Open Monday to Thursday 5:00 to 10:00 P.M., Friday and Saturday 4:00 to 10:30 P.M., and Sunday 4:00 to 9:00 P.M.

You'll recognize the **Parkside Rotisserie and Bar** (76 South Main Street, 331–0003; www.parksideprovidence.com) by the pillows in the windows and the lemon walls, subtly hinting at the "upbeat" Mediterranean cuisine that awaits. Hot off the Labesse Giraudon rotisserie come entrees like top sirloin topped with a crostini of marscapone and Gorgonzola cheese, and roasted chicken with lemon and cashews. Restaurant hours are 11:30 A.M. to 10:00 P.M. Monday to Thursday, 11:30 A.M. to 11:00 P.M. on Friday, 5:00 to 11:00 P.M. on Saturday, and 4:00 to 9:00 P.M. on Sunday.

Olives (108 North Main Street, 751–1200; www.olivesri.com) is known for its crab cakes and Long Island duck. But as you might suspect, this South Main Street restaurant/bar/nightclub has firmly latched onto the martini craze, offering fifty-two varieties of the classic tipple. Among the more unusual concoctions that may fill your frosted glass are a mint chocolate chip martini and an espresso-flavored blend. Dinner is served daily from 5:00 to 10:00 P.M., followed by live blues, rock, and R&B Thursday to Saturday; bar stays open till 1:00 A.M. Tuesday to Thursday and Sunday, till 2:00 A.M. Friday and Saturday. Dinner only on Monday.

At any point along the downtown stretch of South or North Main Street, it's a quick walk down to the river or uphill to the "mile of history" of **Benefit Street.**

Hoofing It around Providence

The ability to experience Providence on foot has always been one of the city's chief virtues: You can easily walk to the State House on Smith Hill, explore Downcity, and cross the Providence River to check out the East Side—all in a single day, if you're feeling ambitious.

Still, it helps to have a little guidance as you make your way from place to place. The Providence Historical Society offers a series of "Summerwalks" that touch upon various aspects of the city's history, a WaterFire tour, and interpretive strolls down Benefit Street and along the riverwalk. Tickets are $12.00 for adults, $6.00 for children ages twelve and under. For more information contact the Historical Society at 110 Benevolent Street, Providence, RI 02906, 331–8575, or visit www.rihs.org.

Besides the East Bay Bike Path, which begins at India Point Park on the East Side, the best place for a walk or jog is on the path running down the wide, tree-lined median of *Blackstone Boulevard,* a street that also has some of Providence's finest homes. For a more serene pastime, you should take a stroll through *Swan Point Cemetery,* a beautiful place where you can walk along to the edge of the cliffs overlooking the Seekonk River. While you're here, look for the headstone marking the final resting places of macabre author H. P. Lovecraft and Civil War General Ambrose Burnside. To cool off after a brisk walk, go to *Three Sisters Cafe* (1074 Hope Street, 273-7230) for some top-notch, home-made Maxmillian's ice cream in thirty-six flavors, including green tea and an assortment of sorbets. Got a late-night ice cream craving? Three Sisters is open 7:30 A.M. to 10:00 P.M. weekdays and 7:30 A.M. to 11:00 P.M. on Friday and Saturday, plus 8:00 A.M. to 10:00 P.M. on Sunday, with longer summer evening hours on the weekends.

Providence's other off-the-beaten-path attractions are scattered throughout the city. To literally get an overview of downtown, find *Prospect Terrace,* a small park on the East Side, at the corner of Cushing and Congdon Streets. To get to the park from Benefit Street, take Meeting Street 2 blocks east to Congdon Street and make a left. In this small patch of green is a statue of Roger Williams, the founder of Rhode Island, who is buried here. From this spot you have a great view of the capitol as well as the tall buildings of the financial district.

The arts are alive and well in Providence—the city is working on creating an arts and entertainment district in the Downcity area—and no more so than at *AS220* (115 Empire Street, 831–9327; www.as220.org), the city's own special breeding ground for innovative and unusual theater and fine arts. At the large AS220 complex on Empire Street, you can find something happening just about any day of the week, thanks to the fact that roughly two dozen artists are in residence and a major theater company performing new plays (the *Perishable Theatre,* 95 Empire Street, 331–2695; www.perishable.org) also calls AS220 home.

In the galleries upstairs and in the *Taquieria Pacifica* (781–TRUK) are a variety of daily free showings by local, usually unknown, artists. The bohemian atmosphere carries over into the cafe, where you can choose from a daily menu of West Coast–style Mexican food. In the evenings there are musical performances ranging from an Appalachian jam session to jazz to intense rock and roll, with a cover charge that rarely exceeds $5.00 to $10.00. Film festivals and poetry slams also are part of the AS220 scene; don't miss the Pork Chop Lounge on Sunday nights at 8:00 P.M.—a comedy "slam" of five-minute acts.

AS220's galleries are open Monday through Saturday, noon to 5:00 P.M. The cafe is open Tuesday to Saturday noon to 10:00 P.M.

While you're downtown and in the mood to be entertained, don't overlook Providence's excellent live music scene. Clubs like *Lupo's Heartbreak Hotel* (79 Washington Street, 272–5876; www.lupos.com) bring up-and-coming national acts as well as second-tier established stars and groups to the historic Strand Theatre. You can catch a good show any weekend, and on most week-

Sullivan Ballou's Grave

Among the graves in Providence's Swan Point Cemetery is that of Major Sullivan Ballou, a member of the Second Regiment, Rhode Island Volunteers, during the Civil War. The monument over Ballou's grave is inscribed with a poignant passage from a letter he wrote to his wife, Sarah, on July 14, 1861, as his unit was preparing to move toward the front. In the letter, Ballou wrote passionately to Sarah of his love of country and sense of duty, yet he also expressed the anguish of knowing he might never see her or their children again.

Ballou ended his letter with a promise that, if he should fall in battle, his family would be reunited in the hereafter: "I wait for you there. Come to me and lead thither my children." Just two weeks later, on July 29, 1861, Ballou was killed in the first major clash of the war, the First Battle of Bull Run, also known as First Manassas.

If you want to read the full text of Ballou's letter, you can find it online at www.sullivanballou.info. The Lysander and Susan Flagg Museum in Central Falls (209 Central Street, 727–7440) has a special Sullivan Ballou room filled with military artifacts from the Civil War and later conflicts. The museum is open on Wednesday and Thursday from 10:00 A.M. to noon, with additional Thursday hours from 2:00 to 4:00 P.M. Admission is $2.00 for adults, $1.00 for seniors and kids.

nights you can take a seat in the Mezzanine or join the scrum on the main floor. For top-shelf local bands, try the *Living Room* (23 Rathbone Street, 521–5200), a landmark on the local club scene.

If the band you're watching goes into a third or fourth encore, you may find your late-night dining choices somewhat limited once you exit the concert hall for the darkened city streets. Fortunately, there's a strange but satisfying diner within walking distance of the Downcity clubs. Late nights, find the trailer housing the *Haven Bros. Diner* (861–7777), open 5:00 P.M. to 3:00 A.M., parked next to Kennedy Plaza by City Hall. It's not unusual to find businesspeople and bikers mingling at the cramped counter there.

Providence's Broadway neighborhood has undergone a mini-renaissance of its own in recent years, perhaps best exemplified by the transformation of the *Columbus Theatre* (270 Broadway, 621–9660; www.columbustheatre.com) from porno house to home of the Rhode Island Independent Film Festival in 2002.

In truth, the 1926 theater—with its vintage suspended marquee, Wurlitzer organ, ornate box office, muraled ceilings, and stained-glass archways—always deserved better than the collected works of Russ Meyer. Inspired by the success of the film festival and the decline of the theatrical porn industry, the theater's longtime owners have taken the Columbus in a polar-opposite direction, hosting film festivals, live performances, and regular showings of independent films.

Across the street, local coffee shop *Nick's on Broadway* (500 Broadway, 421–0286) has been taken over by gourmet chefs and undergone its own meta-

rhodeisland's blackheritage

The first black people in Rhode Island came unwillingly, imported as slaves as early as the mid-seventeenth century. Many of the early fortunes of Providence, Newport, and Bristol were built on the back of the slave trade. Yet black Rhode Islanders began making a mark for themselves even before slavery was abolished in the state: The famous First Black Regiment of Rhode Island fought with distinction during the Battle of Rhode Island in 1778.

The trials and triumphs of black Rhode Islanders are chronicled at the Rhode Island Black Heritage Society Museum (65 Weybosset Street, in the historic Arcade building, second floor, 751–3490). A permanent exhibit, entitled "Creative Survival," documents black history in the state and includes manumission documents, old photographs, and a dress that belonged to Sisseretta Jones, an early black opera singer. The society also presents lectures and special exhibits, such as a recent examination of the *Amistad* story. The downtown museum is open Monday to Friday 9:00 A.M. to 5:00 P.M. and weekends by appointment.

morphosis, with creative spins on standard breakfast fare served countertop in the morning and fixed-price gourmet meals in the evening. Open Wednesday to Saturday 7:00 A.M. to 3:00 P.M. and Saturday 8:00 A.M. to 3:00 P.M. for lunch; call ahead for dinner hours. Artists, attracted to the area by reasonably low rents, hang out at local joints like *Julian's* (318 Broadway, 861–1770; www.julians providence.com) and the *White Electric Coffee Shop* (711 Westminster Street, 453–3007). In the nearby Armory District, the *Hudson Street Market* (68 Hudson Street, 274–4540) is famous for its generous homemade sandwiches.

Wes's Rib House (38 Dike Street, 421–9090; www.wesribhouse.com) might just be the perfect out-of-the-way restaurant. It has great food (barbecued ribs, chicken, and chopped meats) in a genre that's a rarity in New England; the restaurant is open late; and it's located in a desolate part of town that's hard to find.

Wes's implores you to "put some South in your mouth" and has a wood-fired open grill serving up awesome Missouri-style barbecue. You can order ribs by the piece—two to forty—or choose from a number of dinner platters. Try the Show-Me Platter so that you can sample four of the tasty meats; dinners also come with moist corn bread and excellent barbecued beans. If you're really hungry, start with a bowl of Wes's chili—made with meat, of course. Friends from Texas, where they know barbecue, say this is the best they've tasted up North.

To find Wes's Rib House from downtown Providence, take Westminster Street west, passing under Route 10 and over the railroad tracks, then make the second left onto a service road leading into a forbidding industrial park. The

Thursday Night Brings the Arts to Life

Looking for something to do in Providence on a Thursday night? It's not as hard as it might sound, especially if you're here on the third Thursday of the month from March to November. That's the night that the Providence Artrolley (www.gallerynight.info) makes the rounds of the city's art galleries, antiques stores, and performance venues. The free trolley runs continuously from 5:00 to 9:00 P.M. in a loop from Citizens' Plaza (along the riverwalk) through downtown, up College Hill, and down Wickenden Street and Benefit Street. Along the way you can hop off at more than fifteen galleries plus events like poetry slams, dance performances, and plays.

To pass the time on board the trolley, members of the Providence Preservation Society and local celebrity guides are on hand to provide a narrated tour of the city. Free parking is available at Citizens' Plaza on the nights when the trolley is running. For more information on the Artrolley, call 751–2628.

road ends at a parking lot, which belongs to Wes's. The restaurant is in an old factory building. From I–195, take the Route 6 exit (Olneyville), then exit onto Hartford Avenue. Follow Hartford Avenue until it merges with Westminster Street. Take Westminster Street east to Bough Street, make a right, then make a left onto Dike Street. Wes's is 2 blocks down, on your right. Open Monday through Thursday 11:30 A.M. to 2:00 A.M., Friday and Saturday 11:30 A.M. to 4:00 A.M., and Sunday noon to 2:00 A.M.

The **Culinary Archives and Museum** at Johnson and Wales University (315 Harborside Boulevard, 598–2805; www.culinary.org) is a feast for the eyes. The answers to all of your questions about the preparation and consumption of food probably can be found here. One of Rhode Island's best-kept secrets, the Culinary Archives contain more than 400,000 items related to food and hospitality, which incidentally are the major course offerings at Johnson and Wales University.

If a president of the United States ever jotted down a note asking an aide to send out for pizza, the Culinary Archives probably has that note in its collection. Archival documents include a handwritten dinner invitation from Mary Todd Lincoln, vintage postcards featuring restaurants and other food purveyors, and more than 40,000 menus from around the world. Displays feature 4,000-year-old Native American cooking stones, ancient Egyptian and Roman spoons, a bread ring from Pompeii, and a collection of stoves from the nineteenth and twentieth centuries. Since Rhode Island is the birthplace of the diner, naturally the museum includes a diner exhibit; more quirky is a walk-through reproduction of an 1833 New Hampshire country tavern.

In all, the museum—the only one of its type in the world—presents a virtual banquet of more than 300,000 items that any fan of food will enjoy. To get there, take I–95 to exit 18 (Thurbers Avenue). If coming from the north, take a left on to Allens Avenue (Route 1A) when you get off the exit; if approaching from the south, take a right at the end of the exit ramp. Proceed on Allens Avenue (which turns into Narragansett Avenue) until you see a Shell gas station on your left, and make a left turn on Harborside Boulevard. At the bottom of the hill, the museum is in the first building on the left. The Culinary Archives and Museum is open Tuesday through Sunday 10:00 A.M. to 5:00 P.M. (last tour at 4:00 P.M.). Admission is $7.00 for adults, $6.00 for seniors, $3.00 for students, and $2.00 for children ages five to eighteen.

Ask for a sub in Rhode Island, and you're likely to get a blank stare: If it's a sandwich you're after, the word you're looking for is "grinder."

Inquire about a submarine, and chances are you'll get an equally puzzled look. But Providence indeed has its own submarine. The **Saratoga Museum Foundation**—a group working to restore the aircraft carrier USS *Saratoga* as a floating museum at Quonset Point—recently acquired a cold war–vintage Russian missile submarine, now moored at Collier's Point Park and open to the public for tours.

The Juliett 484-class sub that is the centerpiece of the **Russian Sub Museum** was built in the 1950s and designed to fire nuclear-tipped cruise missiles at the East Coast of the United States in the event of war. Later, the sub served in an antiship capacity, targeting vessels like the *Saratoga*.

After being decommissioned in the early 1990s, the sub—designated K-77—was sold to a Finnish entrepreneur and opened as a restaurant in Helsinki; later it served as a Hollywood prop, used during the shooting of the 2002 Harrison Ford thriller, *K-19: The Widowmaker,* the story of the doomed Russian nuclear sub.

After the filming ended, the Saratoga Museum Foundation bought the sub and moved it to Collier's Point, an industrial site on the west side of Narragansett Bay. Tours of the 300-foot sub include visits to the command center, officers' wardroom, and the forward torpedo room, each chockablock with original equipment and intriguing Cyrillic signs and warnings. One of the sub's former battery rooms has been converted to a bunk room for overnight events.

The Russian Sub Museum is open weekdays Memorial Day to Labor Day from 11:00 A.M. to 5:00 P.M. and weekends from 10:00 A.M. to 6:00 P.M. Admission is $8.00 for adults, $6.00 for seniors and military, and $5.00 for kids ages six to seventeen. The sub is located at exit 18 off I–95; go to the end of the ramp, make a left onto Allens Avenue, and follow the signs to the Collier's Point Park entrance, three-quarters of a mile on the right. For more information see the museum's Web site at www.juliett484.org or call 521–3600.

With the opening of the beautiful **Westin Hotel** downtown (One West Exchange Street, 598–8000), Providence finally has a selection of hotels worthy of a city on the rise. However, if you want to be immersed in the history of Rhode Island, there's no better place to stay than the **Old Court Bed and Breakfast** (751–2002; www.oldcourt.com). Located at 144 Benefit Street (perhaps the best-preserved original colonial street in America), the Old Court was built in 1863 as a rectory and sits next to the historic Rhode Island Courthouse. The ten rooms at this rather austere Italianate inn feature private baths and include a full breakfast at rates that are competitive with the big hotels. Rates range seasonally from $115 to $195.

For an even more private place to stay on Benefit Street, ring up innkeeper **C. C. Ledbetter** and book a room at her eponymous bed-and-breakfast (326 Benefit Street, 351–4699; www.ccledbetter.com). Unassuming from the outside—there's not even a sign—the interior of this circa 1780 colonial is brightened with dhurrie rugs, maps (the innkeeper is a professional cartographer), handmade quilts, contemporary paintings, and C. C.'s engaging personality. Start your day with your choice of four kinds of juice, gourmet coffee and tea, fresh fruit, warm bread, and coffee cake, and you'll be ready to take on the sights of the East Side and nearby downtown Providence. Room rates are $95 to $115 nightly.

The neighborhood behind the state capitol won't be written up in travel brochures anytime soon, but this section of Providence is blessed with some lovely colonial and Victorian homes and is slowly being gentrified. Part of that reclamation project is the *State House Inn* (43 Jewett Street, 351–6111; www.providence-inn.com). Located in the shadow of the capitol building, the State House Inn is a well-kept, three-story colonial revival building with ten guest rooms dressed in a country folk art style—not at all what you would expect in the heart of a busy city. But it works, thanks in no small part to the inn's friendly staff, led by innkeepers Frank and Monica Hopton. The inn is fully equipped with air-conditioning, cable televisions, phones, and fax machines, and a full breakfast is included in the room rates, which range from $109 to $149. That's a steal considering you're just steps from the seat of state government and a brisk walk from beautiful Waterplace Park and the rest of downtown Providence.

Douglas Avenue may have been overlooked by the Providence renaissance that has transformed the heart of the city's downtown, but a few urban pioneers are determined to make this thoroughfare near Providence College the city's newest hot spot.

The *Brooklyn Coffee and Tea House* (200 Douglas Avenue, 575–2284; www.brooklyncoffeeteahouse.com) is doing its part for the transformation cause with warm drinks and cool tunes, both served up in a brick-faced former grocery store surrounded by gardens in which caffeinated guests can relax when the weather cooperates.

Brooklyn's set list includes live rock, jazz, and pop; Wednesday is open-mike night, while other nights may feature screenings of silent movies or even a sewing bee. When the music's not playing, you can check out the paintings by local artists, including owner Anthony Demings's rendering of the Brooklyn Bridge that gave the coffeehouse its name. Open Monday to Friday 7:00 A.M. to 1:00 P.M. Also opens select evenings for special events.

East Providence

Just over the Providence–East Providence city line is the best place in Rhode Island to see live comedy. The *Comedy Connection* (39 Warren Avenue, 438–8383; www.ricomedyconnection.com) is located in a former bank building, but the currency here is laughter, not cash. Inside, you can loosen up with a few drinks from the bar, warm up with some local talent onstage, then laugh it up with top regional and national comedians every Wednesday through Sunday night. Showtime is 8:00 P.M., and reservations are required. On Friday and Saturday there is also a 10:15 P.M. show.

Take I–195 to exit 4 (the first exit after the Washington Bridge), and you'll find *Veterans Memorial Parkway,* one of the most pleasant drives in the Providence area. The road begins in a residential area but quickly reaches the Providence Harbor shoreline, where it parallels the route of the defunct Old Colony Railroad line, now the *East Bay Bike Path.* In fact, if you want to take a bike ride on the path, the lot just off Veterans Memorial Parkway is one of the best places to park your car. (For more on the bike path, see the East Bay chapter.)

The road continues on a narrow causeway on the Watchemoket Cove, near the Metacom Country Club, then affords a quick glimpse of the *Fuller Rock Lighthouse* off Kettle Point before reaching the access road for *Squantum Woods State Park,* also traversed by the bike path. Soon Veterans Memorial Parkway merges with Pawtucket Avenue (Route 103); continue south on Route 103.

The road splits and you'll want to bear right onto Bullock's Point Avenue, which will take you through the middle of the village of *Riverside.* Crossing the bike path at the former railroad right-of-way, you'll see on your left an old train station. Until 1948, trains making this stop on the Old Colony Railroad disgorged hordes of summer visitors onto the streets of Riverside.

One reminder of this vanished past is the *Dari-Bee Soft Serve* ice-cream stand (240 Bullock's Point Avenue), a Riverside fixture for more than thirty-five years that boasts the best milkshakes anywhere. Open May 1 until the weather turns chilly.

At one time Riverside was a resort community with grand old hotels that catered to visitors to the Crescent Amusement Park, located near the end of Bullock's Point Avenue by Bullock's Neck. Alas, the once sprawling park was closed and demolished some years ago, and condominiums now stand in the place of the old roller coaster and midway. Just one vestige of the old park remains, but it is worth seeing: the 1895 *Crescent Park Looff Carousel* (www.crescentparkcarousel.com).

Charles I. D. Looff is acknowledged as having been the preeminent master of carousel design, and he favored elaborate, ornate designs in constructing his wooden masterpieces. Rhode Island is fortunate to have a number of Looff-designed carousels, but the best is in East Providence. The Crescent Park Carousel was designed as a showpiece for prospective carousel buyers, so Looff pulled out all the stops in building it. So personal to Looff was this carousel that he carved his own likeness in the decorative panels around the rim. Besides the magnificently carved wooden horses, the carousel is decorated with beveled mirrors, colored glass and jewels, and dainty lights. Organ music plays as the carousel whirls around.

The Crescent Park Carousel is open Thursday to Sunday in the summer from noon to 8:00 P.M., and on off-season weekends. Rides are 75 cents or three for $2.00; there's also a snack bar and gift shop on the premises. Call 433–2828 for information and to confirm hours of operation.

East Providence, by the way, is home to a substantial Portuguese population, one of the more plentiful ingredients in Providence's melting pot. For a taste of spicy chourico and other zesty Portuguese-style dishes, drop by **Madeira** (288 Warren Avenue, 431–1322; www.madeirarestaurant.com), the king of East Providence's Portuguese restaurants. You'll be treated like family at this large, friendly restaurant, which also has an outdoor dining patio and bar in the summer. Open Monday to Thursday 11:30 A.M. to 10:00 P.M., Friday and Saturday 11:30 A.M. to 11:00 P.M., and Sunday noon to 10:00 P.M.

Rhode Island's diverse ethnic population includes an estimated 18,000 people of Armenian descent; there's even a memorial in the North Burial Grounds in Providence honoring the 1.5 million Armenians slaughtered by the Ottoman Empire during World War I. In East Providence, Armenian and Middle Eastern culture is celebrated through food at **Restaurant La Camelia** (92 Waterman Avenue, 434–1225). The decor is simple (relying mostly on traditional music to set the mood), but the service is friendly and attentive, courtesy of chef George Moukhtarian and hostess Guylaine Moukhtarian.

Start with a plate of hummus (blended with garlic, lemon juice, and olive oil) or try the basterma (Armenian pastrami), which will whet your appetite for the steak shish kabob or losh kabob (grilled ground lamb or beef served with cherry tomatoes on a bed of rice or bulgur pilaf). Or, be bold enough to ask George to prepare his rack of lamb (it's not on the menu), which a friend described to me as the most succulent he has ever eaten. *Bon appetit,* or "paree akhorjag," as they say here. Open Monday to Saturday, 5:00 to 10:00 P.M.

Pawtucket

It may be Pawtucket's top tourist attraction, but relatively few people come to see the **Slater Mill National Historic Site** (725–8638; www.slatermill.org). Don't make this mistake, because Slater Mill occupies a key place in the history of the United States.

After conceding defeat in the Revolutionary War, Great Britain was determined to prevent the upstart United States from obtaining the technology needed to join the Industrial Revolution. But the British didn't count on Samuel Slater, an independent-minded man who came to America after managing one of the most progressive mills in England.

Financed by Moses Brown and William Almy, Slater founded the first successful cotton mill in the United States in 1793. The rest, as they say, is history: Building on Slater's success, over the next century American industry grew to such strength that it eventually dwarfed even that of the mighty British Empire.

The Slater Mill complex includes the original *Slater Mill,* a yellow, wooden colonial building sitting over a raceway by the falls in downtown Pawtucket, and the *Sylvanus-Brown House,* built in 1758. Slater Mill contains all of the carding, drawing, spinning, and weaving equipment needed to turn raw cotton into cloth, and museum tours include demonstrations of how each item worked. If the process seems primitive by today's standards, take a look at the spinning wheels and other hand-operated tools in the Sylvanus-Brown House. The rise of the mills soon caused the extinction of such cottage industries.

The *Wilkinson Mill,* the other major structure in the park, is a stone mill built in 1810 by Oziel Wilkinson and considered the birthplace of the American machine tool industry. The mill contains a working nineteenth-century machine shop that is still powered by a 16,000-pound waterwheel.

The Slater Mill complex, which also includes walkways and benches overlooking the powerful waterfall that powered the mills, is located on Roosevelt Avenue in downtown Pawtucket, just north of the intersection with Main Street (take exit 27 off I–95 south, or exit 28 if coming north on I–95). Tours are offered Tuesday to Sunday from 10:00 A.M. to 5:00 P.M. between May 1 and September 30; call for off-season schedule. Admission is $9.00 for adults, $7.00 for seniors, and $6.00 for children ages six to twelve.

Downtown Pawtucket is a little hard to navigate; the city fathers, in their wisdom, decided to make the major city artery into a giant, one-way street. All well and good if you're a local who knows where you're headed; not so good if you're a visitor searching for an unfamiliar shop or restaurant.

Contrary to naysayers from down the river, Pawtucket is not bereft of culture. In fact, as the monument at the corner of Exchange, Goff, and Broad Streets can attest, Pawtucket was featured in the movie *American Buffalo,* starring Dustin Hoffman and Dennis Franz and directed by favorite son Michael Corrente.

The *Sandra Feinstein-Gamm Theatre* (172 Exchange Street, 723–4266; www.gammtheatre.org), founded in Providence as Alias Stage in 1984, earned a fine reputation over the years but was hampered by a cramped location in a part of town (the Jewelry District) more known for nightclubs than fine arts. In 2003, amid a push in Pawtucket to save the city's historic National Guard

Armory, Gamm moved into its new home in the armory annex, a former police garage now converted into a 124-seat theater.

The Gamm presents classic American plays like Arthur Miller's *The Crucible,* Shakespeare, Dylan Thomas, and other works that thrive in an intimate setting. The Gamm has been a central part of an ambitious plan to breathe life into the city's cultural scene. Tickets are $26 to $31 for adults, $23 to $26 for seniors, and $16 for students; shows are Friday at 8:00 P.M., Saturday at 8:00 P.M., and Sunday at 2:00 P.M.

The turreted, Romanesque Pawtucket Armory also is home to the ***Arts Exchange,*** the city's main engine for transforming the 48,000-square-foot building into a downtown arts center. For information on the project, see www.arts-exchange.org. Meanwhile, the ***Pawtucket Arts Collaborative*** (www.pawtucketartscollaborative.org) maintains a small gallery featuring Rhode Island artists at the Blackstone Valley Visitor's Center (175 Main Street, 724–2200; www.tourblackstone.com), a must-stop for any visitor to the region. It's open daily 9:00 A.M. to 5:00 P.M.

Ribbons mark your route to the roof at the ***Rhode Island Rock Gym*** (100 Higginson Avenue, just over the Pawtucket/Lincoln border, 727–1704; www .rhodeislandrockgym.com), an indoor climbing facility where people of all ages and abilities can challenge themselves on a variety of surfaces, from simple vertical walls studded with hand and footholds to a padded, artificial cave with a 70-degree angled ceiling. A total of 10,000 square feet of terrain and fifty walls offer plenty of options for top-roped climbing, lead climbing, and low-level bouldering, including a number of challenging overhangs. A day pass costing just $16.00 (plus $8.00 equipment rental, if needed) lets you climb from 10:00 A.M. to midnight daily; individual and group lessons are also available (call for appointment). The on-site shop offers both equipment rentals and sales.

Good, cheap food you expect from a diner—but ambience and history? Not usually, but the ***Modern Diner*** (364 East Avenue, 726–8390) is a major exception. From the outside, the Modern Diner resembles a big, tan, diesel train engine of the 1940s. Inside, the padded booths and long, polished counter fronting the grill look much the same as they did over half a century ago. The Sterling Streamliner–model diner, a local landmark, also was the first diner in the country to be listed on the National Register.

Did we mention good and inexpensive eats? A delicious burger can be yours for $2.85, while the priciest item on the menu, the Steak Delmonico, will set you back a grand $8.25. The diner is open Monday through Saturday 6:00 A.M. to 3:00 P.M. and Sunday 7:00 A.M. to 2:00 P.M.

For a polar-opposite experience on the same street, check out the ***Garden Grille*** (727 East Avenue, 726–2826; www.gardengrillecafe.com), which claims

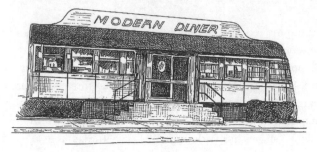

Modern Diner

to be the region's only full-service vegetarian restaurant. Wood-grilled veggie burgers and other healthful delights are served up in a cheerful setting, where patrons can sidle up to a fresh juice bar for a wholesome alternative to the blue-plate special. Dinner entrees include Indonesian rice and tofu, "flame-kissed" vegetables, roasted butternut-squash quesadillas, and wood-grilled pizzas. Open Monday to Thursday 10:00 A.M. to 9:30 P.M.; Friday 11:00 A.M. to 10:00 P.M.; Saturday 11:00 A.M. to 10:00 P.M.; and Sunday 10:00 A.M. to 3:00 P.M. for brunch and 3:00 to 9:30 P.M. for dinner.

Located in a converted 1895 firehouse, the ***Hose Company No. 6*** (636 Central Avenue, 722–7220; www.hosecompanyno6.com) restaurant is intriguing on its own merits. But what has really put the place on the map locally has been the addition of the "hands-on" weekend food-fest and minstrel show known as "The King's Feast."

Perhaps no castle was available, but the old firehouse's stone walls and wood beams provide an appropriate backdrop for this reenactment of a bawdy royal feast. As with themed dinners you may have experienced in Orlando or elsewhere, you eat with your hands or risk being singled out for shame by King Raymond or one of his minions. The meal includes soup and beef stroganoff (the dipping bread helps here), steamed mussels, salad, and roast chicken, along with flagons of ale, white wine, or nonalcoholic cider. The highly interactive show features fools, wenches, and minstrels, and the double-entendre–laden humor is billed as "PG-15."

The King's Feast is presented on Friday and Saturday night, at 7:30 P.M.; tickets are $40 and include the show, food, and drinks (but not tips). Reservations are required: Call Hose Company No. 6 at 722–7220 from Tuesday to Sunday to book. For more information on the feast, see www.freewebs.com/kingsfeastinc. The restaurant is located off exit 2A from I–95; take Route 1A south to the third set of lights, then make a right onto Central Avenue. The restaurant will be on your immediate right.

Pawtucket's ***McCoy Stadium*** is home to Rhode Island's beloved Pawtucket Red Sox (www.pawsox.com), better known as the Pawsox. If you've given up trying to explain to your kids why baseball is so important, bypass the major league millionaires and bring them to McCoy. This is baseball like it used to be, and still oughta be.

The AAA International League farm club of the Boston Red Sox, the Pawsox are a Rhode Island success story writ large. Bankrupt when current owner Ben Mondor bought the team in 1977, the Pawsox regularly outdraw some major league franchises with a combination of reasonable prices, fun family atmosphere, and an excellent ballpark (10,031-seat McCoy was completely renovated in 1999). Like the franchise, the team on the field has been a success, finishing first in its division in 1994 and 1996. Players such as Roger Clemens, Jim Rice, Mo Vaughn, Wade Boggs, and Nomar Garciaparra all have had stints at McCoy before moving on to fame and fortune in the majors.

The high-quality play of young hitters and pitchers aiming for a shot at the big leagues is one attraction; another is the family atmosphere at McCoy. Despite the expansion, the stadium is small enough to be called intimate, and there are no bad seats in the house. In fact, the 1999 remodeling gives fans van-

The Longest Game

The longest game in professional baseball history was played right here at McCoy Stadium beginning (but not ending) on April 18, 1981. Thirty-three innings long, and taking more than sixty-five days to complete, the game ended on a single to left on July 23, 1981, that gave the Pawtucket Red Sox a 3–2 win over the Rochester Red Wings.

The game had gotten off to a rocky start when the stadium lights failed to work properly, but neither fans nor players had an inkling of what they were in for. A Rochester run in the top of the seventh inning was matched by a Pawsox run to tie the game in the bottom of the ninth. The two teams then went another eleven innings without scoring.

An RBI double by Rochester's Dave Huppert put the Red Wings ahead in the top of the twenty-first, but to the chagrin of the Rochester squad and perhaps even some of his own teammates and fans, future All-Star first baseman Wade Boggs tied the game up in the bottom of the inning with an RBI double of his own.

Another eleven scoreless innings passed before, mercifully, the game was suspended at 2–2. The time: 4:09 A.M. on April 19. Pawsox owner Ben Mondor gave season tickets to all nineteen diehard fans who remained in the stands.

More than two months later, the game was resumed at McCoy, and the end came quickly: future big-leaguer Marty Barrett singled with the bases loaded in the bottom of the thirty-third inning for a 3–2 Pawsox win. The game had taken eight hours and twenty-five minutes to play and earned Pawtucket a place in the Baseball Hall of Fame in Cooperstown.

tage points from a left-field tower and a grass berm and bleachers beyond the outfield fence. During batting practice, youngsters "fish" for players' autographs by tying string to cut-up plastic milk containers and lowering programs and baseballs down to the dugouts. Most players happily oblige. The outfield fence is lined with billboards, just like in the old days, and the ramps leading into the stadium are adorned with murals of the Pawsox stars of the past. A tent down the right-field line marks a picnic area where groups can enjoy the game along with a barbecue.

A Pawsox game is a great value, appealing directly to the frugal Yankee heart (that's Yankee as in long-term New Englanders, not the hated Bronx Bombers). Reserved box seats are just $10.00, and general admission tickets are $6.00 for adults and $4.00 for kids and seniors. Hot dogs are about $3.00, and if you come early enough, you can even park for free in the stadium's small lot or on neighborhood streets.

The Pawsox play seventy-two home games between April and early September, and you generally can get tickets right up until game time. McCoy Stadium is located on Columbus Avenue; easiest access is from Newport Avenue/Route 1A or from School Street/Route 114 via Pond Street. Call 724–7300 for ticket information, game schedule, or directions.

Pawtucket's **Slater Memorial Park** is the center of the city's recreational life, featuring baseball fields, tennis courts, pony rides, paddleboats, and a bike path along the Ten Mile River. It also is the site of **Daggett House** (www.members .cox.net/darjan), where eight generations of the Daggett family lived between 1685 and 1894, when the family farm was sold to the city to create the park.

Col. John Daggett and Nathan Daggett both fought in the Revolutionary War, and the Daughters of the American Revolution have restored the house with eighteenth- and nineteenth-century furniture and antiques. Among the items in use or on display are a dress worn by Catherine Littlefield Greene (wife of Gen. Nathaniel Greene) when she danced with Lafayette and a bedspread and quilt owned by Esther Slater. The house is open for tours May to mid-December by appointment as well as for frequent special events. Admission is $2.00 for adults and 50 cents for children under age twelve. Call 722–6931 or 723–0145 to confirm hours or to schedule a tour.

Also in Slater Park is Pawtucket's beautiful **Looff Carousel**, built in 1894. One of the nation's oldest carousels, the Slater Park merry-go-round is of the "stander" variety—the horses go round and round, but not up and down. The admission charge will remind you of the nineteenth century, too: It's just 25 cents (or a donated canned good for charity) a ride. Open daily from Memorial Day to Labor Day 11:00 A.M. to 5:00 P.M.; call 728–0500, extension 252, for information.

On the eastern edge of Slater Park is the ***Ten-Mile River Greenway,*** an embryonic bike path that one day will link the Blackstone River Bikeway and the East Bay Bike Path. A 2.5-mile segment of the path skirts the James V. Turner Reservoir and links the Slater Park segment to an athletic complex off Newport Avenue in East Providence. Future plans call for extending the path north through Ten-Mile River State Park.

Entrances to Slater Park are on Newport Avenue (Route 1A) and Armistice Boulevard (Route 15).

Cranston

The story of the Sprague family is one that a lot of Rhode Islanders, familiar with decades of entrenched political cronyism in state and local government, can relate to. William Sprague turned an old gristmill into a multimillion-dollar cotton manufacturing company in the early eighteenth century and used his wealth as a springboard to the governorship. Following in his namesake's footsteps, William Sprague III spent $125,000 of the family's money to get himself elected governor in 1860 and moved from there to a seat in the U.S. Senate after the Civil War. By the mid-1870s, however, Sprague's lavish spending and financial speculation caused the loss of the family fortune and control of the A & W Sprague Manufacturing Company.

At the height of the Spragues' power, however, the family was worth an estimated $19 million, and its company was the largest in the state and one of the nation's most important firms. The ***Governor Sprague Mansion*** (1351 Cranston Street, 944-9226), built in 1790 and expanded in 1864, contains many examples of fine period furniture, especially in the restored parlor. There also is a collection of Oriental art donated by the Carrington family and a carriage house and stable filled with old carriages, sleighs, wagons, and carts. Tours are $5.00 for adults, $3.00 for children and available by appointment; call for information.

In the same part of Cranston is perhaps the state's most popular in-the-know restaurant: ***Twin Oaks*** (100 Sabra Street, 781–9693; www.twinoaks ri.com). Just across the city line from Providence on Spectacle Pond, Twin Oaks is a local legend, pulling in big, hungry crowds all day long for its huge portions of delicious steaks, chops, seafood, and Italian favorites, all at reasonable prices. Unless you're a Rhode Island "somebody," the challenge here is to get a table, so coming at off-hours is recommended. If you love the tomato sauce—and most diners do—you can take home a jar as a tasty remembrance of your visit. Open Tuesday to Saturday 11:30 A.M. to 1:00 A.M., and Sunday noon to 12:30 A.M. From I-95 north or south, take Route 10 to the Reservoir Avenue

Central Falls

Every state has a community that seems to be the butt of all the local jokes, and the sad fact is that in Rhode Island that place is Central Falls, a heavily industrialized town that has weathered some hard economic times.

Such criticism is more than a little unfair, in my opinion. For example, although Central Fall's main artery, Broad Street, is no Rodeo Drive, it does feature one of the more interesting historic sites in Rhode Island: the Cogswell Tower (727–7474) in Jenks Park.

Built in 1890, the imposing tower was constructed on Dexter's Ledge, a site that played an important role in King Philip's War. From this spot in 1676, a local Indian tribe spotted a colonial raiding party approaching their village and ambushed the attackers along the Blackstone River. Pierce's Fight (named after the commander of the raiding party) ended in a rout, with the doomed colonists fleeing upriver to Cumberland followed by the natives in hot pursuit.

Climb the tower and you'll discover a panoramic view of hardworking Central Falls—not an idyllic landscape, perhaps, but interesting, nonetheless. Afterward, be sure to enjoy one of the restaurants that dot Dexter Street, especially Stanley's (535 Dexter Street, 726–9689), whose onion-slathered burgers were voted best in the Blackstone Valley by *Rhode Island Monthly.*

(Route 2) exit, bear right, make a right onto Pleasant Street, then follow signs to Sabra Street.

Cranston's ***Wein-O-Rama,*** located at 1009 Oaklawn Avenue/Route 5 (943–4990), is another one of those great old roadside attractions that locals love. A big neon sign promises a good, cheap meal, and this restaurant delivers. With a name like Wein-O-Rama, it's no surprise that hot wieners are a staple here, and a flavorful dog is just $1.25. (By the way, these are regular hot dogs, not the miniature, spicy wieners of the New York System shops found throughout Rhode Island.) Also on the menu are inexpensive sandwiches, burgers, and dinners; for instance, a breaded veal cutlet platter, which includes fries and coleslaw, will run you the princely sum of $4.75. Like the food, the decor at the Wein-O-Rama is simple, with a few booths along the windows and a lunch counter with revolving stools. Open Monday to Thursday 7:00 A.M. to 4:00 P.M., Friday 7:00 A.M. to 7:00 P.M., and Saturday 7:00 A.M. to 4:00 P.M.

Campanella's restaurant (930 Oaklawn Avenue, 943–3500) is Cranston's king of calzones: There are seventeen different varieties on the menu, stuffed with ingredients as diverse as tuna, chicken tenders, feta, and swiss cheese, as well as the more traditional meatballs, sausage, mozzarella, and ricotta. Expect to fight the crowds a little on a Friday or Saturday night, but it's well worth the wait when you break into the crust of one of Campanella's golden-brown creations. A variety of pizzas, pasta, salads, and three types of garlic bread fill out the menu. Open 4:00 to 9:30 P.M. on Monday, 11:00 A.M. to 9:30 P.M. Tuesday to Thursday, and 11:00 A.M. to 9:45 P.M. on Friday and Saturday.

Greek food is a bit hard to come by in Rhode Island, which is why I was delighted to stumble across the ***Athenian Restaurant*** (1240 Oaklawn Avenue, 463–6025), located in a nondescript building along a busy stretch of Route 5. There's nothing fancy about the Formica dining-room tables and big chafing dishes of food behind the counter, but this is obviously a popular local place with the workingman's lunch crowd. Orders are taken quickly at the register—another rarity in this often slow-paced state—and the busy manager frequently looks up to greet regulars by name. As for the food, well, I'm a sucker for a good gyro, and the Greek specialties served at the Athenian are served hot and tasty, with generous portions that typically include a big Greek salad covered in feta. Souvlaki, shish kebabs, and spinach pies also are on the menu along with staples like American chop suey and lasagna. Open Monday to Friday 9:00 A.M. to 7:00 P.M., Saturday 9:00 A.M. to 3:00 P.M.

The first time my wife and I tried to find ***Mike's Kitchen*** (170 Randall Street, 946–5320), we literally drove past the restaurant three times without ever spotting it: We ate elsewhere that night.

An Ode to the Ukulele

Anyone who came of age during the 1960s may be forgiven for thinking that the ukulele reached its artistic pinnacle in the hands of pop-culture icon Tiny Tim. But Cranston residents Sue Abbotson, David Wasser, and other dedicated volunteers at the Ukulele Hall of Fame Museum (www.ukulele.org) want you to know that the "uke" is a serious instrument, made famous by such luminaries as Roaring Twenties crooner Cliff Edwards (aka Ukulele Ike) and television pioneer Arthur Godfrey, who preferred the baritone uke.

The Ukulele Hall of Fame Museum stands at the vanguard of the previously unheralded uke subculture: In addition to inducting a total of nine ukulele pioneers into its pantheon, the nonprofit organization sponsors conferences; sells music, videos, and books; and publishes a journal.

An otherwise unremarkable house on Cranston Street (located, by incredible coincidence, down the street from the home of Tiny Tim's longtime manager) enshrines the plaques, ephemera, and rare instruments that make up the Ukulele Hall of Fame Museum while the membership searches for permanent digs. Sue and David welcome visitors who want to learn more about the music that plucks the strings of their heart; for a tour, call 461–1668 or e-mail orders@ukulele.org.

No, we're not directionally challenged: It's just that the restaurant is actually located in the Tabor-Franchi VFW Post, with no outside sign hinting at its dual purpose. But in-the-know locals flock to Mike's despite the modest surroundings because of chef Mike Lapizzere's fine straightforward cooking. Chicken a la Mike is a personal favorite—a fresh egg-battered cutlet stuffed with ham and cheese and baked with lemon and wine. More adventurous diners can try the tripe or other home-style Italian dishes, including squid with tomato sauce or whole stuffed artichokes. Plus there are plenty of the old standards—spaghetti and meatballs, tortellini Alfredo, and shrimp scampi.

The decor may be "1958 suburban patriotic"—as one wag put it—and the bar is run by the VFW, but don't be fooled into thinking that Mike's is some fly-by-night operation. The restaurant has been in business for more than twenty years, and positive word of mouth has generated a huge following. Get there early if you want to avoid a line and a wait (they don't take reservations). Open Monday to Saturday for lunch from 11:30 A.M. to 3:00 P.M. and for dinner Monday and Wednesday 5:00 to 8:30 P.M. To find Mike's, take Route 5 just north of Phenix Avenue; you'll pass a baseball field on your right, and the next right turn is Randall Avenue. The restaurant is in the VFW hall on the corner.

El Tapatio (355 Atwood Avenue; 944–2212; www.eltapatiocranston.com) has some of the best margaritas I've ever had, and the Mexican grub is pretty excellent as well. It's billed as a family restaurant, but with its big flat-panel TVs it's also a great place to hang out on a Sunday afternoon to watch a football game and snack on taquitos and diablo wings. The menu is pretty wide-ranging—even daring—with entrees like enchiladas stuffed with Dungeness crab and an excellent carne asada.

Cranston isn't exactly Rhode Island's most cosmopolitan city—the stereotype is that the town is populated by women with big hair and men with "wicked bad" New England accents. But *Efendi's Mediterranean Bar and Grill* (1255 Reservoir Avenue, 943–8800; www.efendisrestaurant.com) helps put that caricature to rest, with owner Efendi Atma serving up an interesting and challenging variety of Turkish, Middle Eastern, and Mediterranean dishes.

Decor is simple and prices are low, but Efendi manages to transport your senses of taste and smell to another continent (OK, a couple of other continents) with specialties like Isabel's Kapodoyka Pasta—served with a basic pesto sauce, roasted red peppers, kalamata olives, artichoke hearts, pine nuts, and Parmesan cheese—and Izgara Kofte, a Turkish dish with spiced ground beef, parsley, and onions topped with tzatziki sauce. Other menu staples include a variety of shish kebabs, grilled pizzas, and even some classic continental and New England dishes for the less well traveled. Open daily 11:00 A.M. to 10:00 P.M.

Edgewood Manor is a fabulously ornate, 1905 Greek Revival mansion that innkeeper Andrew Lombardi has transformed into a richly appointed bed-and-breakfast (232 Norwood Avenue, 781–0099; www.providence-lodging.com). From the moment you walk into the lobby with its coiffured ceiling and stylish woodstove, every room at Edgewood Manor is a unique visual treat, with decor ranging from art nouveau to Louis XIV. Breakfast is served in an Italian-style dining room with hand-carved walls, and Victorian guest rooms are individually decorated with rare antiques and include Jacuzzi baths and/or working fireplaces.

Edgewood Manor has eight guest rooms, all with private baths. The neighboring Newhall House, an 1892 Queen Anne Victorian, is also operated as a B&B by Lombardi and has six guest rooms, many with fireplaces and Jacuzzi baths. Room rates, including breakfast, range from $129 to $299 nightly.

Located on the border of Providence and the section of Cranston closest to Narragansett Bay, it's a short walk from Edgewood Manor to Roger Williams Park and Zoo. A bit farther south is *Pawtuxet Village,* founded in 1638. A small cluster of historic homes and public buildings, the village is located at the point where the Pawtuxet River meets the bay. (For more information, see the Kent County chapter.)

Johnston

Dame Farm (949–3657) is a reminder of an agrarian lifestyle that, while it flourished until the middle of the twentieth century, largely has been obscured and forgotten in this part of the state. Just 8 miles from the heart of downtown Providence, Dame Farm's mission is to help visitors understand how the food at their local supermarket is grown and harvested.

Owned by the state and operated by four generations of the Dame family, who still live here, Dame Farm raises tomatoes, peppers, eggplant, squash, and some of the state's best corn. Fall is the time for apple picking and, in October, Halloween pumpkins.

Not only can you buy fine produce (90 percent of which is grown on the farm) at reasonable prices, but also the Dames lead educational tours and demonstrate the planting, tilling, tending, and picking that such a harvest demands. Horse-drawn wagon and sleigh rides are offered June to November on Saturday and Sunday, and year-round by appointment.

Dame Farm is located on Brown Avenue, about halfway between Route 6/Hartford Avenue and Route 5/Greenville Avenue. The property is open year-round; the farm stand is open daily July through October, Monday to Saturday 8:30 A.M. to 6:00 P.M. and Sunday 9:30 A.M. to 5:00 P.M.

The eighteenth-century farm is next to **Snake Den State Park,** a large wooded preserve that lies beyond the fields of corn and vegetables. Trails into the oak/hickory forest, skirting two historic cemeteries, ponds, and a swamp, can be accessed on Route 6 by the Department of Environmental Management headquarters and along Brown Avenue.

Amid the auto body shops and modest homes lining Route 128/George Waterman Road in Johnston is a house that stands in sharp contrast to its surroundings. On a small, green patch along the busy road is the **Clemence-Irons House** (38 George Waterman Road, 295–1030; www.historicnewengland.org/visit/homes/clemence.htm), an example of seventeenth-century stone-ender architecture that is unique to Rhode Island.

Taken from a style of home building developed in western England, the Clemence-Irons House was constructed by erecting a massive limestone wall and chimney that anchor the rest of the wooden house. Built circa 1680, the house is one of fewer than half a dozen examples of this style left in Rhode Island. The unpainted exterior of the Clemence-Irons House is a real eye-grabber, while the interior is modestly furnished with a period bed and other pieces.

Listed on the National Register, the house is maintained by Historic New England and is open for tours by appointment. The house is located on Route 128 about 1 mile south of Route 44/Putnam Pike. Open June to October.

OTHER NOTEWORTHY ATTRACTIONS AND EVENTS IN PROVIDENCE AND VICINITY

John Brown House
Providence

Cathedral of St. John
Providence

First Baptist Meeting House in America
Providence

The Providence Atheneum
Providence

The Rhode Island School of Design Museum of Art
Providence

Roger Williams National Memorial
Providence

Roger Williams Park and Zoo
Providence

Convergence Arts Festival
Providence; June

Feast of St. Joseph
Federal Hill; May

While you're in Johnston, don't overlook *Il Piccolo* (1450 Atwood Avenue, 421–9843), an acclaimed Italian restaurant where style and fine cuisine belie the pedestrian, strip-mall locale. Open Tuesday to Friday 11:30 A.M. to 2:30 P.M. for lunch and 5:00 to 9:00 P.M. for dinner.

Places to Stay in Providence and Vicinity

(All Area Codes 401)

PROVIDENCE

C. C. Ledbetter Bed-and-Breakfast
326 Benefit Street
351–4699

The Old Court Bed-and-Breakfast
144 Benefit Street
751–2002

The Providence Biltmore
11 Dorrance Street
421–0700

The Providence Hilton
21 Atwells Avenue
831–3900

The Providence Marriott
1 Orms Street
272–2400

Radisson Hotel Providence Harbor
220 India Street
272–5577

The State House Inn
43 Jewett Street
351–6111

Westin Hotel
One West Exchange Street
598–8000

PAWTUCKET

Comfort Inn
2 George Street
723–6700

CRANSTON

Edgewood Manor
232 Norwood Avenue
781–0099

JOHNSTON

Sky-View Motor Inn
2880 Hartford Avenue
934–1188

Places to Eat in Providence and Vicinity

(All Area Codes 401)

PROVIDENCE

Al Forno
577 South Main Street
273–9760

Angelo's Civita Farnese
141 Atwells Avenue
621–8171

The Blue Grotto
210 Atwells Avenue
272–9030

Cafe Dolce Vita
59 Depasquale Avenue
331–8240

Cafe Nuovo
One Citizens' Plaza
421–2525

Camille's Roman Garden
71 Bradford Street
751–4812

The Capital Grille
1 Cookson Place
521–5600

Casa Christine
145 Spruce Street
453–6255

Caserta's Pizzeria
121 Spruce Street
272–3618

CAV
14 Imperial Place
751–9164

Coffee Exchange
207 Wickenden Street
273–1198

Fellini Pizzeria
166 Wickenden Street
751–6737

Gatehouse Restaurant
4 Richmond Square
521–9229

Haven Bros. Diner
Kennedy Plaza
861–7777

Hemenway's
121 South Main Street
351–8570

Hudson Street Market
68 Hudson Street
274–4540

Julian's
318 Broadway
861–1770

L'Elizabeth
285 South Main Street
861–1974

Mexico
948 Atwells Avenue
331–4985

New Rivers
7 Steeple Street
751–0350

Nick's on Broadway
259 Broadway
421–0286

O-Cha Cafe
221 Wickenden Street
421–4699

The Old Canteen
120 Atwells Avenue
751–5544

The Pot Au Feu
44 Custom House Street
273–8953

Rue de L'Espoir
99 Hope Street
751–8890

Scialo Bros. Bakery
257 Atwells Avenue
421–0986

Three Sisters
1074 Hope Street
273–7230

Walter's Restaurant
286 Atwells Avenue
273–2652

Wes's Rib House
38 Dike Street
421–9090

White Electric Coffee Shop
711 Westminster Street
453–3007

Z Bar and Grille
244 Wickenden Street
 831–1566

EAST PROVIDENCE

Madeira
288 Warren Avenue
431–1322

PAWTUCKET

Hose Company No. 6
636 Central Avenue
722–7220

Modern Diner
364 East Avenue
726–8390

CRANSTON

Caffe Itri
1686 Cranston Street
942–1970

Chelo's Beef Hearth
1275 Reservoir Avenue
942–7666

Twin Oaks
100 Sabra Street
781–9693

Wein-O-Rama
1009 Oaklawn Avenue
943–4990

JOHNSTON

Il Piccolo
1450 Atwood Avenue
421–9843

HELPFUL WEB SITES ABOUT PROVIDENCE AND VICINITY

Blackstone Valley Tourism Council
www.tourblackstone.com

City of Cranston
www.cranstonri.com

City of East Providence
www.eastprovidence.com

City of Pawtucket
www.pawtucketri.com

City of Providence
www.providenceri.com

Providence Chamber of Commerce
www.provchamber.com

Providence Historical Society
www.phs.org

Providence Preservation Society
www.ppsri.org

Providence/Warwick
Convention and Visitor's Bureau
www.goprovidence.com

Town of Johnston
www.johnston-ri.com

SELECTED CHAMBERS OF COMMERCE IN PROVIDENCE AND VICINITY

**Greater Providence
Chamber of Commerce**
30 Exchange Terrace
Providence 02903
521–5000

**East Providence
Chamber of Commerce**
850 Waterman Avenue
East Providence 02914
438–1212

Cranston Chamber of Commerce
48 Rolfe Square
Cranston 02910
785–3780

North Central Chamber of Commerce
1126 Hartford Avenue, Suite 201A
Johnston 02919
273–1310

Kent County and Western Rhode Island

Warwick

Warwick founder Samuel Gorton was an outcast among outcasts, whose belief in individualism apparently so bordered on anarchy that the notably tolerant Roger Williams—himself exiled from Massachusetts—ordered Gorton out of Providence. Gorton and his followers moved south during the 1640s and established their own settlement by the shores of Pawtuxet Cove, naming it after Gorton's protector, the Earl of Warwick.

Warwick's independent spirit once again was on display during the period immediately preceding the American Revolution, when local residents helped attack the grounded British revenue schooner HMS *Gaspee* in 1772. Stuck on a sandbar off present-day Gaspee Point, the ship was set upon by eight longboats full of men furious about the crown's tax-collecting practices. On June 9, 1772, in the first armed conflict of the war, the colonials attacked and captured the ship, offloaded her crew, and burned the *Gaspee* to the waterline. Each May and June, the village of **Pawtuxet** (www.pawtuxet.com) celebrates the first blow for freedom with the **Gaspee *Days Celebration,*** with displays by colonial militia units, craft fairs, dances, and a colonial muster along the Narragansett Parkway (access from

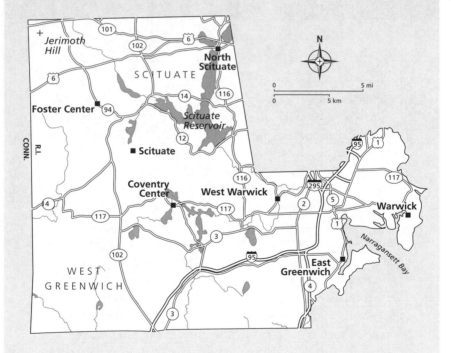

Route 117). For information contact the *Gaspee* Days Committee at P.O. Box 1772, Pilgrim Station, Warwick 02888, 781–1772, or visit its Web site: www .gaspee.com.

Pawtuxet was founded in 1638; the name is the Indian word for "little falls," and the town sits at the spot where the Pawtuxet River rushes over a small natural waterfall before meeting Narragansett Bay. The city of Warwick puts out a handsome handbook describing a comprehensive walking tour of Pawtuxet Village. The tour starts at the Pawtuxet Bridge, which spans the falls, and includes more than twenty homes and public buildings from the seventeenth, eighteenth, and nineteenth centuries. For a copy of the guide, contact the Warwick Economic Development Department's Tourism Office at 3275 Post Road, Warwick 02886; (800) 4–WARWICK; www.visitwarwickri.com.

Off Post Road in Pawtuxet is the entry to the 3-mile ***Pawtuxet River Loop Trail***, which runs along the river's edge to the back of the Rhodes on the Pawtuxet banquet hall on Narragansett Parkway.

The new ***O'Rourke's Bar and Grill*** (23 Peck Lane/Narragansett Parkway, 288–7444) has quickly built a reputation for hosting live Irish bands. The bar is located in one of Pawtuxet's many historic buildings, in this case an 1898 mansard-roofed building with a long history as a commercial center and tavern.

Like most of Rhode Island, Warwick enjoyed a period of prosperity during the Industrial Revolution. Some coastal areas of the town became popular summer destinations during the latter half of the nineteenth century, only to be devastated by the great hurricane of 1938. During the latter half of the twentieth century, Warwick settled into its role as a pleasant suburban community, home to Rhode Island's airport and its major shopping malls.

That said, many of Warwick's best places are along its Narragansett Bay coastline. ***Conimicut Point Park,*** located near the historic villages of Conimicut and Shawomet, offers a breathtaking panoramic view of the bay. The park has a beach and playground but otherwise is relatively small and ordinary, except for one spot. At the very tip of Conimicut Point is a sandbar that curves out into the bay, reaching for the offshore ***Conimicut Point Lighthouse.*** Parking your car at the end of the lot, you can walk out on the sandbar until it narrows to a thin, wet line of sand washed by waves from both sides. (A word of caution: The sandbar is relatively safe for adults in good weather, but storms and even passing ships can cause waves to inundate this fragile spit of land. Nonswimmers and children should not venture too far out.)

Looking straight ahead, you'll see that the sandbar continues, barely submerged, for a few hundred feet more, beyond where even the seagulls can stand. The tide surging madly over the barrier is impressive, and you now understand the need for the small lighthouse that stands watch a little farther out.

From this vantage point, you can look across to the homes lining the western shoreline of Warren and Bristol, down the bay to the wooded outline of Prudence Island and up toward the city of Providence, where the oil tanks of India Point and the skyscrapers of downtown are clearly visible.

Entrance to the park is free and open from dawn until sunset. To get there, take West Shore Road/Route 117 to Conimicut village; look for Economy Road on the east side of the street. Turn onto Economy Road, then bear left onto Symonds Avenue. When you come to Point Avenue, make a right; this will take you directly to the park entrance.

Warwick's Rocky Point Amusement Park was one of the oldest seaside fun parks in America until its sad demise in 1996. The midway has been silenced and the Shore Dining Hall closed down, but a few vestiges of the grand old park remain. One of these is the **Rocky Point Chowder House** (1759 Post Road, 739–4222), which carries on the tradition of serving hot, greasy bags full of Rocky Point's famous clam cakes, along with steaming bowls of chowder—white, red, and clear. The restaurant is open daily 11:00 A.M. to 9:00 P.M.

Farther north on Post Road is, in our opinion, one of Rhode Island's most underrated restaurants. While Providence earns its reputation as one of the premier dining cities in the country, don't overlook Warwick's **Portofino** (897 Post Road, 461–8920). Located in a simple storefront in humble surroundings, Portofino conjures up images of Italy that will quickly make you forget you're on a busy commercial strip. Try the Chicken Sorrentina, sautéed with mushrooms, artichoke hearts, and roasted red peppers covered with melted mozzarella, or indulge in the grilled portobello mushroom—a vegetable entree that even the

Sauce Is the Secret to Bakery Pizza

You need to be careful with your Rhode Island pizza, and that doesn't just mean avoiding spilling sauce on your shirt. Being a native of New York, where we like our pizza thin and cheesy, I was horrified to discover that some Ocean State natives considered thick-crusted, cheeseless pizza a delicacy. Rhode Island's bakery pizza soon won me over, however.

The secret, as you might imagine, is in the sauce, which should be slightly tart and oily enough to impart the proper sensation. As the name implies, you'll primarily find sheets of bakery pizza at neighborhood Italian bakeries, not pizza parlors, although there's no hard-and-fast rule. Bakery pizza is available throughout Rhode Island, but Warwick has more than its share of popular pizza purveyors. For an unexpected treat, visit Antonio's Home Bakery (2448 West Shore Road, 738–3727), or the Italian Bread Box (45 West Shore Road, 737–9842).

AUTHOR'S FAVORITES IN KENT COUNTY
AND WESTERN RHODE ISLAND

Pawtuxet Village	Nathaniel Greene Homestead
East Greenwich	George B. Parker Woodland

most ardent meat eater must respect. Open for dinner Tuesday to Saturday 5:00 to 10:00 P.M. and 3:00 to 8:00 P.M. on Sunday.

Once Samuel Gorton's westernmost settlement, **Apponaug** grew up to become a shipping port involved in manufacturing and molasses-for-rum-for-slaves commerce of the triangle trade, thanks to the protected cove that snakes its way into the center of town. Although Apponaug has become a busy cross-roads in a congested part of Warwick, vestiges of the past remain along Post Road. Next to Warwick's 1894 Town Hall is the **Warwick Museum of Art** (3259 Post Road, 737–0010; www.WarwickMuseum.org), located in the historic Kentish Artillery Armory. Rotating exhibits feature works by regional artists, and the museum also hosts evening dramatic and musical performances, from fla-menco guitar concerts to belly-dancing shows. The museum is open Tuesday to Saturday noon to 5:00 P.M.

Also in Apponaug is the **Crow's Nest**, (288 Arnolds Neck Drive, off Post Road/Route 1 just south of Route 117, 732–6575), an out-of-the-way restaurant that attracts fans of fresh seafood and budget-conscious diners alike. Voted best cheap eats by the readers of *Rhode Island Monthly*, the Crow's Nest also can boast of a nice view of Apponaug Cove and excellent, if straightforward, seafood dishes such as fried clams, stuffed shrimp, baked fish, and broiled lobster. Best of all, you can get a generous portion of fish and chips along with a bowl of creamy, meaty chowder served with three fat, round clam cakes for under $12.

Understandably, the Crow's Nest is a local favorite, and it tends to be busy even on weeknights during the summer. Seniors flock here, as do sailing fam-ilies coming off boats docked at the Ponaug Marina across the street. Free pop-corn at the bar helps pass the time, or you can cross Arnolds Neck Drive and admire the boats and the bay from a small, unmarked boardwalk with built-in wooden tables and seats. The Crow's Nest is open 11:30 A.M. to 10:00 P.M. week-days, 11:30 A.M. to 10:30 P.M. on Friday and Saturday. The restaurant is closed for four weeks beginning mid-January.

The problem with most "museum houses" is that they look and feel like, well, museums. But step through the doors of the 1877 granite-walled Victorian at **Clouds Hill Farm** (884–4550; entrance off Post Road directly across from the Kimberly apartment complex; www.cloudshill.org) and you get the distinct impression that the original owners have simply stepped out and might return at any moment.

Built by industrialist William Smith Slater as a wedding gift to his daughter, Elizabeth, upon her marriage to Alfred A. Reed Jr., this formidable mansion sits on a ledge with fantastic views of Narragansett Bay: On a clear day from the third-floor billiards parlor, you can see all the way to Mount Hope Bay and Fall River. Anne Holst, the current owner, is an eleventh great-granddaughter of Rhode Island founder Roger Williams and a fourth-generation owner of Clouds Hill.

Because the home has remained in the same family for more than a century—a family that Holst describes as "pack rats"—it is stuffed with all the ephemera of everyday life as well as wonderfully ornate period furnishings. Most of the front of the house has been left untouched, including a music room with Egyptian furniture and wall coverings, original curtains, a gas chandelier, and an 1877 Steinway grand piano. Japanese straw matting—used as cushioning and for sound absorption—remains visible under the fine Oriental rugs.

The Java Room, the largest bedroom, is filled with jars and other gifts presented to Reed's father by the king of Siam. A child's bedroom upstairs has bookcases filled with vintage storybooks, and old board games and a rusty train set look as though they've just been played with.

The back of the house still features separate quarters for the maids and household staff, while the basement conceals a highly volatile naphtha-gas system once used to light the house (rare, experts say, since most homes so equipped either burned down or exploded). Even the primitive, telegraph-operated burglar alarm remains.

Clouds Hill Farm is open for group tours by appointment and also for occasional events: The annual candlelight music tour is held on the second weekend of December. Tours include costumed guides and volunteers portraying family members and servants.

Next, take Route 117 east from Apponaug and bear right onto Long Street just after you pass under the railroad bridge. Follow Long Street until it intersects with Buttonwoods Avenue, then continue straight onto Asylum Road. At the end of Asylum Road you'll find one of Warwick's true hidden treasures: **Warwick City Park.** Almost unknown except to locals, City Park is a beautiful, wooded, 126-acre thumb of land thrust between Buttonwoods Cove and Break Neck Cove. Some of the land is given over to ball fields and the like, but much of it remains wooded. Tracing the perimeter of the park is a serpentine jogging and biking path, which affords frequent views of the water as it mean-

Oakland Beach

Like many seaside communities of the nineteenth century, Warwick was blessed to have its share of amusement parks and grand shore hotels—places where people could escape the summer heat in the days when air-conditioning was a distant dream.

One of these icons of a bygone era was Rocky Point Amusement Park, which survived for more than a century before succumbing to bankruptcy in 1996. For the time being, Rocky Point's cavernous Shore Dining Hall still stands watch over Narragansett Bay, but the old park's rides have been sold off.

The smaller amusement park at Warwick's Oakland Beach came to a similar end years ago. Once the site of the grand Oakland Beach Hotel, today this peninsula off Route 117 (take 117 east from Apponaug, past the intersections with Buttonwoods Avenue and Route 113; make a right on to Oakland Beach Avenue) still has a small public beach (better for strolling than swimming) and a cluster of seaside restaurants. Traditional seafood is on the menu at Cherrystone's (898 Oakland Beach Avenue, 732–2532). By the way, actor Brad Pitt ate at Cherrystone's during the filming of *Meet Joe Black* in Warwick.

If you happen to be in town for the Fourth of July, Oakland Beach is one of the best places to view the fireworks around the bay.

ders through forest and up and down some challenging hills (the path makes some sharp turns and can be narrow in spots, so watch your speed).

In Rhode Island, few things say summer like doughboys—the smell of the little balls of dough cooking in a fryer stimulates visions of crashing waves and sunbathers baking in the sun. So it's appropriate that both locations of the famous **Iggy's Doughboys** (889 Oakland Beach Avenue, Warwick, 737–9459; and 1157 Point Judith Road, Narragansett, 783–5608; www.iggysdoughboys .com) are within a Frisbee's throw of the beach.

The original at Oakland Beach has been around since 1924, when it was called Gus's, and claims to be the oldest beach stand in the state. It's a given that on a hot summer evening the lines at Iggy's takeout window will be snaking around the compact brick building, but the sugar-sprinkled doughboys, thick and creamy chowder, and fresh fried seafood are well worth the wait (you can send the kids to the playground next door while you shuffle forward). It's open year-round: Winter hours are Sunday to Thursday 11:00 A.M. to 7:00 P.M. and Friday and Saturday 11:00 A.M. to 8:00 P.M.; summer hours are Sunday to Thursday 11:00 A.M. to 10:00 P.M. and Friday and Saturday 11:00 A.M. to 11:00 P.M.

West Warwick

West Warwick is a small, densely populated former mill town whose downtown is most familiar to Rhode Islanders for its motor vehicle registry office. But West Warwick also has plenty of history: The town is home to the state's first stone cotton mill and Rhode Island's oldest Catholic church (**St. Mary's** on Church Street was built in 1844 and is listed on the National Register).

West Warwick's unassuming **Qué Pasa** (49 Providence Street, 828–7573) is helping to make West Warwick known more for plates of delicious Mexican food and less for license plates. Although its ads boast of "Mexican Food American Style," Qué Pasa has won food lovers over with its more traditional dishes, such as Arroz Yucatan, a seafood dish that includes whitefish and shrimp sautéed in red wine with peas and red peppers and served over rice.

Of course, if you want chips smothered in cheese with salsa for dipping, they have that, too, along with chilled margaritas to wash it down and cut the spice. For dessert, try the fried ice cream covered with honey, whipped cream, and cherries. Open Sunday and Tuesday to Thursday 11:00 A.M. to 10:00 P.M., Friday and Saturday 11:00 A.M. to 11:00 P.M. Closed Monday.

Tangy's Indoor Archery Lanes (1237 Main Street, 826–6262; www .tangysarchery.com), has fourteen lanes open to beginners and experienced

Warwick's Route 2: A Mixed Blessing for Shoppers

Warwick's Route 2 (aka Quaker Lane) is both a blessing and a curse for shoppers. The good news is that the Warwick Mall and the Rhode Island Mall are located on Route 2, both near the junction with Route 113. Numerous major retail giants, from the Sports Authority to CompUSA, also have stores located along the stretch of Route 2 running roughly from Route 113 south to Route 3. Between Route 117 and Route 3 is the Christmas Tree Shops, a year-round mecca for bargain shoppers from across the state. Still farther south is the state's largest movie theater, the Showcase Cinemas, at the interchange with I–95.

The bad news? Traffic—lots of traffic. Especially on weekends, Route 2 can resemble a parking lot, and conditions can be particularly bad where the road narrows just south of Route 113. Best advice for avoiding problems on busy days: To get to the malls, take I–95 south to the Route 113 exit or I–95 to I–295 to the appropriate mall exit. If you then want to visit the stores farther south, jump back on I–95 south one exit to Route 117 west, which soon intersects back with Route 2, or go one more exit to the Route 2 off-ramp, which is where the movie theater and restaurants like Outback Steakhouse, Ruby Tuesday's, and McDonald's are located.

The Station Fire

On the cold night of February 20, 2003, hundreds of patrons were packed into The Station nightclub in West Warwick to see the '80s metal band Great White perform. As the band began playing, a pyrotechnics display lit up the stage, sparking a fire that quickly spread to flammable foam soundproofing materials and to the low roof of the former restaurant building. Within minutes, The Station was engulfed in flames and smoke. One hundred people died, and many others were burned and scarred for life.

Today, nothing remains of The Station building at 211 Cowesett Avenue, but that does not mean the victims have been forgotten. In addition to a huge outpouring of support from Rhode Islanders—each of whom seemed to know someone who was in the club that awful night—and the music community, the victims have been remembered by a makeshift memorial on the nightclub site almost from the moment the flames were extinguished. Drive by the site and you'll see crosses, mementos, and other items memorializing the victims. Plans also are in the works for a permanent memorial for the site. For information contact the Station Fire Memorial Foundation at P.O. Box 513, Coventry, 02816 or visit www.stationfirememorialfoundation.org.

bowhunters alike. The front of the shop is divided between a fifteen-lane, 60-foot target range and a shop selling compound and recurve bows, arrows, and custom strings. During the fall hunting season, there's a wildlife target range where archers can take aim at plastic pheasants, bobcats, deer, and other woodland creatures hiding in an artificial forest.

Lane rentals are $14 per hour for adults and $11 per hour for children. Beginners are welcome, and owner Jim Dean recommends either a $15, fifteen-minute lesson plus fifteen minutes on the lane to get the basics of archery down or a $45, one-hour private lesson ($25 for youths) that allows time to work on bow skills and techniques. Tangy's also runs youth and adult leagues and tournaments. From September through April, open Monday to Friday from 6:00 to 10:00 P.M. and Saturday and Sunday from 1:00 to 5:00 P.M. From May through August, open 6:00 to 9:00 P.M. Tuesday to Friday, Saturday 1:00 to 5:00 P.M.

Scituate

The story of the ***Scituate Reservoir*** is, in some ways, the story of the town of Scituate. Needing a stable supply of drinking water for the city of Providence, the state in 1915 claimed 13,000 acres in the heart of Scituate (whose name comes from a Native American word meaning cold running water) and built a huge dam on the Pawtuxet River. The subsequent filling of the river valley created the largest body of fresh water in the state, but under the waters of the reservoir are the remains of six villages that were condemned in the process. (The residents, happily, were moved out first.)

If you look at a map of Scituate, the reservoir sprawls across town like a giant, crooked letter V. At the right tip of the V is the town of *North Scituate,* located at the crossroads of the Danielson Pike (Route 6) and Route 116. Although it is the largest community in this rural town, North Scituate is a sleepy little place for most of the year. It's always a pleasant place to stroll, and you can easily walk to the picturesque *Horseshoe Dam* from the village center.

The town really comes alive on Columbus Day weekend, however, for the annual *Scituate Art Festival.* Whereas the more famous Wickford Art Festival primarily attracts painters and sculptors, the Scituate festival includes more craftspeople, making for an eclectic group of displays spread around street corners, churchyards, and lawns up and down the streets of town. A drive to the festival is also a good excuse to go leaf-peeping as the local forests explode with color when cool fall weather approaches. Contact the Scituate Art Festival, Inc., at info@scituateartfestival.org or see www.scituateartfestival.org.

About a mile north of the town of North Scituate is the *Seagrave Memorial Observatory* (47 Peep Toad Road), a half minute west of Route 116 on the right side of the road. Here astronomers gather on cloudless nights to gaze at the stars and other heavenly bodies. The observatory, built in 1914 by amateur astronomer Frank Evans Seagrave on the grounds of his Scituate estate, was later purchased by the Amateur Astronomy Society of Rhode Island, now known as Skyscrapers, Inc. (www.theskyscrapers.org).

The observatory has four telescopes, including the historic 1878 8¼-inch Alvan Clark Telescope housed in the observatory dome. On a cloudless night these telescopes are powerful enough to give you a clear view of the rings of Saturn and atmospheric storms on Jupiter, as well as deep-sky objects like nebulae and distant galaxies. Since the club is composed of astronomy buffs, there's always somebody around to tell you what you're looking at.

Skyscrapers is a membership organization that holds regular meetings and outings, but it also opens the observatory to the public every Saturday night. The observatory opens at dusk and stays open for as long as someone wants to use the telescope, sometimes as late as 11:30 P.M. There are other special public events throughout the year, and children are always welcome. Tours can be arranged by appointment.

Route 116 heading south of North Scituate is a great drive, with the silver glint of sun on water a constant companion as you skirt the edge of the reservoir. For breathtaking vistas of the reservoir, you can take the right turn at the Plainfield Pike (Route 14) to the *Ashland Causeway,* a narrow half-mile berm with water on both sides; or keep driving south on Route 116 to Route 12,

A Fall Stroll in Scituate

On a picture-perfect New England autumn afternoon my family took a drive up to Scituate to enjoy the fall foliage, which typically peaks by early to mid-October. Unsatisfied with the view from the car window, we pulled off Route 116 just south of Scituate Avenue (Route 12) into a small parking lot on the west side of the road. Leaving our car, we followed a few small groups of people headed down a well-trodden path under a leafy canopy of gold, red, and orange.

One of the few places around the Scituate Reservoir where human intrusion is permitted (access is otherwise restricted to maintain the purity of the state's drinking-water supply), this wooded road is a fairly easy hike for all but the youngest and frailest travelers, although by the end I was carrying my then three-year-old daughter on my shoulders. From the parking lot, you follow a main trail that proceeds west into the woods and then offers you the choice of turning north toward the dam. Taking this northerly jog will bring you swiftly to Route 12, where you'll exit the woods just at the eastern end of the huge dam that holds back the reservoir waters. There's a cutout on the north side of the road where you can linger for a quick snack or for pictures (my son found a snakeskin on a rock here) before retracing your steps back to your car.

where a right turn takes you to the mile-long *Ganier Memorial Dam,* whose construction created the reservoir. A spillway a little farther east feeds the Pawtuxet River, which meanders south from the reservoir through West Warwick before emptying into Narragansett Bay near the Warwick village of Pawtuxet.

East Greenwich

East Greenwich is a great little town for shopping, dining, or just walking around. Route 1 is Main Street in East Greenwich, yet despite such a central location the town appears in few tourist guides, which tend to focus on nearby Wickford. Don't you make the same mistake, because downtown East Greenwich definitely is worth a visit.

If you want history, East Greenwich has it on Pierce Street (which runs parallel to Main Street) in the form of the *General James Mitchell Varnum House* (57 Pierce Street, 884–1776; www.varnumcontinentals.org). Built in 1773, this mansion belonged to another Rhode Islander who, like the better-known Nathaniel Greene, became a general in George Washington's Continental army. Varnum was the first commander of the Kentish Guards, an elite unit that later was headquartered at the *Armory of the Kentish Guards,* built in 1842 at 80 Pierce Street. Early weapons and a collection of more than 200 posters from the Second World War can be found at the **Varnum Military Museum,** open by appointment at 6 Main Street (884–4110).

The Varnum mansion is fully furnished with period items and is open June through August, Saturday and Sunday 10:00 a.m. to 4:00 P.M. and by appointment.

Walking the streets of town, you will pass many fine antiques stores and bridal shops as well as some interesting specialty stores. The **Robin's Nest Gift Shoppe** (36 Main Street) has a selection of hand-dipped candles and crafts and a huge assortment of Boyd's collectibles (open Tuesday to Saturday 9:00 A.M. to 5:00 P.M., Fridays till 7:00 P.M.), while the **Chocolate Delicacy** (219 Main Street, 884–4949; 800–MRWONKA) threatens your waistline with homemade chocolates, fudge, and truffles. Open Monday to Friday 10:00 A.M. to 6:00 P.M. and Saturday 10:00 A.M. to 5:00 P.M.

The **Green Door** (130 Main Street, 885–0510; www.thegreendoorathome .com) lives up to its billing as "a unique shopping experience"—everything in the store seems to be a one-of-a-kind treasure, from Herend porcelain to vintage tablecloths and owner Susan Swanson's own floral arrangements. The store's disparate offerings are highlighted by a display case full of hand-painted porcelain boxes, called Limoges after their birthplace in France. It's open Monday to Saturday 10:00 A.M. to 5:00 P.M.

As early as 1917 there was a diner at 145 Main Street, and the Worcester Dining Car Company diner that presently houses **Jigger's Diner** (884–5388) was moved here in 1950. For nearly a decade, however, the diner sat stripped and vacant until former owner Carol Shriner renovated it and reopened for business in 1992. On any given day you're likely to find owner Iva Reynhout— who bought the business in March 2000—working the grill in this quaint little spot that is very popular for breakfast and lunch among locals, who will gladly stand and wait for a precious booth or a seat on one of the red stools lining the counter.

Jigger's has excellent omelettes, pancakes, and waffles for breakfast, but the house specialty is its authentic, hot-off-the-griddle Rhode Island jonnycakes. State law allows Jigger's to use the traditional spelling to refer to its jonnycakes (no "h") because they are made from rare white flint corn grown by Iva's father, Rodney Bailey. Open Monday through Friday 6:00 A.M. to 2:00 P.M., Saturday and Sunday 6:00 A.M. to 1:00 P.M., and Wednesday to Monday from 5:00 to 8:00 P.M. for gourmet dinners that defy the pedestrian setting.

The **Savory Grape Wine Shop** (247 Main Street, 866–9463; www.the savorygrape.com) provides a warm welcome to oneophiles and wine novices alike. Owners Jessica and Nino Granatiero have carefully arranged a selection of fine wines (including some of the better wines from Rhode Island and elsewhere in Southern New England) that largely avoids the "same old" labels you'll find in your corner liquor store.

Sure, there are $80 (and up) bottles of wine on the shelves, but equal care has gone into picking the wines on the $11-and-under table. If you're planning to dine at the nearby (and BYOB) Jigger's Diner, the Savory Grape's helpful staff will help you pick out a wine to complement your meal.

Wines at the Savory Grape are uniquely arranged by body, not region, making it easier for nonexperts to shop for the style of wine they prefer. The shop also offers the public a chance to sample something new every Friday and Saturday night, when the shop's private tasting room offers wine and hors d'oeuvres. Open Monday to Saturday 11:00 A.M. to 9:30 P.M. and noon to 5:00 P.M. on Sunday.

Altogether, East Greenwich has more than a dozen restaurants to choose from, ranging from the pizza-and-a-cola offerings at *Frank and John From Italy* (186 Main Street, 884–9751; open Monday to Thursday 3:00 to 10:00 P.M., Friday and Saturday 3:00 to 11:00 P.M.) to the abundance of lunch and breakfast joints like *Audra's Cafe* (315 Main Street, 884–4441), where everything on the menu—from broiled chicken to old-fashioned meatloaf—rings in under $7.50. Open Monday to Saturday 6:00 A.M. to 2:00 P.M. and Sunday 6:00 A.M. to 1:00 P.M. But perhaps the town's most intriguing restaurant is located at the very north end of downtown. The *Post Office Cafe* (11 Main Street, 885–4444; http://pinellimarrarestaurant.com/postoffice.htm) is just what it sounds like: a restaurant in a former post office. In this case, the former post office is a grand brick edifice built in 1934, and the owners have tried to retain as many vestiges of its original function as possible. The acoustics provided by the 20-foot ceiling in the foyer complement the live music on Friday night and for Sunday brunch. Along the walls are the old tellers' cages, their cherrywood finish buffed to a warm glow.

The dining room, in a refurbished mail-sorting area, features an innovative menu emphasizing Northern Italian veal and seafood dishes. Open Tuesday through Thursday 4:30 to 9:30 P.M., Friday and Saturday 4:30 to 10:30 P.M., and Sunday 10:30 A.M. to 2:30 P.M. for brunch.

The owners of the Post Office Cafe also run the *Grille on Main,* a less tony alternative located across the street (50 Main Street, 885–2200; http://pinelli marrarestaurant.com/grille.htm). The publike interior, dominated by wood paneling and large mirrors, is warm and inviting. The menu features sandwiches, pizza, pastas, seafood, and a buttery calamari that's out of this world. The kitchen is open Sunday to Tuesday 11:30 A.M. to 10:00 P.M., Wednesday and Thursday 11:30 A.M. to 11:00 P.M., Friday and Saturday 11:30 A.M. to midnight. The bar is open Wednesday to Saturday until 1:00 A.M.

Even though East Greenwich is one of Rhode Island's most affluent communities, its downtown has not typically been a bastion of fine dining. That has been changing in the last few years, however, and the trend was cemented when the popular but run-of-the-mill Kent Restaurant gave way to **Trattoria Del Corso** (223 Main Street, 398–2905). The creation of young-but-ambitious chef/co-owners Aaron Edwards and Mark Scott, the restaurant has won multiple statewide dining honors during its brief existence.

The menu covers the sweep of Italian cookery, leaning toward the lighter southern cuisine during the summer and the heartier northern dishes in the winter. The quieter upstairs dining room is a joy in the warmer months, when balcony doors are thrown open to let in the cool sea breezes; downstairs is more of a bistro/bar atmosphere. Early bird dinner specials, served Monday to Thursday from 4:30 to 6:30 P.M., include appetizer, drinks, and entrees like grilled salmon and chicken marsala for $18.95 per person. Open Monday to Thursday 4:30 to 10:00 P.M., Friday and Saturday 5:00 to 11:00 P.M.

As you walk toward the south end of downtown East Greenwich, you're liable to notice the aromatic signature of the **Indian Club** (455 Main Street, 884–7100; www.theindianclub.com) before you spy the restaurant itself. The large, popular dining room of this relative newcomer to Main Street features fine Indian cuisine, including a large selection of breads, rice specialties, tandoori dishes, and entrees featuring curried chicken, lamb, beef, and vegetables, as well as more exotic offerings. Open Sunday to Thursday 5:00 to 9:00 P.M. for dinner, Tuesday to Saturday 11:30 A.M. to 2:00 P.M. for lunch, and Friday to Sunday 5:00 to 10:00 P.M. for dinner.

Good Mexican restaurants are a relative rarity in Rhode Island, making **Tio Mateo's** (537 Main Street, 886–1973; www.tiomateos.com) a welcome addition to East Greenwich's dining scene. The storefront location in CVS Plaza is pretty underwhelming, and the bulk of the restaurant's business is take-out. But the small dining room is bright and pleasant, and owner Matt (Mateo) Wronski does the little things right: his cooks are from Hidalgo, homemade and super-fresh ingredients are used in all the dishes, and the prices are right: You'll be hardpressed to spend more than $10 for lunch or dinner here. Open Monday to Thursday 11:00 A.M. to 8:00 P.M., Friday and Saturday 11:00 A.M. to 9:00 P.M.

Completely renovated in 1995, the **East Greenwich Town Hall** (125 Main Street) was built in 1804 and formerly served as the Kent County Courthouse, one of the five original state houses built in Rhode Island. Two other restoration projects have added even more spark and diversity to East Greenwich. For years the once-popular **Greenwich Odeum** movie theater (59 Main Street, 885–9119; www.greenwichodeum.org) was shuttered, killed off by competition from the multiplex that opened just down the road on the corner of Route 401 and Route 2. However, a group of preservationists brought the old vaudeville house back to life as a nonprofit theater featuring performances by national as well as local performers like the Academy Players.

Founder Steve Erinakes, whose family ran the Odeum for more than forty years, describes the present enterprise as total theater, with fare running the gamut from plays to ballet, opera, and live jazz and country music. Recent performances included concerts by folk singers Janis Ian and Patty Larkin and the Rhode Island Comedy Festival. Built in 1926, the 410-seat theater holds performances year-round during the week and on weekends; call for times and ticket prices.

Turning the corner from Main Street onto Queen Street, you'll pass under a railroad bridge and come out on Water Street, which hugs the shoreline of Greenwich Cove and is lined with marinas and restaurants. For fine dockside dining try **Twenty Water Street** (885–3700; www.twentywaterstreet.com), which has a nice deck that's open during the summertime. The formal dining room is open daily during the summer and on weekends during the winter. Open daily 11:30 A.M. to 10:00 P.M. The adjoining **Warehouse Tavern** also serves food and stays open late for libations. Nearby **Harbourside Lobster-mania** (Water Street, 884–6363; www.harboursideri.com) specializes in lobsters, seafood, and steaks and also has drinking and dancing till the wee hours. A pair of outdoor bars provide a local hot spot from April to October. Open Monday to Saturday 11:30 A.M. to 1:00 A.M. and Sunday noon to 1:00 A.M.

Meritage (5454 Post Road, 884–1255) is located on a residential stretch of Post Road just south of downtown East Greenwich, but the environment in this stylish eatery and bar is strictly urban contemporary. The decor is sleek and understated, the kind of place where young, upscale singles meet over grilled pizza and expertly mixed cosmopolitans. Yet prices at Meritage don't require an expense account: the restaurant offers half-price pizzas and appetizers in the lounge during happy hour and late nights every day of the week. Come on Sunday or Monday, and you'll get a bottle of house wine free with dinner for two. Open Sunday to Tuesday 4:30 to 11:00 P.M., Wednesday and Saturday 4:30 to 11:30 P.M., and Friday 4:00 to 11:30 P.M. The bar is open nightly until 1:00 A.M.

Every Rhode Island town has at least one no-frills, high-value restaurant where locals go for seafood and Italian food—a combination that may sound strange to foreign ears, but raises nary an eyebrow hereabouts. In East Greenwich, that restaurant is **Pal's** (43 Division Street, 884–9701).

Located in a residential neighborhood on the water side of Main Street, Pal's has been feeding hungry families for nearly seventy years (Rhode Island

Gov. Don Carcieri, an East Greenwich resident, is a frequent diner). The decor hasn't changed much since the 1930s, and one suspects the same of many of the dinner choices. The deal of the evening is the pasta with meat sauce, meatballs, or sausage (served with bread and soup or salad) for $8.95; the more indulgent may want to go ahead and "splurge" on the $14.95 shrimp scampi with broccoli and mushrooms—the specialty of the house. Open Monday 4:00 to 9:00 P.M., Tuesday and Wednesday 11:30 A.M. to 9:00 P.M., Thursday to Saturday 11:30 A.M. to 10:00 P.M., and Sunday 2:30 to 9:00 P.M.

Like moths drawn to a candle, area residents flock to the neon glow of the *Hilltop Creamery* (5720 Post Road, 884–8753) on warm summer nights. Once, the Hilltop Creamery was a mandatory stop for ice cream before catching a movie at the Hilltop Drive-In across the street. Sadly, the drive-in is now just a memory, but the Creamery lives on. The soft-serve is particularly good here; for a treat try Kay's Famous Torch, a cone-inside-a-cone creation topped with a little American flag. The prices are right, too. You can still get a small cone for under a buck. Open April to October Monday to Thursday noon to 9:00 P.M. and until 10:30 P.M. Friday to Sunday; open till 10:00 P.M. on summer weeknights.

Conquering Jerimoth Hill

People who have climbed Washington's Mount Rainier (14,410 ft.) and Alaska's Mount McKinley (20,320 ft.) to pursue the claim of having stood at the highest point of every U.S. state have long been stymied in their quest by dinky Jerimoth Hill.

Rhode Island's highest point, Jerimoth Hill, stands a grand 812 feet above sea level—and in testament to man's ability to put up barriers more insurmountable than those of the natural world. The summit of Jerimoth Hill is just 100 feet south of Route 101 in Foster, but access to the spot is blocked by private property, and for years the owner adamantly refused to allow hikers to cross his land. The actual summit is owned by Brown University, but the school also refused to cooperate with groups like the Highpointers Club in allowing hikers access to the state's highest spot.

In frustration, the Highpointers (www.highpointers.org) eventually decided to allow members to claim to have conquered Rhode Island's top peak simply by standing next to the Jerimoth Hill sign alongside Route 101.

Prior to his death in 2001, however, property owner Henry Richardson began allowing hikers to climb Jerimoth Hill a few days each year. In 2005, new owners Jeff and Deb Mosley allowed the Highpointers to build a new trail to the summit, and continue to allow access every weekend, marking a new "high point" in relations between the Highpointers and the keepers of Rhode Island's topographic pinnacle.

Despite its industrial theme, the **New England Wireless and Steam Museum** (885–0545; http://users.ids.net/~newsm) sits on a peaceful country lane at Place's Corner, an otherwise obscure crossroads. Devoted to the science of engineering, the museum features exhibits on early radio, telegraph, and television equipment, as well as engines powered by steam, gas, and oil. There's a collection of telegraph machines that were used from the mid-nineteenth century to the early twentieth century, and George H. Corliss steam engines with giant flywheels, built right here in Rhode Island in the 1880s. Each fall the annual **Steam Up** sees the giant engines hissing and spinning as they are turned on in an impressive display of power. The museum is located at 1300 Frenchtown Road and is open by appointment from May to October. Thursday is volunteer day, so call between 9:00 A.M. and 4:30 P.M. to talk with a live person. Admission is $15.00 per adult and $5.00 for children under twelve.

Although East Greenwich has experienced a building boom in recent years, with developments of large executive homes springing up across the landscape, some parts of town retain their rural character. One such place is **Davisville Memorial Wildlife Refuge** (www.asri.org/davis.htm), where you can follow a path along the Hunt River to a small pond popular for fishing in season. To get to the park, take Route 4 south to the exit for Routes 402 and 403, then bear left onto Route 403 (Devils Foot Road). After you come off the highway ramp, the park will be on your right.

West Greenwich

Home to major chunks of the 13,817-acre **Arcadia Management Area** and the 8,319-acre **Big River Wildlife Management Area,** West Greenwich is well known to hunters, hikers, and mountain bikers, but isn't exactly the cultural or culinary hot spot of Rhode Island. Perhaps that's why the sign for the **Big River Inn** (809 Nooseneck Hill Road, 397–2281), located on a dark stretch of Route 3, looks so inviting.

But the hilltop restaurant, built in 1913 as a fine hotel, is more than just the only game in town: The interior is freshly remodeled, and the classic American food—while hardly *haute cuisine*—is fresh, well presented, and satisfying. On many nights, you'll also find a psychic and tarot card reader at a corner table engaged in after-dinner prognostication. Walk-ups are welcome, but it's best to call the restaurant for an appointment if you're looking for feedback on the future that's more detailed than a fortune cookie. Open Monday to Thursday 4:00 to 10:00 P.M. and Friday to Sunday noon to 11:00 P.M. The adjoining bar is open till 1:00 A.M.

Coventry

Rhode Island native Gen. Nathaniel Greene was a Revolutionary War hero of the first rank, but his name is not one you automatically associate with Rhode Island. Greene was George Washington's second in command and played crucial roles in both the Battle of Trenton and the Battle of Yorktown, two decisive victories of the war. After the war the Georgia legislature—grateful to Greene for driving the British out of the state—gave the general a plantation in Savannah, where he moved from his home in Coventry in 1785. Greene died soon afterward and was buried in Georgia, and the Peach State held onto the bulk of Greene's legacy.

Fortunately, Rhode Island got to keep the house where Greene lived for many years and entertained such visitors as Lafayette and General Rochambeau and his French army. The ***Nathaniel Greene Homestead*** (50 Taft Street, 821–8630; www.geocities.com/gmierka/index2.html) strives to educate visitors about Greene's place in Rhode Island history. The Greenes were Rhode Island pioneers: The general's father and brother built and operated one of the first triphammer forges in the country, making iron products such as the doorknobs, hinges, and tools used in colonial homes. The remains of the forge are still visible if you walk down a quiet path behind the Greene house to the banks of the Pawtuxet River. Historians believe the cannon sitting on the lawn of the homestead also was cast in the Greene forge.

Inside the circa 1770 "Spell Hall," period furniture—some passed down from the Greene family—is used to approximate how the rooms might have been furnished in General Greene's time. Some of the artifacts in the house actually belonged to the general and his wife, Catherine Littlefield Greene. After General Greene's death, Catherine, who spent most of the war raising the couple's four children while her husband was off fighting, used the government

Nathaniel Greene Homestead

pension money she was granted to support Eli Whitney's successful development of the cotton gin.

Also on the homestead property is a historic cemetery marking the final resting place of many generations of Greenes, their servants, and their slaves. The Nathaniel Greene Homestead is open from April to October 31 Wednesday and Saturday 10:00 A.M. to 5:00 P.M. and Sunday 1:00 to 5:00 P.M. Tours also are available by appointment. Admission is $3.00 for adults and $1.00 for students. To get to the site, take Route 95 to Route 117 West; just after crossing the town line into Coventry, make a left on Laurel Avenue, cross a small bridge, and make the second left onto Greene Street. Take Greene Street to Taft Street, make a right, and the homestead will be on your left.

As you continue west on Route 117, the congestion that bedevils this narrow road in the more populous part of Coventry finally yields to open country driving. Apart from some old homes and churches, some nice scenery, and a series of reservoirs, there's not much to see along this stretch of road. You drive for 8 or 9 miles before reaching the intersection with Route 102, but your patience will be rewarded.

Take the right onto Route 102 north and proceed about 2 miles to Maple Valley Road. Turn right here, and a short drive brings you to the *George B. Parker Woodland* (1670 Maple Valley Road, 949–5454; www.asri.org/parker.htm), yet another excellent Audubon Society nature preserve. Seven miles of trails begin near the historic Issac Bowen House, built between 1755 and 1795 and now a private residence.

As you follow the trails through this rugged, 600-acre forest, you will notice that the park has an unusual number of artifacts signaling the past presence of man. Back in the 1700s this area was Coventry Center, a small farm community that also boasted a sawmill on the Turkey Meadow Brook. In time, however, the town was largely abandoned, and Coventry Center was reestablished a few miles to the east near a large pond.

Scattered throughout these woods are old cellar holes, the remains of the mill and a charcoal processing site, and rock walls. There's also something rather mysterious: a series of stone cairns that might have been built by local Native American tribes, although that's just a guess. In truth, nobody is really sure who made these curious stone monuments or why. The Parker Woodland is open dawn to dusk.

If you return to the intersection of Route 102 and Route 117, you'll notice a small side street, Old Summit Road. This road leads into the tiny hamlet of *Summit,* once a stop on the New York, New Haven, and Hartford Railroad line. You can still see the right-of-way for the railroad, along with a few historic buildings (the *Summit Baptist Church,* built in 1862, and the *Summit Free*

Library, built in 1891) and the *Summit General Store* (25 Old Summit Road, 397–3366), which claims to be Rhode Island's only real general store. Supporting this assertion is the fact that not only does the store sell groceries, hardware, hay, and feed, but it also serves as the town's post office and video rental store. Open Monday to Saturday 7:30 A.M. to 8:00 P.M., Sunday 8:00 A.M. to 6:00 P.M.

Passing directly behind the Summit General Store is the old right-of-way for the New York, New Haven, and Hartford Railroad. A 15-mile segment of the railbed has been converted to recreational use and christened the *Coventry Greenway,* stretching from the Connecticut border to West Warwick.

The longer unpaved segment of the greenway trail passes over the Moosup River (see page 59) and through the tiny villages of Greene and Summit before reaching Coventry Center, where a paved, 3½-mile segment begins near the Flat River Reservoir and ends near the village of Washington. Plans call for the trail eventually to be linked with the Washington Secondary Bike Path, currently snaking its way southwest on another abandoned rail line in Cranston and West Warwick.

Hikers and mountain bikers can use both the unpaved and paved parts of the trail, while road bikes and inline skaters are obviously limited to the paved portions.

Foster

Rhode Island seemed to have everything it took to make up the quintessential New England state: great ocean beaches, rolling farmland and deep forests, old mill towns and quaint village greens. Only one thing was missing: a covered bridge.

So residents of rural Foster decided to put their town on the map by building Rhode Island's only covered bridge. Alas, no sooner was the bridge finished and dedicated than some teenage vandals came along and burned it down.

The story has a happy ending, though. Seemingly the whole town (including at least one repentant young firebug) pitched in and, with donated lumber and countless volunteer hours, rebuilt the bridge in 1994. A replica of an early nineteenth-century span, the *Swamp Meadow Covered Bridge* crosses Hemlock Brook on a quiet, wooded road near an old mill. To see the bridge, take Route 102 North from the intersection with Route 117 to Route 94, then make a left and proceed north until you reach the Central Pike. Turn left onto this dirt road and the bridge is ¼ mile ahead.

Popular with truckers and families alike, the *Shady Acres Restaurant and Dairy Bar* (164 Danielson Pike, 647–7019) is the best place to stop along Route 6 for a quick meal or ice cream. Located between the Route 94 intersection and the Connecticut border, Shady Acres is an oasis on this sparsely

The Moosup River Railroad Trestle

The railbed of the former New York, New Haven, and Hartford Railroad, cutting across rural Coventry, today serves as the foundation for the Trestle Trail, a hiking and mountain-biking path that offers glimpses of railroad history amid lush wilderness.

While diehard hikers may want to walk the trail from Carbuncle Pond (parking off Route 14) to the Coventry Reservoir (parking off Hill Farm Road near Coventry Center on Route 117), you can take a short hike from the Carbuncle Pond end of the trail to view one of the highlights: the 50-foot-high former railroad trestle that crosses the Moosup River. On a hot summer afternoon this is a great spot to kick back, soak up the sun, and enjoy the beautiful view of the river and forest below, enveloped in near-total quiet and solitude.

It's perfectly OK to come this far and then turn back to your car, or, if you're in the mood, keep going east and you'll pass the small village of Greene and then Summit, where you can get a cold drink at the Summit General Store before heading back.

developed road that runs between Hartford and Providence. Inside there are booths and counter service for patrons who take a seat on the diner stools, while outside there is a screened-in porch and a picnic grove among the shade trees that give the restaurant its name. There's even a small playhouse and swings for the kids to play on while you're waiting for your order from the window. Open Monday 6:00 A.M. to 2:00 P.M., Tuesday through Saturday 6:00 A.M. to 8:00 P.M., and Sunday 7:00 A.M. to 8:00 P.M.

OTHER NOTEWORTHY ATTRACTIONS AND EVENTS IN KENT COUNTY AND WESTERN RHODE ISLAND

Goddard Memorial State Park
Warwick

John Waterman Arnold House
Warwick

Lakeview Amusements
Coventry

Portuguese Holy Ghost Festival
West Warwick; September

Gaspee Days Celebration
Warwick; late May, early June

St. Patrick's Day Parade
West Warwick; March

Steam Up
East Greenwich; September

Scituate Art Festival
Scituate; October

Warwick City Park
Warwick

Places to Stay in Kent County and Western Rhode Island

(All Area Codes 401)

WARWICK

Comfort Inn Airport
1940 Post Road
732–0470

Crowne Plaza Providence
801 Greenwich Avenue
732–6000

Fairfield Inn Providence
36 Jefferson Boulevard
941–6600

Motel 6
20 Jefferson Boulevard
467–9800

Radisson Airport Hotel
2081 Post Road
739–3000

Residence Inn by Marriott
500 Kilvert Street
737–7100

Sheraton Providence
Airport Hotel
1850 Post Road
738–4000

WEST GREENWICH

Best Western Inn
101 Nooseneck Hill Road
397–5494

Classic Motor Lodge
859 Victory Highway
397–6280

The Super 8 Congress Inn
101 Nooseneck Hill Road
397–3381

WEST WARWICK

Comfort Suites
10 Keyes Way
826–1800

Spring Hill Suites by Marriott
14 J. P. Murphy Highway
822–1244

FOSTER

Stone House Motor Inn
162 Danielson Pike
Route 6
647–5850

Places to Eat in Kent County and Western Rhode Island

(All Area Codes 401)

WARWICK

Bugaboo Creek Steak House
30 Jefferson Boulevard
781–1400

The Crow's Nest Restaurant
288 Arnolds Neck Drive
732–6575

Iggy's Doughboys
889 Oakland Beach Avenue
737–9459

Legal Sea Foods
2099 Post Road
732–3663

Portofino
897 Post Road
461–8920

HELPFUL WEB SITES ABOUT KENT COUNTY AND WESTERN RHODE ISLAND

City of Warwick
www.warwickri.com

Pawtuxet Village
www.pawtuxet.com

Providence/Warwick Convention and Visitors Bureau
www.providencecvb.com

Town of Coventry
www.town.coventry.ri.us

Town of East Greenwich
www.eastgreenwichri.com

Town of West Greenwich
www.wgtownri.org

Warwick Online
www.warwickonline.com

SELECTED CHAMBERS OF COMMERCE IN KENT COUNTY AND WESTERN RHODE ISLAND

**Central Rhode Island Chamber
of Commerce**
3288 Post Road
Warwick 02886
732–1100
www.centralrichamber.com

**East Greenwich
Chamber of Commerce**
5853 Post Road
East Greenwich 02818
885–0020
www.eastgreenwichchamber.com

**Rocky Point Chowder
House**
1759 Post Road
739–4222

WEST WARWICK

Cowesett Inn
226 Cowesett Avenue
828–4726

Qué Pasa
49 Providence Street
828-7573

EAST GREENWICH

Cafe Fresco
301 Main Street
398–0027

**Harbourside
Lobstermania**
Water Street
884–6363

Hilltop Creamery
5720 Post Road
884–8753

Jigger's Diner
145 Main Street
884–5388

The Post Office Cafe
11 Main Street
885-4444

Richard's Pub
3347 South County Trail
884–2880

Tio Mateo's
537 Main Street
886–1973

Trattoria Del Corso
223 Main Street
398–2905

**Twenty Water Street
Warehouse Tavern**
20 Water Street
885–3700

FOSTER

**Shady Acres Restaurant &
Dairy Bar**
164 Danielson Pike
647–7019

Northern Rhode Island

The six towns lying north of Providence are linked to the capital city in that they are all part of Providence County. In attitude and atmosphere, however, the northern part of the state is a different world.

The **Blackstone River** dominates the eastern part of Northern Rhode Island, and mill villages dot the riverbanks. If town names like Arnold Mills and Grant Mills point to the region's industrial past, then the French names on mailboxes and storefronts evidence the area's large Acadian population. The river, on the other hand, is named after William Blackstone, a renegade cleric who rode into the area on the back of a bull around 1630 and became the first European to settle here. You won't find any trace of Blackstone's home in Cumberland, however, because the entire hill it once sat upon was leveled and removed in 1886 to make way for the construction of the Ann & Hope Mill.

The western half of this region is mostly rural, with large tracts of forest dotted with lakes, ponds, and reservoirs fed by rivers and streams, some of which were significant enough to support small mill towns of their own. Even native Rhode Islanders rarely venture into the hilly northwestern part of the state except to fish, hike, or hunt. Thanks to the cooler temperatures in the region's valleys and hollows, towns like

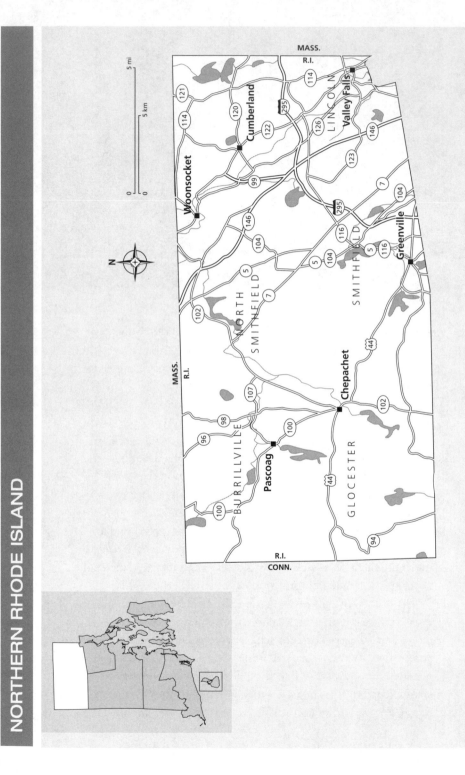

Glocester are famous for declaring school snow days when the rest of the state is getting rain.

One of the best ways to gain an appreciation of this area's place in history is to take a river tour. The **Blackstone Valley Explorer** riverboat departs from a variety of points and offers a unique perspective of the mills, towns, railroads, and grand homes that embraced the river's power during the Industrial Revolution. And although the Blackstone has long been a working river, in many places it still retains its natural beauty.

Among the excursions offered by the Blackstone Valley Tourism Council (www.tourblackstone.com), which operates the forty-nine-passenger riverboat, are the Woonsocket Falls Tour, which covers the mill-dotted riverbank in Woonsocket, and the Valley Falls and Wilderness Tour, which explores less-developed sections of the river in Central Falls, Cumberland, and Lincoln. There are also special fall foliage tours and Haunted River cruises around Halloween. Regularly scheduled tours operate from June through October on weekends and holidays 1:00 to 4:00 P.M. Tours are $10.00 for adults, $8.00 for seniors and children.

In 2000 a newcomer began plying the waters of the Blackstone: the canal boat **Samuel Slater** (www.bedandbreakfastblackstone.com), named for the pioneering mill owner who transformed the river into an industrial power-house. Berthed in Central Falls, the 40-foot canal boat is available for charter and for overnight stays; it sleeps up to four people and includes a full galley, TV, refrigerator, radio, telephone, and head with shower.

Charter rates are $190 for an hour and a half, $75 for each additional hour; the boat can carry up to twelve passengers for charters. Over-night accommodations, which include a full breakfast, are $129 for singles, $179 for doubles, $209 for groups of three, and $239 for groups of four; tack on another $95 for a one-hour river cruise and you can also feast on an optional New England clambake with lobster, shellfish, corn, potatoes, and Portuguese sausage.

The ***Providence & Worcester Railroad*** operates on track laid down in the river valley of the Blackstone, offering yet another way to enjoy some of

AUTHOR'S FAVORITES IN NORTHERN RHODE ISLAND

Blackstone River	Chepachet
Museum of Work and Culture	Diamond Hill Vineyards
Wright's Farm Restaurant	

the region's least-appreciated natural vistas. The Blackstone Valley Scenic Railway offers fall excursion tours between Cumberland and Worcester, Massachusetts; there's also a hugely popular *Polar Express* ride (celebrating the beloved children's Christmas book of the same name, written by Rhode Islander Chris Van Allsburg) in mid-November.

For information on the *Blackstone Valley Explorer,* the *Samuel Slater* canal boat, or the scenic railway tours, contact the Blackstone Valley Tourism Council at 724–2200; e-mail info@tourblackstone.com.

A footnote on Blackstone River attractions: Under the banner of the Blackstone River Valley National Heritage Corridor Commission, efforts currently are under way to expand and link parkland along the river all the way from Worcester, Massachusetts, to Providence. The corridor comprises twenty-five communities lying along 46 miles of the Blackstone River watershed and is intended as a living museum of the industrialization of America. At many of the historical sites in this chapter, as well as elsewhere in this book, you'll notice signs designating the location as part of the corridor. In many cases you'll find interpretive information posted as well. Plans call for a bike path and right-of-way linking many of the places mentioned in this book, including Slater Mill in Pawtucket, the Blackstone River State Park in Lincoln, the Blackstone Gorge Bi-State Park in North Smithfield, and Valley Falls Heritage Park in Cumberland. The Lincoln/Cumberland section of the Blackstone River Bikeway (www.black stoneriverbikeway.com) is already open, with an 8-mile ribbon of pavement starting at Front Street and ending at Manville Road in Cumberland. Visitors also can access the path from the new Blackstone Valley visitor center on I–295. Plans call for the bike path to extend to Woonsocket by 2007. For more information contact the commission at 762–0250 or visit www.dot.state.ri.us/Web Tran/bikeri.html.

Woonsocket

The city of Woonsocket shares Providence's urban setting but is much more firmly tied to the Industrial Revolution than her southern sister. The river waters surging through the Blackstone Gorge made Woonsocket a center for mill industry during the nineteenth century, and the city—actually a melding of six smaller mill villages—remains largely wedded to its industrial heritage. The Providence and Worcester Railroad cuts through the heart of downtown, and unlike many other Rhode Island locales, where the mills have either been abandoned or turned into shops or condos, Woonsocket still has many factories and plants in operation. A recent restoration project has spruced up downtown's business district. The city's North End is noted for its fine early-twentieth-

Ride Those Rapids

The Blackstone River drops an average 10 feet per mile, and although dams and waterfalls control a significant portion of the river's strength, there are still many parts of the river that canoeists will find fun and exciting. The Blackstone has rapids ranging from Class I to Class III (the latter capable of swamping an open canoe if you're not careful), and the occasional stretches of flat water give you the opportunity to enjoy the beautiful scenery.

If you put your canoe or kayak in at River Island Park in downtown Woonsocket, you'll enter a 1,000-foot section of Class I and Class II rapids. City then gives way to forested riverbanks that continue almost to the Manville Dam. Once you portage around the dam, there's another stretch of easy canoeing along forests and past the ruins of the 1872 Manville Mill.

The next portage is at Albion Falls, best viewed from the iron-truss bridges spanning the river. After another portage at the Ashton Viaduct, you'll have a choice of paddling down the river or the parallel Blackstone Canal, which dates from the 1820s. The canal is recommended, since it allows you to avoid the dangerous Pratt Dam area. From Lonsdale the river meanders through a large freshwater marsh and past Valley Falls Pond. At this point you can decide whether to call it a day or take on a series of portages separated by short paddles to reach downtown Pawtucket and Slater Mill— the birthplace of the American Industrial Revolution.

For more information and a copy of an excellent canoe guide for the Blackstone River, contact the Blackstone River Valley National Heritage Corridor Commission, One Depot Square, Woonsocket, 02895; 762–0250.

century homes. For walking tours or other information, stop by the Blackstone River Valley National Heritage Corridor Commission's office, located in the old train station at Depot Square.

To truly experience the grandeur of the North End, book a room at the ***Pillsbury House*** (341 Prospect Street, 766–7983; 800–205–4112; www.pillsbury house.com), an 1875 Victorian mansion transformed by host Roger Bouchard into an impeccable bed-and-breakfast.

The house is a stylistic delight, with great architectural details throughout, notably the original herringbone parquet floors with "Greek-key" edging and dramatic, high-walled parlor. Among the four guest rooms, each with private bath, the White Room on the second floor stands out: It's so fresh-scrubbed it practically dazzles the eyes. The third-floor Country Suite features handcrafted Vermont Country wood furniture.

Snuggled into the second-floor landing is a small work desk with fax and phone for guests to use, and there's also a guest kitchen with a refrigerator, microwave, and sink. Breakfast includes homemade crepes, French toast, quiche, and apple pancakes.

The Pillsbury House is within walking distance of downtown Woonsocket, but finding the house by car is not as simple as it appears to be on a map, so call for directions or check the Web site first. Room rates range from $95 to $135.

River Island Park is a tiny oasis of green in the industrial heart of Woonsocket. From its riverside walk you get a splendid view of the river, the powerful Woonsocket Falls, and the many mills that draw life from the waterway, a neat definition of the city as a whole. Located on Bernon Street, the park is just a stone's throw from Woonsocket's *Market Square,* home of City Hall and Harris Hall, where Abraham Lincoln spoke in 1860.

Also on Market Square is the *Museum of Work and Culture,* equal parts an examination of nineteenth-century mill life and a celebration of the French-Canadian immigrants who helped launch America's Industrial Revolution. The Acadian workers who came down from Quebec to work Rhode Island's mills developed a rich culture and vibrant family life that stood in stark contrast to the grim conditions in which they worked. Housed in a former textile mill, the museum includes rotating exhibits, a re-created church and mill worker's home, a lecture series, and a New Year's Day celebration that re-creates the French-Canadian tradition of visiting family and friends to mark the new year. Open weekdays 9:30 A.M. to 4:00 P.M., Saturday 10:00 A.M. to 5:00 P.M., and Sunday 1:00 to 4:00 P.M. Admission is $7.00 for adults, $5.00 for seniors and students, and free for children under ten (when accompanied by an adult). Market Square, 42 South Main Street (exit 9B off I–295); 769–WORK; www.rihs.org.

Woonsocket: Wieners and Dynamites

Along Main Street in Woonsocket you'll find a half-dozen or so mom-and-pop restaurants vying for business primarily touting two specialties: hot wieners and "dynamite" sandwiches. The wieners, like the ones cooking in the window of the **New York Lunch** (8-½ Main Street, 769–9619), can be found all over Rhode Island. But dynamite sandwiches are unique to Woonsocket.

What's in a dynamite? Think of a sloppy joe with an attitude: The basics are ground beef, tomato sauce, celery, peppers, onions, and hot pepper (dry or wet) served in a torpedo roll, although recipes differ from family to family, restaurant to restaurant. In Woonsocket, you'll find dynamites served at big family gatherings, fund-raiser dinners, and at restaurants such as the **Castle Luncheonette** (420 Social Street, 762–5424), **Main Street 2000** (114 Main Street, 769–2799), and the **Heritage Coffee Shop** (66 Main Street, 765–7639).

High School Hockey Heroes

Rhode Island is a hotbed of hockey, producing such National Hockey League stars as goaltender Chris Terreri, defensemen Mathieu Schneider and Keith Carney, and 1996–97 Rookie of the Year Brian Berard. And nowhere does the passion for hockey burn more brightly than in Woonsocket, home of Mount Saint Charles Academy (800 Logee Street, 769–0310; www.mountsaintcharles.org).

The Mount, as the school is known, is an incubator for hockey talent, and the school is the perennial winner of the state hockey championships. Watching these high school athletes perform is a treat, especially during one of the annual tournaments when top teams from around the region come in to challenge the Mounties. Plus, there's a good chance you'll see a future star in the making; Schneider, Berard, Carney, Chicago Blackhawks goalie Brian Boucher, former New York Islanders goalie (and current general manager) Garth Snow, and many other professional hockey players got their start at the Mount's Adelard Arena.

Even beating the Mounties can be the ticket to success: Former U.S. women's Olympic hockey team goalie Sara DeCosta shocked the state when she led her Toll Gate High School (Warwick) team to a 3–0 shutout over the Mounties during the state championships a few years back, and in 2004 Toll Gate ended Mount Saint Charles's streak of twenty-six straight state championships in a convincing 2–0 sweep. Berard, Schneider, and Carney all played on the men's U.S. Olympic team in Nagano, as well.

After touring the museum, take a stroll across Market Square to ***Ye Olde English Fish and Chips Restaurant*** (25 South Main Street at Market Square, 762–3637), a Woonsocket tradition for more than seventy-five years. Believe me, if you are a fan of classic English-style fish-and-chips, it's worth the drive here no matter where in Rhode Island you are coming from. Goodness knows it's not health food, but the deep-fried delights at Ye Olde English remain delicious despite the switch from cooking in animal fat to low-cholesterol oil a few years back. Opened in 1922 by English immigrants Harry and Ethel Snowden and currently in its fifth generation of family ownership, the fish-and-chips shop expanded to include a dining room back in the '70s but still retains its local atmosphere. Open Tuesday, Wednesday, and Saturday 10:00 A.M. to 6:30 P.M., Thursday 10:00 A.M. to 7:00 P.M., and Friday 9:00 A.M. to 8:00 P.M.

If you're in the mood for a libation, the new ***Vintage*** restaurant and lounge (4 South Main Street, 765–1234; www.vintageri.com), across the street, has a cool upscale bar on the second floor with an outside deck. Open for lunch Monday to Thursday 11:30 A.M. to 2:00 P.M., and for dinner Monday to Thursday 5:00 to 9:00 P.M., Friday and Saturday till 10:00 P.M.

For another on-the-go option for lunch, seek out the ***Castle Luncheonette*** at 420 Social Street (762–5424), where they serve up burgers in a setting straight out of the '50s. Open 10:00 A.M. to 8:00 P.M. year-round. The Castle is one of a few remaining eateries in town where you will find French Canadian favorites such as meat pies and pea soup on the menu.

In the annals of quirky restaurant ideas, **Chan's Fine Oriental Dining,** Depot Square at the junction of Main and Railroad Streets (267 Main Street, 765–1900; www.chanseggrollandjazz.com), deserves a mention. After all, at how many places can you get top-quality live jazz, blues, and country music with your fried rice and egg foo young? Every week owner John Chan brings in performers from around the country, as well as local comedy acts, to entertain diners. The performances are held in Chan's Four Seasons Room, and you can watch the show between trips to the hot buffet and the bar.

If you come just for dinner, you can usually walk right into Chan's dining room, but reservations are required for musical and comedy performances. Ticket prices vary but generally range from $10 to $28, depending upon the performer. Showtime is 8:00 P.M., with an occasional second show scheduled at 10:00 P.M. Chan's is open Monday to Wednesday 11:30 A.M. to 10:00 P.M., Thursday and Sunday 11:30 A.M. to 11:00 P.M., and Friday and Saturday 11:30 A.M. to 12:30 A.M.

North Smithfield

How out of the way is **Blackstone Gorge Bi-State Park**? Well, you can't even get to it from North Smithfield, although most of the park is located within the town's borders: The only access point is in Blackstone, Massachusetts. But don't despair, because finding the 197-acre park is well worth the effort.

To get to the park entrance from Rhode Island, take Route 146A north to St. Paul Street in Woonsocket, making a right at Kennedy's Lunch and crossing the state line into Blackstone, Massachusetts. Make the left at Route 122, then another left onto County Road, which you will take to the end. At the edge of Rolling Mill Dam is a footpath leading down into the gorge.

Known as the hardest working river in America, 400 feet of the Blackstone's 438-foot vertical drop were controlled for waterpower to run the dozens of mills along its path. The stretch of the river within the park, then, is a rare exception; here, the power of the flowing water has cut a rocky gorge and flows unfettered downstream. Blazed trails lead from the parking area through undeveloped woodland and to the edge of the gorge, crossing the state line into Rhode Island along the way.

Also located off Route 146A near Woonsocket is **Wright's Dairy Farm** (200 Woonsocket Hill Road, 767–3014; www.wrightsdairyfarm.com). Wright's is a working dairy with 130 Holstein cows, super-fresh milk, and blueberry muffins that have been voted the best in Rhode Island. Since 1900 the Wrights have been getting up every morning before sunrise to milk their cows, so the milk in the dairy shop is never more than forty-eight hours old. They also sell fresh cream, which is used in the bakery to create delicious pastries. Another favorite: hermits, old-fashioned molasses-spiced cookies with raisins.

Adjacent to the bakery is the dairy barn, where visitors are welcome to stand at an observation window and watch the cows being milked. If you can't make the 4:30 A.M. milking (and who could blame you?) there is another that starts around 2:30 P.M. and continues until dinnertime. Wright's Dairy Farm is open Monday through Saturday 8:00 A.M. to 7:00 P.M. and Sunday 8:00 A.M. to 4:00 P.M. To get there take Route 146A to Woonsocket Hill Road, then head west for ¼ mile until you see the sign for the farm/dairy on your left.

Samuel Slater's mill in Pawtucket is known as the birthplace of the American Industrial Revolution, but it was not Slater's only accomplishment. In 1805 Slater and his partners founded the town of **Slatersville,** which today stands largely intact as the first planned mill community in America. Slatersville is not geared toward tourists; it's just a nice place to spend an hour or so walking around and admiring the old homes on Main, School, and Greene Streets.

In 1807 Samuel Slater sent his younger brother John to buy an old mill and create a planned community in northern Rhode Island. After the plans for Slatersville were laid out, John and his wife, Ruth, moved into the town so that he could oversee the operation of the mill, which he did for the next thirty-five years. The Slaters' modest house, not much different from those of the mill workers, is located on School Street. At the top of a curved drive off School Street is the William Slater Mansion, built in 1854 and belonging to the man who eventually became the sole owner of the Slater Mill.

The village centers on a small, triangular common at the corner of Greene and School Streets. Facing the common is the 1838 Congregational Church with its historic cemetery. If you walk west from the common, you will come to Railroad Street; make a left here and walk to the stone Arch Bridge (built in 1855), and you will have a downriver view of the Slater Mill, also known as the Center Mill. Originally built in 1806, the water-powered cotton mill burned and was rebuilt in 1826.

Slatersville is located at the junction of the Providence Pike (Route 5) and Victory Highway (Route 102); you can also get there by taking the Route 146A exit off of Route 146 in North Smithfield. Also on Victory Highway in Slatersville is **Gator's Pub and Restaurant** (1402 Victory Highway, 769–2220; www.gatorspub.com), a casual place where you get a sandwich or a simple, family-style meal on the outdoor deck, or work off a beer or two on the beach volleyball court out back. Open 11:30 A.M. to 1:00 A.M. daily (kitchen stays open till midnight on weekends).

If you tell a Rhode Islander that you are going to catch a movie at the ***Rustic Drive-In*** (Route 146, 769–7601), you may get some funny looks. That's because the Rustic once showed X-rated movies. For the past decade, though, the Rustic has been packing in young families and couples on a budget with prices that are an incredible bargain in these days of $10 movie tickets. For about $17 per carload, you can enjoy a double feature on any of the drive-in's three screens. Second-run movies just out of the expensive theaters are the rule, and the Rustic pulls in more than its share of family films.

The window speakers are long gone, but patrons can tune in the sound-track on their car radios. The playgrounds and miniature railroads typical of the drive-ins of yore are also missing, but the Rustic's snack bar still offers a wider variety of food and snacks than your standard movie theater, including burgers and clam cakes.

The last drive-in theater in Rhode Island, the Rustic is a landmark on Route 146, with its giant neon marquee pointing the way to the box office. The Rustic gets very busy on warm summer nights, so come early and bring a portable radio and a blanket or lawn chairs so that you can sit outside. (You can bring your own snacks and drinks, too.) The Rustic Drive-In is open nightly during the summer and on weekends and holidays during the spring and fall.

Burrillville

The Rhode Island Red may have a monument in Adamsville (see Newport County chapter), but the state's real shrine to chicken is ***Wright's Farm Restaurant*** at 84 Inman Road off Route 102 in Nasonville (769–2856; www.wrightsfarm.com).

Family-style chicken dinners are a Rhode Island tradition, and nobody does it bigger or better than Wright's Farm. Diners have just two choices: all-you-can-eat roasted chicken ($10.25 for adults, $5.95 for children ages two to ten, free for kids under two) or the steak dinner ($18.00). Skip the steak: It's the tender, moist, falling-off-the-bone chicken that makes Wright's Farm famous, along with heaping side dishes of fresh-cut french fries, pasta with homemade tomato sauce, and crisp salads topped with an excellent house Italian dressing (it's all-you-can-eat on the side dishes, too).

The restaurant is tremendous, with six dining rooms that can accommodate 1,600 people, but the decor is bright and inviting, the service fast and friendly, and the place is immaculate. This impressive operation is the result of more than forty years in business—plenty of time to work out any kinks.

Wright's Farm is extremely popular with Ocean State natives, so expect a wait even with all those tables. A large bar, festooned with carved and painted chickens of all shapes and sizes, is a nice place to pass the time, or you can check out the gift shop (which, surprisingly, is somewhat light on chicken souvenirs) or try your luck at the keno games that run constantly in the lounge. Wright's Farm is open Thursday and Friday 4:00 to 9:00 P.M., Saturday noon to 9:30 P.M., and Sunday noon to 8:00 P.M.; no credit cards accepted.

The northwest corner of Rhode Island is occupied by one of the state's most out-of-the-way places, the *Buck Hill Management Area.* One of the many undeveloped tracts managed by the state, Buck Hill is teeming with wildlife and is a great place to get acquainted with Rhode Island's still-abundant natural heritage.

Marked trails surround a marsh and follow old roads across both the Massachusetts and Connecticut state lines. Along the way you are bound to see some of the ducks and waterfowl that reside in the marshes and ponds. A sharper eye is required to spot the owls, pheasants, deer, foxes, and wild turkeys that also make Buck Hill their home. Plan on spending a couple of hours here, especially if you come in the early spring or early fall, when the days are cooler and the insect population less oppressive. (Beware: Late fall and early winter is hunting season.)

The entrance to the Buck Hill Management Area is an unmarked gravel road on the right side of Buck Hill Road, approximately 2³⁄₁₀ miles from the intersection with Route 100/Wallum Lake Road. Also in Burrillville are two other state-owned nature preserves worth exploring: the *Black Hut Management Area* (enter off Spring Lake Road, which intersects with Route 102 in Glendale, just south of Wright's Farm) and the *George Washington Management Area* and the adjacent *Casimir Pulaski State Park,* with access from Route 44/Putnam Pike near the Bowdish Reservoir in Glocester, 5 miles west of the junction of Route 44 and Route 102. Both the Washington and Pulaski Parks have beaches for freshwater swimming.

Southeast of Buck Hill on Route 100 near Pascoag is *White Mill Park* (568–4300), a pleasant stop for a picnic lunch or a brief ramble in the woods. A picnic pavilion overlooks the Wilson Reservoir, while a pretty arched bridge crosses a waterfall to a series of hiking paths, one of which will take you to the crumbling remains of the worsted mill that operated here from 1895 through the 1960s.

Gourmet cooks will tell you that preparing a meal can be more fun than eating it. You can put that theory to the test at the *Old Aaron Smith Farm* in Mapleville. Hosts Richard and Claudette Brodeur welcome groups of six or more to enjoy an evening of eighteenth-century cooking and fine dining at their circa 1730 farmhouse. The Brodeurs will teach you how to prepare such traditional seasonal dishes as braised duck and Cornish game hens with chestnut stuffing, roasted in an old cast-iron stove and served in the house's formal dining room.

You can snack on the appetizers you have prepared and quench your thirst on homemade lavender punch or calendula nectar or bring your own wine.

All the food you prepare and eat for your four-course meal is organically grown and raised on the farm (in season), and all dinners include appetizers, entree, dessert, and beverages. The Brodeurs also are happy to give you the recipes so that you can try these dishes at home.

The Old Aaron Smith Farm is located at 264 Victory Highway, which intersects with Route 102 just south of Lapham Farm Road (568–6702; www.aaron smithfarm.com). Workshops/dinners are available Friday to Sunday and upon request; reservations required. Dinner prices range between $42 and $52, plus gratuity. BYOB.

Just thinking about a doughboy can raise your cholesterol count. Consisting of a slab of dough deep-fried in oil and coated with powdered sugar, doughboys are a flagrant violation of any sensible dietary plan—but worth the indulgence. These Rhode Island favorites occupy a place of honor at **Mr. Doughboy** (1950 Bronco Highway, 568–4897), a classic roadside attraction that lures travelers on Route 102 through Glendale with a restaurant, a miniature railroad, go-karts, batting cages, and miniature golf. You will be amused, and the kids will love it. Open Monday to Saturday 5:30 A.M. to 7:00 P.M. (till 10:00 P.M. in the summer) and Sunday 6:30 A.M. to 8:00 P.M.

The rambling, circa 1774 **Western Hotel** on the Old Douglas Turnpike (610 Douglas Pike, 568–6253) has a long history as a way station on the former stagecoach run between Providence and Worcester, a dance hall, and today, a restaurant and tavern. Step through the old saloon-style doors for family-style pizza, grinders, chowder, or a cold one at the bar. Open Tuesday to Thursday and Sunday from 11:00 A.M. to 11:00 P.M., and until 1:00 A.M. on Friday and Saturday (kitchen closes at midnight).

Glocester

The village of **Chepachet** is the heart of Glocester, the crossroads of three major state roads (Routes 102, 44, and 100) in a town that remains largely undeveloped. Despite its busy main street, however, Chepachet retains much of its charm.

A variety of antiques stores, many in historic homes and buildings, are clustered in the center of Chepachet. An 1814 mill standing beside the Chepachet River is home to the **Stone Mill Antiques & Craft Center** (1169 Main Street, 568–6662; www.stonemillantiquesdesign.com). European furnishings, china, glassware, jewelry, and primitive furniture predominate. Open Saturday and Sunday 11:00 A.M. to 5:00 P.M.

Across the street is the ***Old Post Office*** (1178 Main Street, 568–1795), where owner Jere Henault has done such a convincing restoration job that at least once a week somebody comes in looking to mail a letter. (Jere sends them to the new post office down the road.) The collection, which includes merchandise from about a dozen dealers, includes lots of toys and '50s Americana, estate jewelry, books, and a kitchen room in the back that will remind you of Grandma's. The Old Post Office is open Thursday through Saturday 11:00 A.M. to 5:00 P.M. and Sunday noon to 5:00 P.M.

The ***Brown & Hopkins Country Store*** (1179 Putnam Pike, 568–4830; www.brownhopkins.com) also has two floors of antiques, but there's much more to the story than that. First opened in 1809, Brown & Hopkins is the oldest continually operated country store in America. Many authentic touches remain, including a creaky, wide-beamed wooden floor, an old potbellied stove, and an open-beamed ceiling.

As in any good country store, display cases in the front of the building are crammed with penny candies. Staples like flour and rice no longer dominate the shelves (except for a forty-pound wheel of Vermont cheddar), having been replaced by crafts and collectibles; gourmet coffee and pastries are sold from behind the counter.

Upstairs, the rooms on the second and third floors have been arranged to give the feel of an old country home, with a twist: Everything is for sale. In one room, a long antique table is set with early American stoneware, another is set up like a bedroom, while miniature Christmas trees adorned with handmade decorations fill another. Brown & Hopkins is open Monday to Saturday

Brown & Hopkins Country Store

10:00 A.M. to 5:00 P.M. (open until 7:00 P.M. on Thursday) and Sunday noon to 5:00 P.M.

If you need to take a breather, cross the bridge over the Chepachet River to the town fire station. An unmarked path leads along the river to a pretty pond covered with lily pads. There's a good spot to sit right where the pond swells over an old dam and the waterfall gurgles into the stream below. Or just settle into one of the benches at the pocket park on the other side of the bridge, closer to Main Street.

Another old Main Street business, the *Job Armstrong Store* (1181 Main Street) has been restored as a headquarters and small museum by the Glocester Heritage Society (www.glocesterheritagesociety.org). On display are medical artifacts from the Civil War, a drum and uniform from the Chepachet Cornet Band, and displays on the history of the Dorr Rebellion, an 1842 suffrage revolt led by Chepachet resident Thomas Dorr.

The museum is open Saturday 11:00 A.M. to 3:00 P.M. and by appointment; call 568–1866.

The *Stage Coach Tavern* (1157 Putnam Pike/Route 44, 568–2275; www .stagecoachtavern.com) is another Chepachet building with a storied past. Originally built in the early 1700s as a private home, the building was in use as a tavern in July 1842 when Thomas Dorr—the duly elected governor of Rhode Island—began his rebellion against incumbent governor Samuel King, who refused to step down. In quelling Dorr's revolt, King's troops shot through the door of the tavern, set up headquarters in the building, and didn't leave until the end of the summer.

Once a stop on the stagecoach run between Providence and Connecticut, the Stage Coach Tavern is still luring travelers with a fine selection of seafood, steaks, pasta, and poultry. The house specialty is prime rib, which you can order Governor Dorr–style—smothered with sautéed mushrooms and onions the way old Thomas liked it. The tavern in the same building has a local atmosphere. Open Wednesday and Thursday noon to 9:00 P.M.; open till 10:00 P.M. Friday and Saturday and till 8:00 P.M. Sunday. The bar is open until 1:00 A.M. daily, with lighter tavern food available when the dining area is closed; full menu is available in the bar when the dining room is open.

Finally, Chepachet is home to one of the state's unique public celebrations—the annual *Ancients & Horribles Parade* (www.glocesterri.org/parade .htm). Held on the Fourth of July, the parade is described by one local resident as the "anti-Bristol" parade. (For a description of the far more traditional Bristol Fourth of July parade, see the East Bay chapter.) Rather than marching bands playing patriotic themes, local iconoclasts build floats and dress up in costumes parodying the news of the day and skewering local politicians. Anyone who

Dorr's Rebellion

Critics who bemoan the sorry state of Rhode Island politics need to put their complaints in perspective: At least the state's present-day political battles don't include actual gunfire. Such was not the case during the brief but all-too-real Dorr's Rebellion of 1842.

Unlike most states, Rhode Island never replaced its colonial charter—dating back to 1663—after the Revolutionary War. The upshot was that through the 1840s, only property owners could vote. Leading a group of disenfranchised citizens, Thomas Wilson Dorr launched a reform campaign to give the vote to all male citizens. Both Dorr's group and the state legislature drafted versions of a new constitution, but it was Dorr's that emerged victorious in a referendum.

Governor Samuel King's sitting government declared the Dorr constitution illegal. Undaunted, Dorr's party held elections and named Dorr governor in 1842. King refused to step down and called out the militia to crush Dorr's government. There were a handful of armed clashes between Dorr's supporters and the state militia, but Dorr was unable to raise enough popular support to defeat King. Dorr was captured and sentenced to life in prison in 1844.

While Dorr lost the rebellion, his ideals soon triumphed. In 1843 the state adopted a new constitution expanding the vote to non-property owners, and Dorr himself was released from prison after serving just one year. The Dorr Rebellion also led to an important Supreme Court decision that gave Congress and the president the power to determine each state's lawful government.

takes the time to make a costume can join the procession, which in past years has included everything from impersonators dressed as Rhode Island politicians to a float depicting Mike Tyson's infamous ear-chewing bout with Evander Holyfield. It's a wicked good time.

Don't call **Grace Note Farm** (969 Jackson Schoolhouse Road, 567–0354; www.gracenotefarmweb.com) a bed-and-breakfast: First, owner Virginia Sindelar wants guests who are interested in experiencing all the farm and the surrounding countryside (dubbed the "Rhode Island outback") have to offer. And second, guests are offered more than just breakfast when they stay, including meals that feature recipes that are as old as the 1730s farmhouse itself.

Sindelar is restoring the house in reverse, replacing modern fixtures, wherever practical, with antiques, right down to the doors to the guest rooms. The suite and a separate guest cottage are among the most attractive accommodations; the former can sleep a large family with its two double beds, loft, and single bed, while the rustic cottage has a fine view of the brook running through the property and the horses running through the corral.

The inn's common room shares the great view through large windows on two sides, one of the few concessions to modernity in the house. The array of activities available to guests is impressive, starting with riding on the trails snaking out from this working horse farm. Sindelar estimates that there are 150 miles of trails in this northern corner of Rhode Island, including some that cross through undeveloped Pulaski State Park and into neighboring Connecticut. The trails also are used by hikers, snowmobilers, snowshoers, and snowmobilers, and guided excursions can be arranged through Grace Note Farm. The less adventurous will perhaps gravitate toward a carriage ride through the woods, followed by a massage delivered on-site by a licensed therapist. Rates are $100 per person per night (kids twelve and under are half price); guests are welcome to bring and board their own horses.

Spice up your trip through rural Rhode Island with a stop at the **Cherry Valley Herb Farm,** located at 969 Snake Hill Road, 4½ miles from the intersection with Route 116 (647–3614; www.cherryvalleyherbfarm.com). There are eight aromatic herb gardens you can wander through on this fifty-acre farm, and a quaint shop is located in a big red barn that has everything you need to prepare your own herbal teas, potpourri, herb wreaths, and arrangements. Cherry Valley even holds classes if you want to learn more about cooking or designing with herbs.

There also is an abundant selection of herbs to choose from, with fresh plants available from April to September and dried herbs sold year-round. If the children are getting bored, they can go outside for a peek at the farm's cows while you browse among the cookbooks, candles, bath oils, teapots, and dried flowers.

The shop is open Thursday through Saturday 10:00 A.M. to 4:00 P.M. and Sunday 1:00 to 4:00 P.M.; closed the month of February.

Cumberland

The town of Cumberland occupies the rural northeastern corner of Rhode Island. Flanked by the Blackstone River and the city of Woonsocket, most of Cumberland's attractions are found along Route 114, also known as Diamond Hill Road, named after the town's most prominent topographical feature.

Route 114 is a pleasant, two-lane paved country road running through mixed farms, woodland, and small clusters of homes. From Route 295, travel north from exit 11 (the last exit in Rhode Island) until you see the jolly flags fronting the store at **Phantom Farms** (2920 Diamond Hill Road, 333–2240; www.phantomfarms.com), a farm stand featuring local produce and pies and pastries stuffed with fruit from the orchard out back. There's a sunny porch out-

Faith Forged by Fire

The monks of the former Our Lady of the Valley monastery, located on Diamond Hill Road in Cumberland, believed in the virtue of hard work. So much so, in fact, that they themselves quarried much of the granite used to build their church and quarters after arriving here from Canada in 1900.

Unfortunately, the monks also built in wood (despite having been driven out of Nova Scotia by a devastating fire at their former abbey). In 1950 a blaze that began under a stairwell in the guest house destroyed both it and most of the church, prompting the monks to relocate once again—this time to Spencer, Massachusetts, where they remain to this day.

However, the monks left behind a lovely piece of property, whose 400 acres can be enjoyed via public hiking and horse-riding trails. The former monastery also is home to the Cumberland Public Library (1464 Diamond Hill Road, 333–2552; www.cumberlandlibrary.org), which occupies some of the surviving monastery buildings, including the cloisters and chapter room. The grounds are open daily from dawn till dusk; the library is open Monday to Thursday 9:00 A.M. to 8:00 P.M., Friday and Saturday from 9:00 A.M. to 5:00 P.M., and Sunday from 1:00 to 4:00 P.M.

side where you can indulge your sweet tooth and admire the farmhouse amid the apple trees. Open year-round, 6:30 A.M. to 6:00 P.M.

About a quarter mile north of Phantom Farms is the unassuming entrance to one of Rhode Island's best-kept secrets, ***Diamond Hill Vineyards*** (3145 Diamond Hill Road, 333–2751 or 800–752–2505; www.favorlabel.com). Keep a sharp eye or you'll miss the small sign on the right (east) side of the road, which leads to a narrow gravel track through the woods, ending at the winery.

Located in a charming circa 1780 farmhouse surrounded by flowers and grapevines, the tasting room/gift shop is a cozy space where, like as not, the person pouring the wine will be one of the owners. Pete and Claire Berntson, with an able helping hand from winemaker son Allan, daughter Chantelle, and son-in-law Stephen, have been growing Pinot Noir grapes on their small farm since 1976, producing an eclectic variety of wines including vintages made from apples, peaches, raspberries, and blueberries. The wines are reasonably priced, and the Berntsons will make up an attractive gift basket for you to take home.

The gazebo outside the vineyard house is the perfect spot to uncork a bottle and relax in this peaceful, bucolic setting. Diamond Hill Vineyards is open Thursday to Saturday noon to 5:00 P.M. and Tuesday to Sunday noon to 5:00 P.M. in November and December.

Proceeding north on Route 114 soon brings you to Nate Whipple Highway/Route 120. If you make a right turn here and proceed about half a mile, you will see Sneetch Pond Road on your left, just past an old church. Turn here to find **Pentimento** (322 Sneetch Pond Road, 334–1838), an antiques shop in the historic village of Arnold Mills. Located in a beautifully restored former granary building, the shop's outside deck alone makes it worth a stop. The owner will let you bring a bag lunch to eat on the deck after you shop. Shaded by an elm tree that grows through cuts in the wooden floor, the platform hangs over a small waterfall on the Abbott Run River, inviting you to linger with your repast. Open Wednesday to Saturday 11:00 A.M. to 5:00 P.M.

You might want to spend a few minutes longer in **Arnold Mills,** an interesting village that has largely been overlooked by the passage of time. This is an old farming village that got its name from a gristmill built in 1745 by Amos Arnold. (The foundation of the old mill can be seen behind Pentimento.) Later, Arnold Mills was involved in a number of industries, including boat-building, an odd (although successful) choice for a landlocked town.

After that glory period, Arnold Mills slipped back into its previous role as a sleepy backwater, but visitors can still appreciate the community's old homes, churches, and mill pond. Across the street from Pentimento are the remains of an 1825 water-powered machine shop. On your way back out of town, look for the circa 1750 Amos Arnold House on Sneetch Pond Road.

If Diamond Hill actually were made of diamonds, it would have disappeared under an army of pickaxes long ago. In fact, the area gets its name from a mile-long exposed vein of quartz, formed eons ago by mineral-rich water running through a fracture in the earth's crust. Once a ski area, **Diamond Hill Town Park** (Route 114) today provides a wealth of hiking trails over steep terrain, with excellent views of the surrounding countryside from the top of the hill. During your hike look for the massive stone anchors that once held the ski lifts in place. The park explodes with color as the leaves turn in autumn and is a year-round attraction for rock climbers.

At the base of the hill is a band shell set by a small stream, the site of occasional concerts and other town activities. The section of the park on the east side of Route 114 is by far the most popular with visitors, but the bulk of the parkland actually is accessed by a narrow corridor on the west side of the road.

Directly across the street from the park entrance is the **Ice Cream Machine** (4288 Diamond Hill Road/Route 114, 333–5053), home of some of the best homemade ice cream in the state. Nicely landscaped, with painted wooden cows grazing in a small enclosure on a hillside overlooking the parking lot, the Ice Cream Machine promises a wide variety of flavors fresh out of the churn. The cookie dough and maple walnut are wildly popular, and the mint chocolate chip is so minty that it's like biting into a frozen peppermint patty. For a real indulgence try the Diamond Hill Sundae, a mountainous four scoops of ice cream topped with whipped cream and nuts. Open

April to October. Hours are Sunday to Thursday 11:00 A.M. to 8:00 P.M. and Friday and Saturday 11:00 A.M. to 9:00 P.M. in the spring and fall. In the summer it's open daily from 11:00 A.M. to 10:00 P.M.

The *Valley Falls Heritage Park* also is located on Route 114, but it is on the southern end of the road (3½ miles south of Route 295, where Route 114 is called Broad Street) in the community of Valley Falls, right across the Central Falls city line.

To their everlasting credit, local preservationists and civic officials a few years back took a decrepit, debris-strewn former mill site and creatively turned it into an interpretive park on the Industrial Revolution. Today the park on the east side of Mill Street (turn at Cumberland Town Hall) is laced with curved walkways and sturdy bridges and has plaques explaining the significance of the river and the surrounding ruins.

In this unique park, all the forces that drove nineteenth-century industry are gathered in one place. Before you are the Blackstone River and the waterfall, flanked by still-standing mill buildings and spanned by an old bridge. Crossing the river downstream is a railroad trestle, still used by the Providence and Worcester Railroad. Finally, below you are the remains of an old mill complex, including remnants of the raceways and turbines that powered the looms. The park is open dawn to dusk.

In the name of progress, the site of William Blackstone's riverside homestead in present-day Valley Falls was flattened in 1886 to make way for the giant Ann & Hope Mill. However, progress also dictated the demise of most of Rhode Island's large textile mills, and in time employment in the service and retail industries replaced mill jobs as the backbone of the economy. So it seemed only fitting when, in 1953, the old mill in Cumberland was converted to the first Ann & Hope department store.

Smithfield

Powder Mill Ledges Wildlife Refuge is a small nature preserve with three trails meandering through reclaimed farmland and hardwood forests and leading to a pond where muskrats and great blue herons have been spotted. You can walk the circuit at a comfortable pace in about an hour and a half, then stop at the headquarters of the *Audubon Society of Rhode Island,* which is located here. The society maintains an extensive library on natural history and operates a gift shop, as well as conducting tours of its half dozen or so refuges around the state.

The Audubon Society headquarters and library are located adjacent to the parking lot for the Powder Mill Ledges Wildlife Refuge at 12 Sanderson Road/Route 5, just south of the intersection with Putnam Pike/Route 44

(949–5454; www.asri.org). It's open Monday through Friday 9:00 A.M. to 5:00 P.M.; and Saturday noon to 5:00 P.M.

Despite the cars whizzing by on nearby Route 295, an air of serenity pervades the grounds of the *Smith-Appleby House*, a twelve-room farmhouse near Georgiaville Pond. Originally built as a one-room "stone-ender" in 1696, the house later was grafted onto a larger structure moved here from Johnston in the early 1700s to form the present building. The deed for the property was given by Rhode Island founding father Roger Williams to John Smith.

Unlike many of the other historical homes in the area, the Smith-Appleby House has been completely furnished, so visitors can get a good idea of what the everyday lives of the Smiths and Applebys—who lived in the house from 1696 to 1958—must have been like. An old settee and piano dominate the sitting room, while antique teapots and crockery line shelves in the keeping room. A "smoke room" on the second floor of the house was used to cure meat.

Also located on the seven-acre site is a caretaker's cottage and the tiny shack that once was the Smithfield train depot. Across a small stream lies an old cemetery. The Smith-Appleby House is the headquarters of the Historical Society of Smithfield, which occasionally runs special events such as socials and May breakfasts that feature members dressed in period costumes. Tours are available from May to December by appointment and cost $3.00. Call 231–7363 or visit www.smithapplebyhouse.org for more information.

The Smith-Appleby House is located at 220 Stillwater Road, off Route 116 just south of the intersection with Route 7. The house is on your right after the Route 295 underpass.

If you've worked up an appetite, check out the nearby *Kountry Kitchen* (10 Smith Avenue, 949–0840), where the big portions, reasonable prices, and friendly service are excelled only by the views of Hopkins Pond. Open Sunday

Rhode Island's Apple Capital

Smithfield is known locally as Rhode Island's apple-picking capital, with a bunch of orchards located in the vicinity of Greenville.

Whether you're looking for the perfect pie filling or something to crunch on the spot, you'll find a wide variety of apples at the orchards of Appleland Orchard (135 Smith Avenue/Route 116, 949–3690) and pick-your-own at Jaswell's Farm (50 Swan Road, 231–9043; www.jaswellsfarm.com). Spend an hour or so straining for that perfectly symmetrical fruit at the top of the tree and carting around baskets overflowing with green and red orbs, and your family is sure to leave with sore arms and big smiles.

to Thursday 6:30 A.M. to 2:00 P.M. and Friday and Saturday 6:30 A.M. to 8:00 P.M. For family dining with a touch of class, open the door to the **Greenville Inn,** an Italian restaurant that makes a tender, juicy chicken Française and a tasty chicken Lorenzo with artichoke hearts, mushrooms, black olives, and diced tomatoes. Every entree from pasta to prime rib is priced less than $20 (36 Smith Avenue, 949–4020). Dinner hours are 4:00 to 10:00 P.M. Monday to Thursday, 4:00 to 11:00 P.M. Friday and Saturday, and noon to 10:00 P.M. Sunday.

Smithfield also is home to one of the last of a vanishing breed: an original **A & W Drive-In Restaurant** (Putnam Avenue/Route 44, just west of the Apple Valley Mall; no phone), complete with car service and classic cheeseburgers, fries, and milkshakes.

Lincoln

You can set out from the Smith-Appleby House on a nice country drive that also has some intriguing historic sites along the way. Making a right turn from the Smith-Appleby House onto Stillwater Avenue, head south until you come to Lime Rock Road, where you will make a left. Enjoy the rural landscape as you head east; after you cross Route 123/Albion Road, the name changes to Wilbur Road. At this point start keeping an eye out for the **Jedediah Smith Homestead** on your left, just before the intersection with Route 246. At the stop sign at the intersection with Route 246, look to your right and you will notice the white facade of the **North Tollgate House,** currently the home of the **Blackstone Valley Historical Society** (1873 Old Louisquisset Pike, 725–2847). Built in 1807, the tollhouse was the fee collection point on the north end of the old Louisquisset Pike (Route 246).

Crossing Route 246, you will be dazzled by the limestone quarries and white buildings of the historic **Conklin Limestone Quarry** (334–2330; www.conklinlimestone.com), established in 1640 and the oldest continually operated industry in the United States. Chunks of gleaming limestone taken from this still-active quarry are piled up right to the roadside. For a look at Lincoln's mineral wealth in a more pristine setting, visit the Nature Conservancy's **Lime Rock Preserve** (take 246 north, then turn left on Wilbur Road; go ½ mile and look for a small parking lot on the right). The 130-acre preserve features limestone ridges, marble deposits, woods, swamps, streams, and views of the Lincoln reservoir.

Farther along Lime Rock Road, on your right side, you will see a sign for Mowry's Tavern. The old inn, built in 1686 and now a private home, sits close to the road and is shaded by a row of ancient trees.

Turn left onto Simon Sayles Road; the next intersection is Route 126. Cross straight over and proceed down Cullen Hill Road until you see a sign pointing left down Lower River Road to the entrance to ***Blackstone River State Park.***

As you emerge from your car in the small lot under the Route 116 bridge, you might be tempted to ask, "What park?" And indeed, the charms of the Blackstone River State Park are not readily apparent, and no signs guide your way. But as you walk north on a well-worn footpath, details start to emerge. On your right you can hear the sound of rushing water, and through the trees you catch glimpses of the Blackstone River making its way south to Pawtucket.

Soon enough you see a side path and a small wooden bridge to your left and make a startling discovery: another body of water flowing in quiet obscurity through the woods. You have found a remarkably well-preserved section of the Blackstone Canal, built in the early nineteenth century to move goods down the river from Worcester, Massachusetts, and Woonsocket to Pawtucket and Providence.

Farther along there is an overlook where the remains of an old canal lock are plainly visible. Another viewing platform offers a great look at the waterfall, whose rumbling is audible through the woods long before it comes into view.

From the parking lot the trails following the old canal towpath south actually extend much farther—6 miles in total—and a 3³⁄₁₀-mile section beginning on Front Street in Lincoln has been resurfaced as a premier biking and recreational trail. When completed, the Blackstone River Bikeway will stretch for 17¹⁄₁₀ miles, linking the East Bay Bike Path (see the East Bay chapter) to the Massachusetts border north of Woonsocket. Also on the south side of the parking lot, facing the canal, is the ***Kelly House,*** built in 1820 by Wilbur Kelly, a Providence ship captain who backed the construction of the canal. The Kelly House is now the ***Captain Wilbur Kelly House Museum*** (333–0295), which features exhibits on Rhode Island's transportation history, from canals to interstates. Open April to October, 9:00 A.M. to 4:30 P.M..

Waterfall in Blackstone River State Park

If you're tempted to linger a while in Lincoln, you can truly immerse your-self in local history at the ***Whipple-Cullen Farmstead*** bed-and-breakfast, located on nearby Old River Road (99 Old River Road, 333–1899). Ten gener-ations of Whipples and Cullens (hosts John and Barbara Cullen are the latest) have lived in this post-and-beam farmhouse since 1736. A continental break-fast before a crackling fireplace—one of eight in the house, including some in guest bedrooms—is included with your stay, and guests will find the architec-tural heritage of the house revealed at every turn, from beehive ovens to pine-plank floors and colonial mantels and moldings. Four guest rooms, with shared baths, are available for $80 nightly.

The town of Lincoln holds onto its rural character despite the fact that the town's borders touch those of Provi-dence. This fact is evident at ***Lincoln Woods State Park*** (723–7892; www .riparks.com/lincoln.htm), especially on a winter ride through the forest on horseback, courtesy of ***Sunset Stables*** (722–3033; www.sunsetstablesri.com). Guided trail rides are offered year-round; the park also is known for its freshwater beach and picnic areas.

The ***Lodge Pub and Eatery*** at 40 Breakneck Hill Road (Route 123, 725–8510; www.thelodgepub.com) captures the town's bucolic essence with its road-house exterior and whimsical hunting-lodge decor, featuring moose-heads and sconces made of snowshoes hanging from the walls.

There's a whiff of adventure on the menu, as well: In addition to the stan-dard burgers and steaks, and family-style chicken, you'll find a variety of house specials like grilled chicken breast mari-nated in maple syrup. The salad bar is fresh, extensive, and complemented by a selection of homemade dressings,

albionfalls

One of the prettiest spots along the entire Blackstone River is at Albion Falls, best reached by taking Old River Road in northern Lincoln to School Street, just north of the Kirkbrae Country Club.

The Albion Bridge crosses the river just downstream from the powerful Albion Dam, built in 1916 to power the Albion Mill, which today survives as a condominium complex. From the center of the bridge you can enjoy the sight and sound of the falls as well as the peaceful wooded surroundings. Or, you can walk along a dirt path between the river and the still-active tracks of the Providence and Worcester Railroad to the west side of the dam, where you can see the old headrace that allowed the river waters to rush through a narrow passage and turn the gears at the mill. Eventually, the Blackstone River bike and jogging path now under construction farther south will come through this spot, as well.

While you're in the area, take a quick stroll through Albion village, another of the Blackstone Valley's well-preserved mill towns.

including an exceptional chunky bleu cheese. A small bar offers live music Wednesday, Thursday, and Friday. Open Monday through Saturday 11:00 A.M. to midnight and Sunday noon to 10:00 P.M.

There was a time when the Great Road was the only land link between Lincoln and Providence and when the house and farm belonging to Eleazer Arnold were the only sign of civilization for miles around. Much has changed since then, but the *Eleazer Arnold House* remains as a reminder of those quieter times.

Perhaps the best example of Rhode Island stone-ender construction extant, the circa 1687 Eleazer Arnold House, located at 449 Great Road, is open to visitors by appointment. The house is a veritable museum of historic architecture, from the massive stone wall and fireplace whose stones were taken from nearby quarries, to the original and reconstructed paneling in the downstairs rooms, to the peaked attic, where the original beams that framed the house are still visible. Even the flaws of the old building are fascinating: The attic is adorned by graffiti left by former work crews, including a painter who labored here in 1911. For information call Historic New England (617–227–3956; www .historicnewengland.org/visit/homes/arnold.htm).

Continuing west on the Great Road from the Eleazer Arnold House will bring you to *Chase Farm,* another bit of the Blackstone Valley National Heritage Corridor and an important piece of preserved open space in Lincoln. Walking and hiking trails meander over the sparsely wooded landscape at this old farm, and locals say the best thing going on at the 118-acre Chase Farm in winter is sledding on the rolling hills that dot the property. Facing the Great Road near the Chase Farm entrance is the historic *Hannaway Blacksmith Shop* (671 Great Road, 333–1100), where smithies demonstrate their art and conduct tours one Sunday a month, and *Hearthside House* (677 Great Road, 726–0597; www.hearthsidehouse.org), a stonefaced Federal mansion built in 1810. This National Register home was recently opened to the public, mostly

OTHER NOTEWORTHY ATTRACTIONS AND EVENTS IN NORTHERN RHODE ISLAND

Lincoln Park
Lincoln

Lincoln Woods State Park
Lincoln

William Blackstone Memorial
Cumberland

Ancients & Horribles Parade
Glocester; July 4

Woonsocket Autumnfest
Woonsocket; October

HELPFUL WEB SITES ABOUT NORTHERN RHODE ISLAND

Blackstone Valley National Heritage Corridor, www.nps.gov/blac/

Blackstone Valley Tourism Council
www.tourblackstone.com

City of Woonsocket
www.ci.woonsocket.ri.us
www.woonsocket.org

Town of Burrillville
www.burrillville.org

Town of Cumberland
www.cumberlandri.org

Town of Glocester
www.glocesterri.org

Town of Lincoln
www.lincolnri.org

Town of North Smithfield
www.northsmithfieldri.com

through events like a Christmas open house and monthly open houses on Saturdays from 1:00 to 4:00 P.M. Call for further details and schedule of events.

Apart from a few pilots and daredevils, very few people are even aware of the existence of ***North Central State Airport,*** and therein lies its charm. A terminal building and hangars dating from the '50s and '60s line the airfield, and the airport is surrounded by woodlands. The quiet is broken only occasionally by the sound of a Cessna or Piper taking off or landing. It's a reminder of a time when flying was a simpler, more seat-of-the-pants affair.

Places to Stay in Northern Rhode Island

(All Area Codes 401)

WOONSOCKET

Holiday Inn Express and Suites
194 Fortin Drive
769-5000

Woonsocket Motor Inn
333 Clinton Street
762-1224

NORTH SMITHFIELD

Hilltop Inn
797 Eddie Dowling Highway
762-9631

Quality Inn
355 George Washington Highway
232-2400

GLOCESTER

Grace Note Farm
969 Jackson Schoolhouse Road, Pascoag
567-0354

Lakeside Motel
66 Putnam Pike, Route 44 Harmony
949-3358

White Rock Motel
750 Putnam Pike
Route 44, Chepachet
568-4219

SMITHFIELD

Comfort Suites
1010 Douglas Pike
231-6300

LINCOLN

Lincoln Marriott Courtyard
636 George Washington Highway
333-3400

**Whipple-Cullen
Farmstead B&B**
99 Old River Road
333–1899

Places to Eat in Northern Rhode Island

(All Area Codes 401)

WOONSOCKET

Castle Luncheonette
420 Social Street
762–5424

**Chan's Fine
Oriental Dining**
Depot Square
765–1900

**Ye Olde English Fish and
Chips Restaurant**
25 Market Square
762–3637

GREENVILLE

The Greenville Inn
36 Smith Avenue
(Route 116)
949–4020

The Kountry Kitchen
10 Smith Avenue
(Route 116)
949–0840

BURRILLVILLE

Mr. Doughboy
Route 102, Glendale
568–4897

Wright's Farm Restaurant
84 Inman Road
769–2856

GLOCESTER

Chester's Restaurant
102 Putnam Pike, Harmony
949–1846

Stage Coach Tavern
1157 Putnam Pike
Chepachet
568–2275

FORESTDALE

The Village Haven
90 School Street
762–4242

CUMBERLAND

Davenport's Restaurant
1070 Mendon Road
(Route 122)
334–1017

Ice Cream Machine
4288 Diamond Hill Road
333–5053

Tuck's Food & Spirits
2352 Mendon Road
658–0450

LINCOLN

The Lodge
40 Breakneck Hill Road
725–8510

NORTH SMITHFIELD

The Beef Barn
1 Greenville Road
762–9880

SELECTED CHAMBER OF COMMERCE IN NORTHERN RHODE ISLAND

Northern Rhode Island Chamber of Commerce
6 Blackstone Valley Place, Suite 301
Lincoln 02865-1105
334–1000

The East Bay

The three Bristol County towns known collectively as the East Bay—Barrington, Warren, and Bristol—each have a unique character that, despite their proximity, makes them easily distinguishable.

Of the three, Bristol is the largest and best known, thanks to the town's famous Fourth of July parade and its involvement in America's Cup yachting. Warren is a quiet New England seaside town, while Barrington serves primarily as an upscale bedroom community for the city of Providence.

Adding vitality to all three towns is the ***East Bay Bike Path*** (www.riparks.com/eastbay.htm). Built on the right-of-way of an old railroad line, the path winds its way 14½ miles from India Point Park in Providence to downtown Bristol. Along the way, bikers, strollers, and in-line skaters pass through East Providence, Barrington, and Warren.

About half of the path's length is in Providence and East Providence, but we give it prominence in this chapter because the path is a great alternative to driving if you want to see the best that Bristol County has to offer. The Barrington stretch passes through the cool, wooded confines of ***Haines Memorial State Park*** (253-7482; www.riparks.com/haines.htm; a good place to park your car), offering occasional glimpses of the town's beautiful homes as it proceeds south to skirt ***Brickyard***

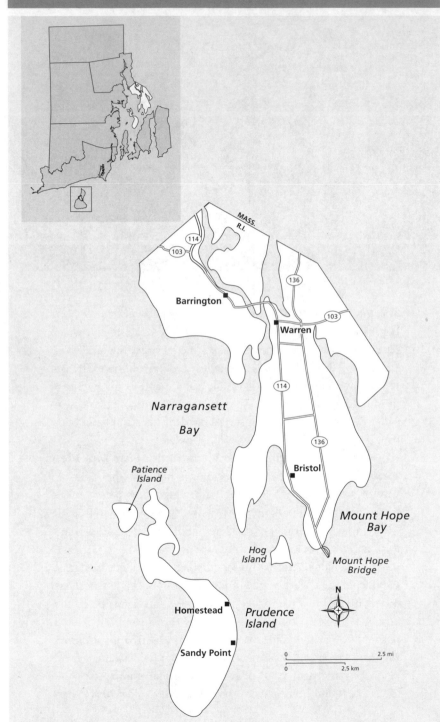

Pond. One of the most beautiful spots on the route is where the path crosses the Barrington River just north of Route 114, bringing riders onto the small peninsula that comprises the towns of Warren and Bristol.

In Warren the setting for the bike path changes from woods to suburbia, then passes right through the heart of downtown, gently curving behind Town Hall and past an inviting Del's lemonade stand. Lock up your bike here and enjoy all the attractions of Warren that are just a few steps away.

The path hugs the shoreline after passing over the Bristol town line, affording an excellent (though occasionally breezy) view of Narragansett Bay. The route then briefly moves back inland, where you can choose to make a detour into *Colt State Park* or continue to the terminus at *Independence Park* on Bristol Harbor. Once again, your location puts you within easy walking distance of downtown sites, shops, and restaurants.

By car, the best approach to Bristol County is to take I–195 east to Route 114 south, which takes you along and then across the Barrington River before narrowing to become Main Street in Warren. The name changes again (to Hope Street) once you enter Bristol, but Route 114 remains the main drag in both Warren and Bristol. Most of the attractions in this chapter are in close proximity to Route 114, although a few in Bristol are located off Route 136 (Metacom Avenue), which runs parallel to Route 114 before the two roads merge near the southern tip of the peninsula, just before the Mount Hope Bridge.

Barrington

As you drive south on Route 114, you're likely to be distracted by the beautiful views of the Barrington River to your left. A little-known nature preserve on the northbound shoulder of the road offers even better vistas. *Osamequin Park* is a forty-two-acre bird sanctuary wedged between the road, a pond to the south, and the Hundred Acre Cove section of the Barrington River to the east. There is a small network of trails and elevated walkways over the marshes that allow you to stroll from the small parking area directly down to the beach or around the property to the pond and a dam. Waterfowl abound.

Part of the reason the park is relatively unknown is that drivers heading south on Route 114 tend to whiz by without ever seeing it. (Even heading north it's easy to miss.) To get there from the southbound lanes, take the first left after the sign for the Zion Bible College exit, making a U-turn, which will take you a short distance north on Route 114 to the park, which is on your right. Better yet, wait until you're headed back north at the end of the day to stop, when you can catch the sunset reflecting off the water. Osamequin Park is owned by the town of Barrington; call the town recreation department (247–1900) for information.

Barrington's Brickyard Pond

Brickyard Pond in Barrington looks for all the world like a sliver of natural beauty, carefully preserved so that even the town's founding fathers might recognize it if they were to return. In fact, they would not: Brickyard Pond did not even exist until the 1940s.

If the first settlers remembered the area at all, it would be for the large clay deposits found here. From the seventeenth century on, the Brickyard Pond site was the source of clay for brickmaking. For almost one hundred years, a succession of brick manufacturing firms dug deeper and deeper into the earth, until all the clay was gone.

In 1943 the Barrington Steam Brick Company shut down for good, and the former clay pits filled with water to form Brickyard Pond, creating the pretty views enjoyed today by thousands of people passing by on the East Bay Bike Path.

As you proceed south on 114, you'll pass Barrington's medieval-style **Town Hall** (283 County Road, 247–1900) on your left, built in 1888 on a foundation of natural boulders. Past the Town Hall, Route 114 intersects with the East Bay Bike Path (watch out for runners, bikers, and strollers!) and takes a sharp jog east to cross the Barrington River. If you make your first right after the bridge onto Barton Avenue, you'll find the **Tyler Point Grille** (32 Barton Avenue, 247–0017; www.tylerpointgrille.com), an acclaimed seafood and Italian restaurant adjacent to the Barrington Yacht Club. The restaurant is open nightly for dinner 4:30 to 10:00 P.M., Friday and Saturday 4:30 to 11:00 P.M., and Sunday 4:30 to 9:00 P.M.

Warren

Continue following Route 114 south, and two small bridges will bring you to downtown Warren. Although southern neighbor Bristol gets more attention, Warren is a gem of a New England seaside community that should not be overlooked.

Ravaged by the British during the Revolutionary War, Warren rebounded to prosper as a shipbuilding center and as home to Rhode Island's largest whaling fleet during the nineteenth century. The Industrial Revolution took hold when the whaling business dried up after the Civil War, but Warren remains essentially the small town that it was at the turn of the century.

Dominating Main Street (Route 114) is the **1890 Town Hall** (514 Main Street, 245–7340; www.townofwarren-ri.gov), with a facade featuring an intricate, unusual carving of the Wampanoag sachem Massasoit, an early friend to the white settlers of this area. The "Sowams" referred to in the carving is the

name of the large native settlement that existed here by the banks of the Warren River. After being exiled from Massachusetts, Roger Williams lived at
Sowams before moving north to found Rhode Island. There's a plaque at the
foot of Baker Street marking the spot of **Massasoit Spring,** the supposed site
of Sowams (Barrington also claims to be the location of the village).

Also hard to miss on Main Street is the imposing **George Hail Library**
(530 Main Street, 245–7686; www.georgehail.org), named for an early Warren
industrialist. From the outside, the massive stone construction and stained-glass
windows give the building the appearance of a medieval fortress church. The
interior, restored to its original 1889 beauty and watched over by a portrait of
Hail, remains a cozy haven for local bibliophiles. Upstairs there is a small
museum focusing on Warren history: The collection includes melted window
glass from the Baptist Meetinghouse burned by the Redcoats in 1778; old fire
buckets and ship models; and scrimshaw and ships' logs that recall the town's
whaling heyday of the 1840s. The museum is open Wednesday from 2:00 to
4:00 P.M. and by appointment; the library itself is open Monday to Thursday
10:00 A.M. to 8:00 P.M. and Friday and Saturday 10:00 A.M. to 5:00 P.M.

The **Delekta Pharmacy** (496 Main Street, 245–6767) is known for its cabinets. Not the dark-stained wood cabinets cluttered with old apothecary bottles
that line the walls (although they were here when the pharmacy opened in
1858). No, it's the coffee cabinets—also known as a milkshake or a frappé,
depending upon your state of origin—that are the Delekta's claim to fame.
Owner Eric Delekta, whose family has run the pharmacy since the 1940s, brews
the coffee syrup every morning, and Warren residents and savvy bike path veterans alike make the pilgrimage here.

A true throwback, the Delekta is the kind of pharmacy that you usually
only read about nowadays, with an old-fashioned soda fountain dominating the
front of the store and medicine and sundries lining the shelves in back. The tin
ceilings are original, as are the gaslight globes hanging in the windows. Open
Monday to Friday 8:00 A.M. to 6:00 P.M., Saturday 8:00 A.M. to 4:00 P.M, and Sunday 8:00 A.M. to noon.

If the coffee cabinet's close cousin—coffee milk—is the state drink (and
the state's General Assembly says it is), then Rhode Island's unofficial state junk
food undoubtedly is the hot wiener. At **Rod's Grill** (6 Washington Street,
245–9405), they serve armfuls of these little fire-red hot dogs (known affec-
tionately as "gaggers") right off the grill to a jam-packed lunchtime crowd.
Open Monday, Wednesday, and Saturday 6:30 A.M. to 4:00 P.M.; Tuesday and
Thursday 6:30 A.M. to 7:30 P.M.; Friday 6:30 A.M. to 6:00 P.M.; closed Sunday.

Farther north on Main Street is the circa 1840 **Baptist Church in Warren**
(407 Main Street, 245–3669), actually the third Baptist house of worship to stand

on this spot. (The first was burned by—you guessed it—the British.) The congregation's first minister was James Manning, who also started a Latin school that later became Brown University.

At the corner of Main Street and Miller Street, the former Lyric Theatre has been reinvented as the *Imagine Gift Store* (5 Miller Street, 245–4201; www .imaginegiftstores.com). From the festive exterior to a procession of painted cows, the store virtually explodes with vibrant color and personality. Step through the door and you are greeted by a '50s-style ice-cream parlor full of frozen treats and penny candy. The back of the old theater has been transformed into three floors of unique gifts, from gourmet foods to "Fresh Produce" clothing. Open Monday to Saturday 10:00 A.M. to 6:00 P.M., Sunday noon to 5:00 P.M.

Between Main and Water Streets is a series of quiet historic streets that could have been lifted straight out of a Victorian-era stereograph. The short walk to the river anywhere between Wheaton Street and Liberty Street yields a fascinating mix of architectural styles from the eighteenth and nineteenth centuries. Particularly lovely is the area around Church and Baker Streets. Look for the towering white columns fronting the *First Methodist Church* (25 Church Street; 245–8474; www.gbgm-umc.org/warrenri), built in 1845 and based on a design of Sir Christopher Wren. Across the street, sitting between Church and State Streets, is a small commons centered on a veteran's memorial and a Civil War–era cannon.

At 59 Church Street is *Maxwell House,* a circa 1755 colonial-style home with an herb garden, a large central chimney, and twin beehive baking ovens. The home is operated by the Massasoit Historical Association and is open Saturday from 10:00 A.M. to 2:00 P.M. and by appointment, and for occasional cooking demonstrations and colonial craft displays. Call 245–0392 for more information.

The oldest *Masonic Temple* in New England can be found on nearby Baker Street. Built in 1798 and still used for meetings by the local Masonic Lodge, the Federal-style building (Baker Street, 245–3293) was constructed

AUTHOR'S FAVORITES IN THE EAST BAY

East Bay Bike Path	Blithewold Mansion and Gardens
Downtown Warren	Haffenreffer Museum of Anthropology
Prudence Island	

using beams from British frigates sunk in Newport Harbor. You can call for a tour to get a closer look at the twin Ionic doors and the hall's elaborate, hand-painted Egyptian murals. The **Warren Fire Museum** (38 Baker Street), located at the Narragansett Steam Fire Engine Company station, features historical artifacts from the 250-year-old department and exhibits of old fire-fighting equipment, including "The Little Hero," a hand-operated water pump purchased in 1809. Call the fire chief's office at 245–7600 to view the collection.

The Greek revival **St. Mark's Episcopal Church** (21 Linden Street, 245–3161; www.stmarkswarren.org), designed by famed local architect Russell Warren, broods alongside Linden Street with its Ionic portico and canted double doors. The 1829 church is guarded by two stone lions, and an old bell sits on the lawn.

Wharves, many dating from the Revolutionary War period, line Water Street, along with historic homes, small shops, and restaurants. One of the latter is **Wharf Tavern** (215 Water Street, 245–5043; www.wharftavernri.com), for over forty years a landmark situated on the Warren River. At least six varieties of lobster dishes are served here (check out the Lobster Extravaganza on Monday and Tuesday nights), as well as a wide range of other seafood, steaks, pasta, and poultry. The moorings that surround the restaurant attract diners from sea as well as land. Even if you don't come to eat, take a few minutes to walk out on the restaurant's dock, open to the public, for a great view of the river. Open Monday to Thursday 11:30 A.M. to 9:00 P.M. and until 10:00 P.M. Friday and Saturday; open 10:30 A.M. to 9:00 P.M. on Sunday, including Sunday brunch. The lounge, which features live music on the weekend, stays open later.

The *Vista Jubilee* is proof that the sea remains intrinsic to Warren's character. Built here, the 350-passenger ship is operated by **Bay Queen Cruises** (461 Water Street, Gate 4, 245–1350 or 800–439–1350 in Rhode Island; www.bay queen.com). It leaves the docks at the foot of Miller Street for four- and six-hour tours of Narragansett Bay. Passengers can enjoy a variety of lunch and themed dinner cruises, including holiday parties and dinner dances on weekends.

The cruise is a great way to see the state from the inside looking out, as the *Vista Jubilee* offers spectacular views of Prudence Island, Jamestown, and the Newport Bridge.

Lunch cruises are $30 for adults, $23 for children; brunch cruises are $33 for adults, $28 for children; and dinner cruises are $39 (adults only).

No walking tour of Warren would be complete without a stop in at least one of the town's dozens of antiques shops, located mostly on Main Street, Child Street (Route 103), and Water Street.

The commercial fortunes of Water Street have ebbed and flowed in recent years but currently seem to be on an upswing. **Summerwood** (57 Water Street,

855–1751; http://summerwood.cc) is a beautiful store filled with Indian statuary, Indonesian masks, and teak game tables and other furniture. Open Tuesday to Friday 10:30 A.M. to 5:30 P.M. and Saturday 10:00 A.M. to 5:00 P.M. ***Meeting House Antiques*** occupies a circa 1790 corner store (47 Water Street, 247–7043) and specializes in Early American primitive antiques.

At 125 Water Street, the historic Warren mainstay the Nathaniel Porter Inn has been reborn as the ***Nat Porter Restaurant*** (289–0373; www.natporter .com). Some of the formal New England ambience has been stripped away in favor of a decor makeover and a modern menu emphasizing market-fresh ingredients, although the cozy feel of an old tavern still remains. Open Tuesday to Sunday 5:00 to 10:00 P.M. Another old Water Street standby, Bullock's, has yielded to ***Stella Blues*** (50 Miller Street, on the corner of Miller and Water, 289–0349; www.stellabluesri.com), a moderately upscale restaurant/pub serving a menu of seafood, sandwiches, and Italian specialties and live music on Thursday nights—a virtual must for an eatery that gets its name from an old Grateful Dead tune. Open Sunday to Thursday 11:30 A.M. to 9:30 P.M., Friday and Saturday 11:30 A.M. to 10:30 P.M. (Late-night denizens will be happy to note that the bars at both the Nat Porter and Stella Blues keep serving libations until 1:00 A.M.)

Tucked away behind the ***Tav Vino*** restaurant (a wine tavern, if you hadn't guessed; 245–0231) on the water side of Water Street, is one of Warren's true culinary treasures: the bright and cheerful ***Three Rivers*** (267 Water Street, 289–2067). This upscale breakfast (and lunch) spot, the brainchild of owner Nancy O'Connell, occupies an airy, whitewashed building resembling a boat shed right along the Warren River. An outdoor deck is popular in the summer, but the atmosphere here is warm all year-round. "Egg-and-bacon" eateries are a dime a dozen in the East Bay, but Three Rivers stands apart with its sophisticated morning menu, serving favorites like a portobello mushroom stuffed with spinach, pesto, and scrambled eggs and homemade sweet corn and black bean fritters. Open Wednesday to Sunday 7:00 A.M. to 2:00 P.M.

On Main Street you'll find ***Yankee Consignment*** (446 Main Street, 245–6569), specializing in antique and used furniture.

At the address where for years Casala's Market sold groceries to local residents, John Devine has opened ***Water Street Antiques*** (149 Water Street, 245–6440), which features a large selection of art deco furniture and lighting and a slightly racy collection of old pinups. Open daily noon to 5:00 P.M. More upscale is ***Wren & Thistle Antiques*** (19 Market Street, 247–0631; www.wren andthistle.com), which in addition to glassware and fabric has a broad selection of fine china that's worth perusing. Open Tuesday to Sunday 11:00 A.M. to 5:00 P.M. Owner Jackie Williams also runs a one-suite bed-and-breakfast upstairs with huge windows overlooking a private garden. Room rate is $120 per night. Books are the item that stands out at *Ancestral Antiques* (462 Main Street, 245–2129), which also features furniture, china, and costume jewelry.

Warren's *India* restaurant (520 Main Street, 245–4500) boasts a pair of the East Bay's best dining spaces: a sunken outdoor courtyard for the summer months and a traditional Indian dining room with cushioned floor seating before a stage where live jazz is performed on Friday and Saturday evenings. Suffused with the scent of incense and curry, India provides a transcendent dining experience. Open Sunday to Thursday 11:00 A.M. to 10:00 P.M. and 11:00 A.M. to 11:00 P.M. Friday and Saturday.

The *Second Story Theatre* (28 Market Street, 247–4200; www.2ndstory theatre.com) is first-rate: Founded by Trinity Repertory veteran Ed Shea, this is a professional operation that just happens to reside in a small town. With one hundred seats surrounding a minimalist set, the focus is on dialogue-intensive works like *Death of a Salesman, Of Mice and Men,* and *A Streetcar Named Desire.* (In 2003's production of *Salesman,* the only prop was Willy Loman's battered suitcase.)

The performance space occupies most of the second story of an old union hall, but downstairs is a piano lounge and bistro that exemplify Warren's emerging sophistication as an arts, dining, and cultural center for the East Bay. Copper-covered tables and a half-moon bar highlight a warm dining room serving an adventurous menu, while a brightly decorated piano lounge invites theatergoers to relax on couches and comfy chairs with a glass of wine before or after the show. Shows are generally Thursday to Saturday at 8:00 P.M., with Sunday matinees at 3:00 P.M.; tickets are $20. The bistro is open 6:00 P.M. to midnight on show nights.

On Warren's Child Street, the nineteenth-century *Cutler Mills* (www.cutler mills.com), once a textile manufacturing center, has been renovated to include retail space, artist's lofts, and recreational facilities. Closest to the street you'll find *The Market at Cutler Mills* (137 Child Street, 247–0021), an organic food market that holds cooking classes and wine and cheese tastings; to-go meals can be enjoyed at tables inside or out. Open Monday to Saturday 9:00 A.M. to 8:00 P.M., Sunday 9:00 A.M. to 6:00 P.M. The sleek *Imago* art gallery (16 Cutler Street, 245–3348) exhibits the works of local artists and hosts occasional poetry readings and other public events. Open Tuesday to Saturday noon to 4:00 P.M.

By far the crowning glory of the Cutler Mills complex, however, is the transformation of the mill's old boiler room into the *Basically British Tea Room* (16 Cutler Street, 245–0072). A combination of traditional tea shop and antiques store, Basically British is tucked away inside the mill complex, through a rough metal gate and a garden-like summer courtyard where live bands occasionally play. Inside, the once sooty industrial space has been whitewashed and carefully spruced with stained-glass windows and velvet drapes to create a surprisingly intimate atmosphere, full of interesting nooks and crannies and stuffed with British culinary delicacies and antiques large and small. Owner Fab Goldberg and her attentive staff offer guests a choice of dozens of teas, including exotics such as Russian Corovan and Moroccan Mint, served alongside sweet and crunchy scones accompanied by clotted cream and strawberry jam (a full lunch menu also is available). Basically British is truly one of the great "finds" in the East Bay, and a must-see if you are in Warren. Open Sunday to Thursday 11:00 A.M. to 6:00 P.M., Friday and Saturday 11:00 A.M. to 11:00 P.M.

For our last two stops in Warren, you need to leave downtown. From Main Street/Route 114, proceed north of Town Hall to Child Street/Route 103, and make a right. Follow Child Street until you cross a small bridge over the Kickemuit River, proceeding approximately ½ mile to Long Lane. Make the right here and continue until Long Lane ends at Barton Avenue; proceed east (left) on Barton Avenue to Touisset Avenue; make a right, and follow this road until you come to the Touisset fire station, on your right. Pull into the fire station parking lot, and you'll find the trailhead for the **Touisset Marsh Wildlife Refuge** (949–5454; www.asri.org/touisset.htm).

A seventy-acre nature preserve, the Touisset Wildlife Refuge features open meadows, as well as paths that cut through forest and open up onto salt marshes, a small inlet (Chase Cove), and the banks of the Kickemuit River. Along the well-marked trail you can see an abundance of wildlife, especially in the marsh area that is home to herons and egrets. The trail crosses a small brook, and at high tide it can get quite muddy, so pack some water-resistant footgear if you come. One main trail circles the periphery of the property, while several smaller paths allow access to the interior. Open dawn to dusk year-round.

Rhode Island has such an abundance of fine Italian restaurants that the big cities like Providence and Newport can't contain them all. Surrounded on all sides by fast-food joints, the **Tuscan Tavern** (632 Metacom Avenue/Route 136, 247–9200; www.tuscantavern.net) is an island of casually elegant dining in the heart of suburbia. Inside this classic Tuscan villa, the main dining hall is ringed with bright murals that offset the burnished wood interior; a half-circle counter frames a huge oven used to make pizzas, calzones, and bruchetta. The adjoining bar is dominated by a stone fireplace.

Like the decor, the menu is sophisticated without being stuffy, and prices are reasonable (most entrees are under $20). Popular Northern Italian entrees include a generous Palazzo grilled pork tenderloin in a caramelized onion sauce; Vitello Dante, topped with mushrooms, spinach, mozzarella, and marsala wine; and Pesce Adriatica—cod with lobster cream sauce. Open Monday to Thursday from 11:00 A.M. to 9:30 P.M., Friday and Saturday from 11:00 A.M. to 10:30 P.M., and Sunday from 11:00 A.M. to 9:00 P.M.

Bristol

Despite its somewhat isolated location, Bristol has never been a backwater. Founded in 1680, the town briefly served as headquarters for Lafayette during the Revolutionary War, when town fathers paid a ransom in cattle and sheep to keep a British naval squadron from leveling the place. In the eighteenth and early nineteenth centuries, a number of seafaring Bristol residents made their fortunes in the infamous triangle trade, running molasses, rum, and slaves between America, Africa, and the West Indies. The great homes lining Hope Street, including Linden Place, an impressive Federal-style mansion, are the lasting legacy of this prosperous (if morally questionable) period for the town.

The collapse of the triangle trade nearly ruined Bristol, but the town bounced back to become a shipbuilding center of world renown from the late 1800s on.

Shipbuilding still is a vital part of the local economy, but today Bristol's main claim to fame has more to do with the Stars and Stripes than with semaphore flags. The town's annual *Fourth of July parade* (www.july4thbristol ri.com) has made Bristol nearly synonymous with patriotic celebration in southern New England. Held since 1785, the parade today is an extravaganza of bands, floats, Clydesdales, mummers, and fireworks that attracts thousands of spectators. The red, white, and blue stripe painted down Hope Street attests to the fact that the parade is serious business hereabouts, and many folks stay in town from the time the church bells ring at 6:00 A.M. to signal the start of festivities, until long after the last of the fireworks have boomed across the bay.

Nearly as legendary as the parade are the traffic tie-ups associated with it; even the bike path gets clogged, although it remains one of the better ways of getting into town for the big show. Fortunately, the town begins celebrating weeks in advance, with festivals and free concerts to get you into the patriotic spirit without having to brave the big holiday weekend crowds. If you plan to stay at one of the handful of inns located downtown during the holiday, make your reservations well in advance—as in years, not months.

Stand on the deck of the *Audubon Society of Rhode Island's Environmental Education Center* (1401 Hope Street, 245–7500; www.asrieec.org) and look to your right, and you'll see houses. Look to the left, and there's a line of condos marching downhill to the edge of the East Bay Bike Path. No doubt,

Bristol's "Patriotic Exercises"

Beginning with the first observance in 1785 (conducted by Revolutionary War veteran Dr. Henry Wright), many of Bristol's early Independence Day celebrations contained elements at once strange and familiar to those of us who associate the Fourth of July with fireworks and backyard barbecues. Although the day was marked by cannon fire, music, and dancing, the centerpiece of Bristol's patriotic celebrations during the seventeenth and eighteenth centuries was more solemn: a prayer service held at one of the town's many houses of worship.

While most people from outside Bristol know only about the Fourth of July parade—officially the "Grand Military, Civic, and Fireman's Parade"—the town has proudly clung to the traditional "Patriotic Exercises" that have marked Independence Day since colonial times. Each year, prior to the parade, residents gather at Colt Memorial School in downtown Bristol for a ceremony that includes prayers, the singing of the national anthem, and the award of a U.S. flag to the Bristol native who has traveled the greatest distance to be home for the parade.

The parade itself has been held almost every year since 1834, except for a few years in the nineteenth century when the town was hit by hard times and could not afford to pay for the official procession (also, the 1881 parade was canceled because of the assassination of President James Garfield). Today, as many as 10,000 marchers take part in the parade as it proceeds along its 3-mile route through downtown Bristol.

the land you're standing on would be condos, too, had a generous property owner not donated the twenty-eight-acre parcel to the Audubon Society.

Opened in July 2000, the Environmental Education Center helps guide visitors on a virtual and real-life tour of some of Rhode Island's major wildlife habitats, including farmland, meadows, wetlands, and Narragansett Bay. A kid-friendly exhibit hall includes a display on the nighttime denizens of local cornfields (the hall is lit by flashlight), and a 500-gallon aquarium represents wetland life, teeming with fish like killies and lumbering horseshoe crabs. The star of the show, however, is a life-size, 33-foot-long replica of a Northern Atlantic Right Whale, cut away so visitors can pop their heads inside to check out the whale's blubber, baleen, and internal organs.

The center's main building sits on a sloping hillside and serves as the terminus for a 7/10-mile trail that passes through many of the same habitats described in the exhibit, ending at the shore of the bay. The path weaves through a meadow and cornfield, briefly through forested land, and crosses a freshwater wetland via a wooden boardwalk before intersecting with the East Bay Bike Path (racks are provided for those who want to combine a bike ride with their visit). The boardwalk continues through a salt marsh before stopping at the water's edge.

The Environmental Education Center and walking trail are open daily 9:00 A.M. to 5:00 P.M.; Sunday winter hours are noon to 5:00 P.M. Admission is $6.00 for adults, $4.00 for children ages four to twelve, and free for children under age four.

Rearing up over the east side of Route 114 are a pair of copper bulls, which mark the entrance to **Colt State Park** (253–7482; www.riparks.com/colt.htm). The park, a sprawling 464-acre recreation area carved out of the former Colt estate, features bike paths, beaches, and a 3-mile shoreline drive with magnificent sunsets. A "National Path to Fitness" trail, 6 miles in length, features exercise stations for both children and adults. A farmers' market operates on Friday afternoons in the spring and summer.

Just south of the park but before you enter downtown Bristol, look for Poppasquash Road on your right. Turn here and follow the road around Bristol Harbor (slowing to enjoy the view across the water to downtown Bristol) to **Coggeshall Farm Museum** (253–9062; www.coggeshallfarm.org).

Coggeshall's raison d'être is to re-create the life of a typical Rhode Island coastal farm family of the 1790s, and it involves a lot more than dressing the staff in period costumes. All the vegetables and herbs grown here, as well as the livestock, are what would have been raised by a family of the eighteenth century, and the products of the farm are used in demonstrations for visitors. Depending on what time of year you come, you'll find workers shearing sheep, tapping maple trees for their sap, pressing cider, or working the smithy's forge. It's best to call ahead to schedule your visit to coincide with one of the farm's many special events, topped by the annual Harvest Fair (held the third week of September). The fair features traditional music and games like tug-of-war and— a big hit with the kids—pumpkin-seed spitting contests. Open Tuesday through Sunday 10:00 A.M. to 4:00 P.M. October through March and 10:00 A.M. to 6:00 P.M. April through September. Admission is $3.00 for adults and $2.00 for seniors and children ages six to fifteen; additional fees charged for special events.

Farther down Poppasquash Road is the **Point Pleasant Inn** (333 Poppasquash Road, 253–0627; www.pointpleasantinn.com). Drive to the end of the road, through the stone gates with the PRIVATE PROPERTY sign, and turn left at the P/P sign.

For anyone who ever drove through an upscale neighborhood and wondered what it would be like to live in one of those homes, this is your chance to find out. The first floor of this elegant brick and clapboard manor house has everything you'd expect from a fine waterfront home: a library/TV room, dining area with views of Poppasquash Cove and downtown Bristol, and a great room accessed through double doors at the end of a long, paneled hallway. The doors open onto a bright room with two walls of windows overlooking

Antiquing along Hope Street

Nearby Warren's antiques stores may get the lion's share of the attention, but Hope Street in Bristol also has a nice selection of shops for collectors and treasure-hunters.

Stoneware and china are among the "antiques, gifts, and curiosities" preferred at Muzzie's Attic (407 Hope Street, 253–0814). Alfred's (331 Hope Street, 253–3465) has a fine collection of mahogany furniture, china, crystal, and silver. Robin Jenkins Antiques (278 Hope Street, 254–8958) specializes in indoor and outdoor furniture from the eighteenth, nineteenth, and twentieth centuries.

Just east of Hope Street, toward the harbor on State Street, is another pair of antiques shops with distinct reputations. You won't find Western wear at Jesse-James Antiques (44 State Street, 253–2240), but owners Jesse Miranda and James Dumas say their low consignment fees mean low prices and a quick turnover in their stock of furniture, glassware, collectibles, and textiles. Across the street, the Center Chimney (39 State Street, 253–8010) is the only shop in town selling estate jewelry, from rings to brooches to necklaces.

Farther north on Hope Street is Dantiques (676 Hope Street, 253–1122), where owners Dan and Chris Manchester collect all the merchandise they acquire from estate sales around the region. They have a wide variety of antique furniture as well as collectibles like inkwells, perfume bottles, and paperweights.

the water; a corner couch invites you to linger a while, and a telescope is available for tracking sailboats or zeroing in on the Bristol waterfront.

Upstairs, both hallways and guest rooms are graced with original oil paintings of horses, rustic landscapes, and nautical scenes. Each room has its own unique character, particularly the Narragansett Suite with its all-leather sitting area and the Bristol Harbor room with its private deck overlooking the pool.

The inn also has a basement sauna, game room, and gym. All-inclusive rates range from $525 to $625 nightly and include lodging, breakfast, cocktails, snacks, and use of the tennis courts, kayaks, and bikes. Open late April to early November.

Downtown Bristol is a stroller's paradise. Hope Street (Route 114) is unusual in that one side of the street is lined with shops, while grand old homes line the other. Best known of the latter is *Linden Place* (500 Hope Street, 253-0390; www.lindenplace.org), the Federal-style-with-a-flair mansion of the DeWolf and Colt families. Linden Place is open Thursday through Saturday 10:00 A.M. to 4:00 P.M. and Sunday noon to 4:00 P.M., May 1 to Columbus Day. It is also open from noon to 6:00 P.M. every day from the second Monday in December to December 31, except December 24 and December 25. Admission is $5.00 for adults and $2.50 for children under age twelve; additional fee is charged during the Christmas season, when the mansion is decorated according to various holiday themes, such as "The Night Before Christmas" or "Christmas in Miniature." The Linden Place Fourth of July picnic, which includes breakfast, lunch, and a bird's-eye view of the parade from the mansion lawn, is a hot ticket ($40 for adults, $25 for children).

Linden Place is nice to visit, but if you wonder what it would be like to be a guest in such a grand old home, you have a couple of choices: the **Bradford-Dimond-Norris House** (474 Hope Street, 253–6338; www.bdnhouse.com) and the **Rockwell House Inn** (610 Hope Street, 253–0040; www.rockwellhouse inn.com), are architecturally similar to the DeWolf mansion, though in more modest proportions.

Known as the "Wedding Cake House," the circa 1792 Bradford-Dimond-Norris House is named for a former deputy governor, governor, and sugar magnate, respectively. Originally a two-story building, a third floor was added after the Civil War, giving the house its confectionery appearance. Now a bed-and-breakfast owned by Lloyd and Suzanne Adams, the house is steeped in history and colonial trappings, and the quiet garden veranda is a favorite spot for breakfast or just to relax and read a book. The Bradford-Dimond-Norris House has four guest rooms with rates ranging from $125 to $200 per night.

Most inns boast about being romantic, but the Rockwell House has the history to back up the claim. The "Courting Corner" at the back of the house—a cozy alcove warmed by a stone fireplace—was built by Charles Rockwell for his daughter, June, after she was jilted by a ne'er-do-well suitor. Happily, the concept was a success: The daughter's eventual husband proposed to her before the fire, and many other couples have gotten engaged in the Courting Corner over the years.

Innkeepers Debra and Steve Krohn also put out a full gourmet breakfast, and the location means you can walk to almost everything the town of Bristol has to offer. The four guest rooms all have private baths and range in price from $150 to $249.

Other prominent Hope Street buildings include the **1880 Town Hall** and the 1883 **Burnside Memorial,** honoring native son and Civil War general Ambrose Burnside. A courtyard next door to the Burnside building contains a memorial to Bristol's war dead; the building itself now houses the **Bristol Visitor's Center,** open daily 11:00 A.M. to 4:00 P.M.

Sam's Restaurant & Pizzeria (149 Bradford Street, 253–7949) reminds me of the pizza joints of my youth, with simple stools facing a Formica countertop, huge, low-slung freezers holding unknown treats, and pictures of the owner and his family pasted on every available vertical surface. In the corner,

Burnside's Sideburns

Civil War general Ambrose Everett Burnside's battlefield prowess was less than legendary: Burnside is remembered more for his facial hair than for his skill in facing the enemy.

A veteran of the Mexican War, Burnside moved to Rhode Island in 1853 and opened a factory to manufacture a breech-loading carbine that he designed, but he was forced to sell the business when the government failed to give him a military contract.

When the Civil War broke out, Burnside rose quickly from command of the First Rhode Island regiment to a succession of more significant posts, culminating in his being named commander of the Army of the Potomac—the standard-bearer for the Union Army—in 1862. But Burnside's career as a commander was uneven; earlier successes leading smaller groups of men were followed by blunders as head of larger units.He resigned from the army in 1865.

Burnside's limited military successes were enough to help get him elected governor of Rhode Island three times, but his most lasting legacy sprung from his copious facial hair, trimmed into bushy muttonchops. Pundits switched the syllables of Burnside's last name and dubbed the style "sideburns."

Momma sat sorting through piles of soda cans for recycling, while the younger generation worked in the kitchen.

This storefront pizzeria on a Bristol side street intrigued me because it advertised Sicilian pizza, which from my early memories involved a thick, puffy crust with crispy edges and lots of cheese and sauce. Alas, Sam's pizza is more the pan-baked, medium-crust variety found throughout Rhode Island, but the good news is that it's an exceptional example of the genre. My daughter and I sat down at the counter and ordered a large pizza with "melted mozzarella cheese" off the menu, intending to bring some home; instead, we wolfed down practically the whole, delicious sheet.

Sam's has been successful since 1947 by treating customers like family, chatting us up even though we were immediately spotted for nonregulars. For a taste of simple hospitality and great pizza, the restaurant is open Wednesday to Saturday 11:00 A.M. to 10:00 P.M. and Sunday 11:00 A.M. to 9:00 P.M.

Bristol in some ways is Rhode Island in microcosm; everybody knows everyone else, many residents have lived here their whole lives, and most would never dream of leaving. A walk around the town commons, located just a block east of Hope Street (either State Street or Church Street will get you there), provides some insight into the sense of community that local residents share. In the center of the grassy commons is the town bandshell, right next to an extensive children's playground. There is a ball field where, for generations, young sluggers have been hitting foul balls into the fieldstone back wall of the *First Baptist Church,* built in 1814 and topped with a chubby, open-sided bell tower that still rings residents to services on Sunday mornings. Next to the church, in a neat line fronting on High Street, are two other community cornerstones, the old *Byfield School* and the *1817 Bristol County Courthouse,* which housed meetings of the Rhode Island General Assembly from 1819 to 1852.

Another historic building on High Street is the *William's Grant Inn* (154 High Street, 253–4222; www.wmgrantinn.com), located in an 1808 colonial/Federal home in a quiet neighborhood in Bristol's historic district. The inn has five rooms decorated with period furniture and antiques, and there's a quiet patio and garden out back, complete with goldfish pond. Breakfast, included with the price of a room, includes Portuguese French toast, New Zealand bacon and egg pie, and blueberry pancakes whipped up by innkeepers Diane and Warren Poehler. Rooms with a private bath are $99 to $199.

East of Hope Street is Thames Street and the Bristol waterfront, where shipbuilders still ply their trade and an array of eateries wait to tempt your palate and quench your thirst. Directly across from Independence Park and the end of the East Bay Bike Path is a restaurant that's a favorite with Bristol residents, *S.S. Dion* (520 Thames Street, 253–2884; www.ssdion.com). With tongue-and-groove walls adorned with nautical knickknacks and photos, S.S. Dion is an unpretentious setting in which to enjoy generous portions of well-presented seafood, especially the swordfish dishes for which owner Steven Dion and his staff are best known. Open Monday to Saturday 5:00 to 9:00 P.M.

For equally good food in a more casual setting, roll your bike up to the front door of *Quito's* (411 Thames Street, 253–4500), a cozy clam shack located on a pier on Bristol Harbor at the south end of Independence Park. If you want table service, step inside the tiny dining room; otherwise, order your fried or baked fish, legendary clam cakes, or seafood stew or chowder from the take-out window and grab a table on the dock. Beer and wine—rarely found at your run-of-the-mill clam shack—also are served. Open Monday to Saturday 11:30 A.M. to 9:00 P.M. and Sunday 11:30 A.M. to 8:00 P.M. during the summer; closed Monday during the winter.

Just past Quitos are a number of new additions to the Bristol waterfront, starting with a boardwalk that runs along the edge of a former mill complex now converted to luxury condominiums and ends at the door of the acclaimed DeWolf Tavern. A stroll along the boardwalk affords a good look at the past and future of Bristol, not to mention the great views of Bristol Harbor.

DeWolf Tavern (259 Thames Street, 254–2005; www.dewolftavern.com) is part of Bristol's historic legacy and the town's cutting edge. Located in a circa

King Philip's War

If you've ever wondered why Native Americans never tried to push the early European settlers back into the sea once they realized that the newcomers intended to take away their lands, the answer is: They did. Unfortunately for the native population, however, the effort was too little, too late.

By the time the Pilgrims landed in Plymouth, Massachusetts, in 1620, native tribes like the Wampanoag, Patuxet, and Narragansett had already been ravaged by a series of epidemics, unwittingly introduced by the earliest European explorers. These plagues, which continued on and off throughout the seventeenth century, killed 75 percent of the Wampanoags; other tribes were completely decimated.

While early relations between the white settlers and the Native Americans were harmonious, by the 1660s the English craving for land brought the settlers into conflict with the weakened but still formidable native tribes. After the English poisoned his brother Wamsutta (Alexander) in 1661, the surviving son of the great Wampanoag sachem Massasoit, Metacomet (Philip), began preparing for a war to drive the white settlers out of New England.

Lasting from 1675 to 1676, King Philip's War was the Native Americans' last, best chance to reclaim their homelands. At a war council at Mount Hope (Montaup), Philip united tribes that for generations had fought each other, including the Nipmuc, Pocumtuc, and Narragansett, and fighting broke out across Massachusetts, Rhode Island, New York, and Connecticut. Early raids and battles favored Philip's forces. But the English trapped the Narragansetts in their swamp fortress near Kingston, Rhode Island, in December 1675 and nearly wiped out the tribe. In early 1676, Philip led a series of raids on English settlements, burning Providence and Warwick, among other towns. But he lost a valuable ally in April when Canonchet, the leader of the Narragansetts, was captured and executed. After a losing battle at Turner's Falls in Connecticut, Philip's tribal alliance fell apart, and the English eventually trapped Philip at Mount Hope in August 1676.

Betrayed by an informer, Philip was shot on August 12, and his severed head was put on display at Plymouth. With him died the last hope of the native New England tribes, which by the beginning of the eighteenth century had almost ceased to exist on their former lands.

1818 warehouse building built from granite ship's ballast, the restaurant offers an interesting fusion menu designed by chef Sai Viswanath, who incorporates Indian flourishes into his New England American dishes. Diners are literally surrounded by history, including panels of nineteenth-century graffiti uncovered during recent renovations. The restaurant's upstairs deck is perhaps the best spot for fine waterfront dining in the East Bay. Open Monday to Saturday 5:00 to 10:00 P.M., Sunday 5:00 to 9:00 P.M. (bar open till midnight except on Sunday).

For more casual fare accompanied by a selection of draft beers, the nearby **J.G. Goff's Pub** (251 Thames Street, 253–4523) has a pair of waterfront decks and an expansive menu of appetizers and sandwiches. Open 11:30 A.M. to 1:00 A.M. daily (kitchen closes at 10:00 P.M. Sunday to Thursday, 11:00 P.M. on Friday and Saturday).

A 1932 Narragansett Brewery truck garage on Thames Street has been thoroughly renovated to become the home of **Redlefsen's Rotisserie and Grill** (444 Thames Street, 254–1188; www.redlefsens.com), formerly located on Hope Street. A two-sided gas fireplace, a variety of warmly finished wood and stained-glass windows, and a large skylight make the interior of this eclectic, European-style restaurant cheerful and inviting. The roomy bar side is awash in yachting memorabilia and decor, and Redlefsen's pours a unique selection of tap beers you aren't likely to find at your local tavern, including Worsteiner, Spaten Munchen, Pilsner Urquell, and Franzickaner Weisbar.

The German beers salute the heritage of owner Walter Guertler, who also hosts a lively Oktoberfest each fall, complete with lederhosen-clad dancers and singers, sauerbraten, and festival beers. Although Wiener schnitzel is the specialty of the house and German and Alsatian dishes are popular, the menu draws inspiration from around the world. Open for lunch Monday to Saturday 11:30 A.M. to 2:30 P.M. and for Sunday brunch 10:30 A.M. to 2:30 P.M.; open for dinner Monday to Thursday 5:00 to 9:30 P.M., Friday and Saturday 5:00 to 10:00 P.M., and Sunday 5:00 to 9:00 P.M.

For a cold pint of ale or lager after a brisk workout on the bike path, there's no better place than **Aidan's Pub,** located a couple of blocks south of S.S. Dion on the corner at 5 John Street (254–1940). A neighborhood bar and restaurant that does not feel the need to hit you over the head with shamrocks to prove its Irishness, Aidan's pours a number of hearty brews from its taps, the perfect companion to the pub's excellent fish and chips, bangers and mash, and corned beef. Open daily 11:30 A.M. to 1:00 A.M.

Few would use the word "handsome" to characterize the infamously arbitrary and notoriously slovenly Judge Roy Bean, but that's the best way to describe the **Judge Roy Bean Saloon** (1 State Street, 253–7526). Little expense was spared in constructing the bar/restaurant's pair of exquisite, hand-carved bars, and owner Aidan Graham has lavished fine wood, brickwork, and expensive glass both inside and out.

J. R. Bean's packs them in Wednesday to Saturday with live music downstairs, a pair of pool tables at "Jersey Lilly's" on the second floor, and a dance hall on the top floor.

Judge Bean was said to favor his fellow Irishmen when handing down decisions in his frontier Texas courtroom, so he'd probably pass favorable judgment on the menu at this Bristol nightspot, which features a variety of pub fare and an iced Irish coffee topped with whipped cream. Open Monday to Thursday 4:00 P.M. to 1:00 A.M., Friday to Sunday noon to 1:00 A.M.

Occupying a small storefront on State Street is one of Rhode Island's most acclaimed new restaurants, **Persimmon** (31 State Street, 254–7474; www.persimmonbristol.com), where chef/owner Chempe Speidel works his culinary magic. Open Tuesday to Sunday 5:00 to 9:00 P.M.

Nearby, at the end of Constitution Street, is the gateway to one of Rhode Island's most out-of-the-way locales, **Prudence Island** (www.prudenceisland .us). The Prudence Island ferry (253–9808) leaves from the docks here. You also can call **Shaw's Water Taxi** to get to Prudence Island from Newport (683–2021).

Located in the heart of Narragansett Bay, Prudence Island is big enough (6½ miles long, 1⅜ miles wide) to make you wonder why it never was developed like its sisters to the south: Aquidneck Island (Newport, Middletown, and Portsmouth) and Conanicut Island (Jamestown). The bulldozer's loss is our gain, though, as Prudence remains an isolated oasis just minutes by boat from the state's most densely populated areas.

Home to about 150 year-round residents and a large deer population, Prudence begs to be explored on foot, especially since large chunks of the island are accessible only by gravel roads (hardier souls could try a mountain bike). Most points of interest are along the island's main drag, Narragansett Avenue, which runs parallel to the eastern shoreline. About a mile south of the ferry landing at Homestead is the **Sandy Point Lighthouse,** built in 1851 and overlooking a small adjacent beach. Another half mile brings you to the beginning of a nature trail, which accesses the **Heritage Foundation of Rhode Island parkland** in the center of the island. Continue south to reach **South Prudence State Park,** established on the site of an abandoned naval base.

The **Narragansett Bay National Estuarian Research Reserve** is based on Prudence Island and comprises Prudence, Patience, Hope, and Dyer Islands. Prudence Island visitors can drop in to the reserve's learning center, located at 55 South Reserve Drive (683–6780).

The more adventurous can head north from the ferry to explore the undeveloped Pine Hill area, which includes a beach at Sandy Beach Road. A grassy cart path extends from here to the northern tip of the island, at **Providence Point.**

Prudence Island is a nice place for a little outdoor activity, but be forewarned: There are no restaurants and only two small stores (**Marcie's General Store** on Narragansett Avenue at the ferry landing and **Freddy's** by the lighthouse). Prudence Park, located on the island's west side, has some nice

Victorian homes, while the island's still-functioning one-room schoolhouse is on Broadway.

Thanks to the large deer population, Lyme disease–bearing ticks also are an unfortunate hazard for hikers on Prudence Island, so wear long pants.

As you travel south from downtown Bristol on Hope Street/Route 114, you'll be tempted to look right to catch occasional glimpses of Bristol Harbor. Instead, keep an eye out to your left. At the corner of Burnside Avenue, you'll see the hull of the *Defiant,* an America's Cup trial boat built in Bristol. Turn here and you'll be at the doorstep of the ***Herreshoff Marine Museum.***

As Bristol is to sailing, the name Herreshoff is to yachts. It was here that five generations of the Herreshoff family built some of the world's fastest and most beautiful wooden vessels, from the eight consecutive America's Cup–winning yachts of the late nineteenth and early twentieth centuries to the patrol torpedo boats of the Second World War. The museum, housed in the company's former manufacturing plant, tells the story in scores of photos and with the gleaming hulls of the fifty or so boats on exhibit.

Inside, you can run your hand along the elegant and graceful lines that mark the designs of "the Wizard of Bristol," Captain Nat Herreshoff, and his progeny. Amid the great sailing vessels, don't miss the *Thania,* used in the filming of the movie *The Great Gatsby,* and the *Sprite,* Nat Herreshoff's personal boat and the oldest catboat in America.

Across Burnside Street from the Herreshoff exhibits is another tribute to racing yachts, the ***America's Cup Hall of Fame*** (One Burnside Street, 253–5000; www.herreshoff.org). Included in the hall are America's Cup memorabilia, photos of all of the winning captains, and models of the hulls of every Cup winner.

The Herreshoff Marine Museum and the America's Cup Hall of Fame are open daily May through October from 10:00 A.M. to 5:00 P.M. Admission is $8.00 for adults, $7.00 for seniors, and $2.00 for students; children under twelve are free.

The ***Lobster Pot Restaurant and Gallery***'s name betrays its humbler origins as a family-oriented seafood joint. They've been serving fresh seafood here for more than seventy years, but about a decade ago the Lobster Pot underwent extensive renovations and emerged as an upscale eatery. It's been a successful transition; many Ocean State residents call the Lobster Pot the best seafood restaurant in the state. Lobster, swordfish, and a raw bar are prominent features. Expansive windows offer a panoramic view of upper Narragansett Bay and Hog Island and Prudence Island; an outdoor patio offers similar vistas.

If the Lobster Pot's high ceilings and bright atmosphere remind you of an art gallery, that's because it is one: Seascapes and other works from Rhode Island, national, and international artists adorn the walls and are for sale, along with a selection of fine jewelry. The Lobster Pot is located at 119 Hope Street/

thepriceof pragmatism

People in Rhode Island complain as much about their politicians as anyone anywhere else, if not more so. But every so often, local pols' inbred Yankee pragmatism temporarily outweighs the bureaucratic impulse.

Case in point: In 1998 state officials were in a quandary over the tolls collected at the Mount Hope Bridge. Seems the 30 cents per car being collected wasn't enough to maintain the tollbooths, let alone make a profit for the state.

Predictably, some lawmakers proposed raising the tolls to a level that would cover the cost of collecting them. In some places, that would have been the end of the matter.

But after not too much discussion, the state came up with a surprising, common sense alternative: eliminate the cost by eliminating the tollbooths. Even more shockingly, that's exactly what the state did. So as you drive across the Mount Hope Bridge totally free of charge, perhaps you should toss a token of gratitude to that most unusual of beasts: the pragmatic politician.

Route 114 (253–9100). Open Tuesday to Sunday for lunch and dinner, 11:30 A.M. to 9:00 P.M. on weekdays, 11:30 A.M. to 10:00 P.M. on Saturday, and noon to 9:00 P.M. on Sunday.

There's a touch of California at Bristol's ***Blithewold Mansion and Gardens,*** 101 Ferry Road/Route 114, just north of the Mount Hope Bridge (253– 2707; www.blithewold.org). Towering over the other trees in the mansion's "enclosed" garden is a 100-foot giant sequoia, the largest redwood tree east of the Rockies. Planted in 1911, the tree grows about a foot each year and is the highlight of just one of the many beautiful gardens at Blithewold. The former estate of a Pennsylvania coal magnate, Blithewold has thirty-three acres of gardens centered on a forty-five-room mansion resembling an English manor house. The mansion, built in 1908, sits before a sloping lawn that affords a terrific view of Narragansett Bay.

Many of the plants, shrubs, and trees at Blithewold convey the spirit of the Orient as well, reflecting a turn-of-the-century passion for Asian horticulture. In one garden stands a Chinese toon tree, the first ever planted in America; another corner of the estate has been turned into a Japanese water garden, with an earthen bridge that crosses a pond to a tiny island, a maple tree, and a decorative Japanese lantern. The grove of yellow bamboo on the property actually was something of a mistake of fortune: The bamboo originally was planted simply to provide garden stakes, but it began growing beyond all expectations. Today the bamboo stalks grow to more than 20 feet tall, and visitors can follow a trail through the grove.

Tours of the mansion are available mid-April to Columbus Day Wednesday to Sunday from 10:00 A.M. to 4:00 P.M., but the grounds are open for self-guided tours year-round from 10:00 A.M. to 5:00 P.M. Admission is $10.00 for adults, $8.00 for seniors and students; children under age seventeen are free. The mansion also is open most of the month of December for an annual Christmas exhibit.

If you're thinking that this would be a lovely part of the state in which to linger for a while, you're in luck: Kathryn and David Swanson have converted the top floor of their home at 150 Ferry Road into a charming guest suite. The main bedroom at the *Swanson House* overlooks the perennial gardens on this 1.5-acre property; there's also a smaller second bedroom and a dressing room that's a big hit with the brides who overnight here for their weddings at nearby Blithewold or Mount Hope Farm.

Guests of the Swanson House are welcome to relax under the trellis on the terrace out back or stroll the quiet property; downtown Bristol is just a mile away, and the walk to town can be broken up with a visit to the Herreshoff museum or a number of antiques shops. Room rates are $150 nightly, double occupancy (for continental breakfast, add $25), plus $75 for a third person. For more information call 254–5056.

Proceeding south, you reach an intersection where you can either go straight across the bridge or turn left and head back north on Route 136. Make the left.

As you bounce down the seemingly endless wooded road leading east to the *Haffenreffer Museum of Anthropology* (Tower Street off Metacom Avenue/Route 136, approximately 2 miles north of the Mount Hope Bridge), it's easy to forget that you're on a peninsula measuring about 3 miles across at its widest point. Your jaunt through the woods is rewarded, however, as the trees part and the road ends at the museum grounds overlooking Mount Hope Bay, with a lovely view of downtown Fall River and the Braga Bridge. A grassy hillside slopes down toward the bay—a nice place for a picnic lunch on a sunny day.

The museum itself is located in part of an old dairy farm, converted in 1928 to house brewing magnate Rudolf Frederick Haffenreffer's personal collection of Native American artifacts. Today the museum is operated by Brown University and contains ceremonial clothing, pottery, weapons, and jewelry representing not only the Wampanoag tribe native to this area but also other native cultures from throughout the United States, South and Central America, and around the world. The Plains Indians collection is especially extensive.

Extending south of the museum buildings to Mount Hope Point is the crowning jewel of the Haffenreffer property: 435 acres of history-filled forest, swamp, and shoreline highlighted by *King Philip's Chair* and nearby Cold Spring, the spiritual center of Wampanoag life and the seat of government for King Philip. Philip led his tribe into a disastrous final conflict with the white settlers of Rhode Island and Massachusetts, and he was killed in Mirey Swamp in

1675 in the final act of a war that saw the near-annihilation of the Wampanoags.

The museum and grounds are open Saturday and Sunday 11:00 A.M. to 5:00 P.M. from September through May and Tuesday to Sunday 11:00 A.M. to 5:00 P.M. from June through August. Museum admission is $3.00 for adults, $2.00 for seniors, and $1.00 for children under twelve. Call 253–8388 for information or visit its Web site: www.brown.edu/facilities/haffenreffer.

Contiguous with the museum property is the 127-acre **Mount Hope Farm** (250 Metacom Avenue, 254–5059; www.mounthopefarm.com), recently saved from development and now open to the public for hiking and biking. This farm, which is more than 300 years old, includes a 1745 colonial home where George Washington stayed with Deputy Governor William Bradford in 1789. More recently, this was the home of the Haffenreffer family, whose legacy includes the Cove Cabin, a log building with great views of the Mount Hope Bridge and Seal Island, a refuge for harbor seals. The Cove Cabin is used for public events, including lectures and an annual jazz and lobster festival in August.

Mount Hope Farm offers endless options for exploration, and the best way to experience it all is to stay at the **Governor Bradford House** bed-and-breakfast, located in the heart of the property and featuring eight guest rooms under its gambrel roof. The public spaces of the inn are delightful, including the Haffenreffer Room with its baby grand piano and bay window looking into the garden, and the Isaac Royal Room with its ancient gaming table and nautical decor. Every room seems to have its own story, such as a guest bedroom that has a trapdoor under the bed where the owners—who made their fortune selling beer—may have stashed booze during Prohibition. B&B room rates are $125 to $275 per night.

OTHER NOTEWORTHY ATTRACTIONS AND EVENTS IN THE EAST BAY

Barrington Town Hall Barrington	**Colt State Park** Bristol
Bristol Art Museum Bristol	**Historical and Preservation Society Museum** Bristol
Bristol Train of Artillery Bristol	**Bristol Fourth of July Parade** Bristol
Charles W. Greene Museum Warren	**Old-Fashioned Family Clambake** Warren; July

The Bradford House is just one lodging option: There are also rooms available in a rustic Haffenreffer family guest cottage and in the former cabana facing the pool. Each offers a great starting point for exploring the estate, beginning with an 1880s barn that once was used as a gym and still contains vintage shuffleboard paddles and pulleys from an old gym set (the barn is now used for wedding receptions and other events). Nearby coops house a variety of pheasants and Rhode Island Reds (including Charlie the rooster), and cows graze in the adjacent fields. Walking paths lead to spring-fed ponds, old rock walls and foundations, a monument to King Philip's War, and the rocky shoreline of Mount Hope Bay. The grounds of the Mount Hope Farm are open 8:00 A.M. to 3:00 P.M. during the winter and until 5:00 P.M. during the summer. Tours of the Governor Bradford House are conducted May to October, Wednesday to Saturday from noon to 4:00 P.M.

Back on Route 136 and heading south, keep an eye out for Mount Hope Avenue on your left and a small sign for ***Tweet Balzano's Family Restaurant*** (180 Mount Hope Avenue, 253–9811; www.tweetsrestaurant.com). Ever since Tweet and Millie Balzano opened the place in the 1950s, this has been the Bristol mecca for generous seafood and Italian dinners served family style and at a reasonable price (entrees are under $16 except for an occasional twin-lobster special). Open Monday to Thursday 4:30 to 10:30 P.M., Friday and Saturday 11:30 A.M. to 11:30 P.M., Sunday 11:30 A.M. to 10:30 P.M.

A short drive farther and you'll reach the end of the Bristol peninsula; fortunately, the ***Mount Hope Bridge*** awaits to carry you over Mount Hope Bay to Portsmouth. As you pass over this narrow, two-lane span, drive slowly to admire the architecture that won the designers international acclaim when the bridge was built in 1929. The bridge is especially pretty on a warm summer night, when all the old lampposts are lit in silent accord with the lights dancing on the waters below.

Places to Stay in the East Bay

(All Area Codes 401)

BRISTOL

Bradford-Dimond-Norris House
474 Hope Street
253-6338

King Philip Inn
400 Metacom Avenue
253-7600

Rockwell House Inn
610 Hope Street
253-0040 or
(800) 815-0040

Swanson House
150 Ferry Road
254-5056

William's Grant Inn
154 High Street
253-4222 or
(800) 596-4222

WARREN

Wren & Thistle B&B
19 Market Street
247-0631

HELPFUL WEB SITES ABOUT THE EAST BAY

Bristol Phoenix
www.bristolri.com

East Bay Tourism Council
www.eastbayritourism.com

Online Bristol
www.onlinebristol.com

Town of Barrington
www.ci.barrington.ri.us/

Discover Bristol
www.discoverbristol.com

Town of Warren
www.townofwarren-ri.gov

Places to Eat in the East Bay

(All Area Codes 401)

BARRINGTON

Tyler Point Grille
32 Barton Avenue
247–0017

BRISTOL

Aidan's Pub
5 John Street
254–1940

DeWolf Tavern
259 Thames Street
254–2005

J.G. Goff's Pub
251 Thames Street
253–4523

Judge Roy Bean Saloon
1 State Street
253–7526

Leo's Ristorante
365 Hope Street
253–9300

The Lobster Pot Restaurant and Gallery
119 Hope Street
253–9100

Persimmon
31 State Street
254–7474

Quito's
411 Thames Street
253–4500

Redlefsen's Rotisserie and Grill
444 Thames Street
254–1188

S.S. Dion
520 Thames Street
253–2884

Tweet Balzano's Family Restaurant
180 Mount Hope Avenue
253–9811

WARREN

Basically British Tea Room
16 Cutler Street
245–0072

Delekta Pharmacy
496 Main Street
245–6767

The Market at Cutler Mills
137 Child Street
247–0021

Nat Porter Restaurant
125 Water Street
289–0373

Rod's Grill
6 Washington Street
245–9405

Stella Blues
50 Miller Street
289–0349

Tav Vino
267 Water Street
245–0231

Three Rivers
267 Water Street
289–2067

Tuscan Tavern
632 Metacom Avenue
247–9200

Wharf Tavern
215 Water Street
245–5043

SELECTED CHAMBER OF COMMERCE IN THE EAST BAY

East Bay Chamber of Commerce
www.eastbaychamber.org
16 Cutler Street
Warren 02885
245–0750

Newport

The mansions of the Gilded Age are the siren song for Newport visitors. But while the elegant "cottages" of the Vanderbilts and Astors are well worth a visit, don't let them lure you away from Newport's many other treasures.

By the time the mansions off Bellevue Avenue were built, Newport already had been a thriving seaport and intellectual center for more than 200 years. Until a prolonged British occupation stunted the city's progress during the Revolutionary War, Newport rivaled New York and Boston in importance. To this day Newport deserves much more than its reputation as a playground for the rich and famous.

Even those who come to town seeking the history of this old seaport tend to gravitate toward Thames Street, which means that neighborhoods like *Easton's Point* can be overlooked. Yet the Point section of Newport has as much history packed into a few small streets as just about any other place in America.

Founded by Quakers, most of the Point's quiet streets are either numbered or named after plants, trees, or geographic features, since Quaker theology frowned upon such "man-worship" as naming things after people or artificial objects. One exception is Washington Street—the Quakers' Water Street was

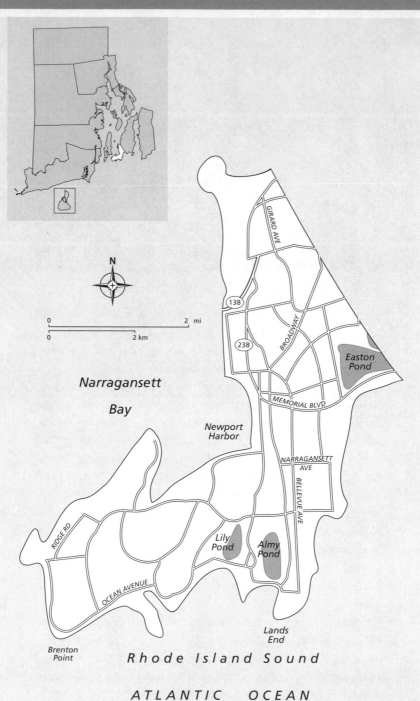

N

0   2 mi
0   2 km

Narragansett

Bay

GIRARD AVE

138

238

BROADWAY

Easton
Pond

MEMORIAL BLVD

Newport
Harbor

NARRAGANSETT
AVE

BELLEVUE AVE

RIDGE RD

Lily
Pond

Almy
Pond

OCEAN AVENUE

Lands
End

*Brenton
Point*

Rhode Island Sound

ATLANTIC OCEAN

rechristened after the Revolution in honor of the war's greatest hero.

Washington Street runs along the water roughly from the Newport Bridge to the parking lot of the Newport Visitor and Information Center, and many of the Point's finest homes, spanning centuries of history and changing architectural styles, line this beautiful avenue. Most famous of these is **Hunter House** (54 Washington Street, 847–1000; www.newport mansions.org), built in 1748 and considered the finest example of Georgian architecture in North America. Unlike many of its Newport neighbors, the Hunter House was spared destruction by the British during the occupation, probably because the owner was a staunch supporter of the Crown. When the British left town, so did the house's Tory owner, and Hunter House became the headquarters for Admiral de Ternay, commander of the French fleet dispatched to help the colonists in their fight against the British. Later, Senator William Hunter bought the house and lived there for forty-four years, and it's his name that stuck.

Hunter House was the first property restored by the Preservation Society of Newport County and features a fine collection of period furniture made by the Townsends and Goddards, the Newport cabinet-making families (and in-laws) whose work has sold for as much as $13 million at auction. Stepping through the ornate front door is a step back into a world of eighteenth-century luxury. Open 10:00 A.M. to 5:00 P.M. on weekends in April and October, daily from June through September. Admission is $10.00 for adults and $5.00 for children ages six to seventeen. It is closed in May.

In sharp architectural contrast to Hunter House is the **Sanford-Covell Villa Marina** (72 Washington Street, 847–0206; www.sanford-covell.com), a circa 1869 Victorian summer home with a magnificent, 35-foot entrance hall. Whether arriving by land or sea, guests (and their pets) at the Sanford-Covell Villa

acityoffirsts

Newport bills itself as America's First Resort, but municipal boasting doesn't stop there. According to the Newport County Convention and Visitors Bureau, Newport also can claim America's first:

ferry service, begun in 1657

gas streetlights, installed in 1803

circus, hosted in 1774

female newspaper editor, lighthouse keeper, and telephone operator

passenger airline service, with regular flights to and from New York

public roller-skating rink

auto race, in 1895

arrest for speeding, in 1904 (the driver was barreling through town at 15 mph)

open golf tournament, international polo match, and National Lawn Tennis Championship

synagogue

church steeple

AUTHOR'S FAVORITES IN NEWPORT

Easton's Point	Fort Adams
Rose Island Lighthouse	Apple & Eve Newport Folk Festival
Newport Casino	August
Hall of Fame Tennis Championships and Enshrinement	JVC Jazz Festival
July	August
Touro Synagogue	Black Ships Festival
	July

Marina are welcome to stay in rooms in the stately house, which has a bayfront saltwater swimming pool off the porch in back. Rates in season are $180 to $350, including continental breakfast and complimentary afternoon port and sherry in the parlor; off-season rates range from $95 to $250.

Across the street from the Sanford-Covell property, at the corner of Washington and Willow Streets, is the *Church of Saint John the Evangelist,* a fine Gothic parish church built of stone in 1894.

The *Stella Maris Inn* (91 Washington Street, 849–2862; www.stella marisinn.com) represents yet another architectural style. Originally called Blue Rocks, this French Renaissance–style mansion was built in 1861 as a private home and later sold to the Sisters of Cluny, who used it as a convent and renamed the house Stella Maris, or "Star of the Sea." Now a bed-and-breakfast, the inn has eight guest rooms with views of either the bay or the lovely garden out back. The wide, white porch that fronts the house invites you to linger over breakfast and enjoy the cool salt air. Weekend room rates are $175 to $195 in the high (summer) season and $125 to $150 off-season; rooms are $125 to $150 on summer weekdays and $95 to $110 off-season.

Directly across Washington Street from Stella Maris is *Battery Park,* a local secret that offers one of Newport's best bay views. Take a break from your stroll through the historic Point and watch the traffic passing over (cars and trucks) and under (boats and windsurfers) the *Newport Bridge* looming to the north. To the south is *Goat Island,* which currently is cluttered with hotels and marinas, but during World War II was used to manufacture and store thousands of highly explosive torpedoes.

Shielded from view by the bulk of the Hyatt Regency Newport, Goat Island's *Pineapples on the Bay* is an unpretentious waterfront cabana bar—

appropriately, located adjacent to the hotel pool—that's open to the public during the summer season.

Not only does Pineapples offer some elbow room when the rest of Newport is jammed with tourists, for the price of a cocktail it provides sweeping views of the bay, the bridge, and sunsets over the West Bay. In addition to tropical drinks, Pineapples serves a variety of appetizers, salads, burgers, and sandwiches, with Ben & Jerry's ice-cream pops and frozen candy bars for dessert.

For an after-dinner romantic stroll, follow the short gravel path nearby to the small lighthouse that stands watch over the north end of the island. Pineapples is open June to September, 11:00 A.M. to 9:00 P.M.; call the Hyatt at 851–1234 for more information.

Battery Park in the Point section also affords an excellent view of Rose Island and the historic ***Rose Island Lighthouse*** (www.roseislandlighthouse .org). The Rose Island Lighthouse Foundation invites guests to stay overnight at the lighthouse, located on a tiny (18.5-acre) island in the middle of Narragansett Bay. Actually, it's more of a challenge than an invitation: The lighthouse, built in 1869 and restored in 1993, has no running water, no maid service, and no electric appliances. You bring your own food and make your own bed. Everything in the guest quarters is manually operated, from the ice-cream maker to the washing machine to the alarm clock, with the goal being "to see if modern man can manage a few days having to pump his own water," explains Foundation executive director Charlotte Johnson. When guests are done with their chores, they are free to explore the one-and-one-half-acre lighthouse property and walk the shoreline of Rose Island, which is cluttered with old Navy buildings and populated mainly by seabirds. Nightly rates range from $165 to $195 and vary seasonally. For $700 to $2,000 (depending upon the time of year), you can even become the keeper of the week, tending to the lighthouse while staying in a modern apartment on the building's second floor. From November to

Rose Island Lighthouse

April, the foundation conducts weekend seal-watching tours that combine a lighthouse visit with observations of harbor seals on nearby Citing Rock.

For the less intrepid, the foundation also operates a museum at the lighthouse, which reproduces the life and lodgings of a turn-of-the-century lighthouse keeper. The museum is open 10:00 A.M. to 4:00 P.M., and the Jamestown ferry makes regular stops at the island between July 1 and Labor Day; the Rose Island Lighthouse Foundation provides launch services to guests the rest of the year. Write to the Rose Island Lighthouse Foundation at P.O. Box 1419, Newport, 02840, or call 847–4242 for more information.

Leaving Washington Street via any of the "tree" streets (Elm, Poplar, Willow, Walnut, Chestnut, Cherry, and Pine) allows you to sally past a virtually unbroken line of colonial homes, the feature for which the Point probably is best known. At 29 Elm Street is the aptly named **Third & Elm Press** (846–0228; www.third andelm.com), whose wares doubtless would have been familiar to eighteenth-century Point residents: woodblock prints, Christmas cards, and notepaper. Drop by and you'll likely find owner Ilse Buchert Nesbitt, a former typesetting and book-design instructor at the Rhode Island School of Design, hard at work with one of her nineteenth-century letterpresses. Along with drawers full of manual type, the big old presses occupy much of the floor space in the shop. Open Tuesday to Saturday 11:00 A.M. to 5:00 P.M., and by appointment.

The **Rhumbline** restaurant (62 Bridge Street, 849–3999) is the Point's hidden gem. Modestly set amid a row of colonials on a side street lit by gas lamps, the restaurant's cheery interior—all light woods and white tablecloths accented by stained-glass panels—provides a welcome harbor from a winter night's chill or any time of year. The open and congenial atmosphere extends from the tavern in the rear to the main dining room, where the lack of pretense is belied by a sophisticated menu presenting regional comfort food with gourmet flair. Whether you choose the Rhumb Burger stuffed with Gorgonzola and herbs or the osso bucco, pan-roasted salmon, or cassoulet (a stew made with navy beans, duck confit, garlic sausage, and smoked ham), you're bound to leave warm and satisfied. Open Tuesday to Thursday 5:00 to 10:00 P.M., and until 10:30 P.M. on Friday and Saturday; open Sunday for brunch from 10:00 A.M. to 2:00 P.M. and for dinner from 5:00 to 10:00 P.M.; closed Monday.

Newport on Foot offers a walking tour of the Point April to October; price is $8.00 for adults and free for children under twelve. Call 846–5391 for more information.

Right on the edge of the Point district, across the street from the **Newport Visitor and Information Center,** is one of the town's real treasures, **Cardines Field.** One of the oldest baseball parks in the country, Cardines Field is a wonderful place to spend a warm summer evening appreciating the labors of ballplayers who still do it for the love of the game. Built in 1936, Cardines is home to the New England Collegiate Baseball League's Newport Gulls, who play twenty-three home games in the stadium during June and July. Most games start at 6:35 P.M.; individual tickets are $4.00 for adults, $2.00 for seniors and military, and $1.00 for children under twelve. Call 845–6832 or 877–77–GULLS or check the Web site at www.newportgulls.com for more information.

Like Fenway Park in Boston and Wrigley Field in Chicago, the stadium itself is as much an attraction as the game. The bleachers are set on a fieldstone foundation, while a green, wooden pavilion wraps around the corner of Marlborough Street. Beyond the high outfield fence stands a line of fine colonial homes, repeatedly dented over the years by home runs off the bats of local heroes as well as baseball legends Jimmie Foxx and Satchel Paige, both of whom played here in their younger days.

Although ticket prices at Cardines Field are nominal, for the price of a beer, you can see the game for free from the back patio of adjacent ***Mudville's Pub*** (8 West Marlborough Street, 849–1408), a sports bar crammed with memorabilia from the Celtics, Bruins, and Red Sox. Open 11:30 A.M. to 1:00 A.M. daily; excellent food, including a thick, meaty clam chowder, is served until 11:00 P.M. on weekdays and 11:30 P.M. on Friday and Saturday.

From Mudville's it's just a short walk to the heart of downtown Newport, with its historic Brick Market, wharves, and colonial homes as well as fine restaurants, shops, and pubs. Many of these attractions are geared to Newport's phenomenal summer tourist trade, but there are still a few odd and overlooked gems waiting to be discovered.

Unlike almost everything else on Bowen's Wharf, ***Aquidneck Lobster*** (846–0106), located at the end of the dock, past the Chart House Restaurant, is no tourist trap. Its "facade" is a loading platform, and your "guides" are brawny, bearded men with greasy smocks who usually are too busy to acknowledge

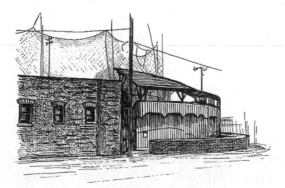

Cardines Field

Not a Road, and Not an Island: What's with That Name?

When it comes to place names, Rhode Island is a state of confusion. Properly noting that most of the state is not an island at all, visitors are often stumped by the Ocean State's curious moniker (which in fact is an abbreviation of the state's full name—the State of Rhode Island and Providence Plantations).

Here's the story: When Italian explorer Giovanni Verrazano sailed up the East Coast in 1524, he came upon a triangular island, which he noted was about the size of the Greek island of Rhodes. He was actually referring to Block Island, but the early settlers of modern-day Rhode Island thought Verrazano was talking about Aquidneck Island, where Newport is located. So they renamed Aquidneck Island "Rhode Island."

Later, the islands in Narragansett Bay were united politically with the plantation settlements that stretched south from Providence along the east and west sides of the bay—thus giving Rhode Island its extra-long appellation.

your presence. But you didn't come to see *them*; you came for the lobsters.

Inside huge green holding tanks are as many as 30,000 lobsters, pulled from local waters and unloaded at the docks here for distribution to the restaurants of Newport and the rest of Rhode Island. There are blue lobsters, orange lobsters, and albino lobsters. There are little chicken lobsters, and occasionally giant, twenty-five-pound monsters that are seventy-five to one hundred years old.

Evan Smith, vice president of marketing of the Newport Visitors and Convention Bureau, likes to bring guests to Aquidneck Lobster to give them a taste of the "real" Newport. Although this is a working fishing center, visitors are always welcome. There always is a selection of super-fresh seafood on ice, and, of course, the lobsters are for sale. Open daily 6:30 A.M. to 5:30 P.M.

From yachts to schooners to powerboats to catamarans, there are many options for tourists who want to charter a boat or book an excursion to explore Newport Harbor and Narragansett Bay. One of the more unusual, however, is the **Rumrunner II,** which in summer departs daily from Bannister's Wharf in downtown Newport (dockside, 847–0299; office, 849–3033 or 800–395–1343; www.cruisenewport.com).

With its numerous unpopulated islands and hidden coves, Narragansett Bay was an active center for bootlegging liquor during Prohibition. Under cover of darkness, small, fast boats like the *Rumrunner II* would venture out past the 12-mile limit to meet ships from Canada and the West Indies and load up their decks with cases of alcohol. To avoid the Coast Guard on the way back to shore, rumrunners would use camouflage, superior speed, and knowledge of local waters. But sometimes their luck ran out: In one famous 1929 incident, the Coast Guard fired on an escaping rumrunner, the *Black Duck,* killing three men and wounding another.

With Roaring Twenties music in the background (and complimentary Black Duck Rum cocktails on evening cruises), the *Rumrunner II* crew mixes Prohibition lore with the standard descriptions of bay sites, including the Newport mansions, Rose Island, and Jamestown. Once powered by triple 500-horsepower engines capable of 60 miles per hour, the 1929 Elco motor yacht *Rumrunner II*— originally built to the specifications of two New Jersey bootleggers—was retooled for the more modest needs of tourist excursions but still manages a breezy 30 knots, permitting the tour to cover a lot of water in an hour and a half. The East Passage Express Tour, departing Memorial Day through Labor Day at 11:30 A.M., 1:30 P.M., and 3:30 P.M. (call for spring and fall schedules), is $18 per person and includes complimentary juice and soda; children under twelve are $13 and a 10 percent senior citizen's discount applies. The Smuggler's Cocktail Cruise departs at 5:30 and 7:00 P.M. and costs $25 per person.

Newport's Gilded Age "cottages"—the mansions lining Bellevue Avenue and surrounding streets—are smack in the middle of the beaten path. Most of

Nordic Newport

Could Rhode Island have been discovered almost 500 years before Columbus "sailed the ocean blue"? Some Norwegian scholars think that the Vikings, led by Leif Ericsson, actually sailed up Narragansett Bay, and that Ericsson's fabled "Vinland" in fact was coastal Rhode Island. Some of the geographic details of the area match the descriptions of Ericsson and his brother, Thorwald, who also spent time in Vinland. Believers point to evidence such as Bristol's "singing rocks" (read about Tiverton's Speaking Rocks in the Newport County chapter) and the discovery of an ancient battle-ax in North Kingstown in 1889; skeptics say that Ericsson's Vinland probably was farther north.

Legend also has it that Newport's Old Stone Mill, located in Touro Park at the corner of Bellevue Avenue and Mill Street, was built by the Vikings. The purpose and origin of this odd circular structure, with its arched stone walls, is a mystery. Some say it is a mill dating to the seventeenth century, while some scholars and local residents insist that Ericsson built it during his stay in Vinland about the year A.D. 1000.

What do you think? You can weigh the evidence as you walk around the small park, open daily until sunset—then perhaps retreat to the bar at the Hotel Viking (where else?) to ponder it some more.

the well-known mansions, including the Breakers and Chateau-sur-Mer, are maintained and operated by the Preservation Society of Newport County (849–9900), whose tours and activities tend to reflect the genteel surroundings.

On the other hand, the independently operated and less well-known **Belcourt Castle** (657 Bellevue Avenue, 846–0669; www.belcourtcastle.com) has a deserved reputation for quirkiness. Belcourt Castle hosts an array of unusual special events, including a ghost tour, murder mystery nights, candlelight tours, and medieval banquets.

Belcourt, a reproduction of King Louis XIII's hunting lodge at Versailles, claims to have more ghosts per square foot than anywhere else in Newport, if not the country. Among the spirits you may encounter during the two-hour Ghost Tour are the Monk, who always appears in close proximity to a wooden seventeenth-century German statue, and a screaming ghoul who haunts a fifteenth-century suit of armor in the ballroom.

Regular tours of Belcourt Castle are from 9:00 A.M. to 4:00 P.M. Belcourt is open daily during the summer, and Friday to Monday in the winter; call for spring and fall hours. Admission is $12.00 for adults, $8.00 for seniors and college students, $7.00 for children thirteen to seventeen, and $5.00 for children ages six to twelve. Kids under age six are free. The Ghost Tour is conducted Thursday to Saturday in the spring, summer, and fall at 5:00 P.M. and costs $18 per person (not recommended for young children); candlelight tours set off at 6:00 P.M. Friday to Monday and also cost $18 per person. Belcourt Castle is closed during the month of January.

Speaking of ghosts, Newport has plenty of 'em, as detailed in Eleyne Austen Sharp's book, *Haunted Newport*. This old town is a hotbed for bloodsuckers, too, if you take vampire scholar Christopher Rondina's word for it; he calls New England "The Transylvania of the Western World." Austen Sharp and Rondina help headline a quirky newcomer on the city's cultural calendar: **Haunted Newport Month.**

First held at Halloween in 1999, the celebration of things spooky in Newport features lectures, ghost tours to sites such as Belcourt Castle and the Cliffside Inn (home to the ghost of artist Beatrice Turner), psychic readings, graveyard tours, a Harry Potter day, and a haunted carousel ride. **Ghost Tours of Newport** (841–8600; www.ghostsofnewport.com) conducts spooky tours of the city's historic districts from April through October (including nightly from May 1 through Halloween). The ninety-minute tours include stops at graveyards, creepy Blood Alley, and the reputedly haunted former headquarters of General George Washington. Tickets are $18 for adults, $10 for kids.

Illustration may be one of America's most public forms of art—what, for instance, could be more immediately accessible than a Norman Rockwell cover

Lights, Camera, *Amistad!*

Visiting downtown Newport not only is a step back into history, it's also a visit to a movie set—specifically, the set of the Steven Spielberg 1997 epic, *Amistad.*

Spielberg and his cast and crew spent nearly the entire month of March 1997 in Newport filming key scenes for *Amistad,* the true story of an 1839 slave rebellion and the trial that followed. Courtroom scenes, featuring actors Matthew McConaughey, Anthony Hopkins, and Morgan Freeman, were filmed inside Newport's 1739 Colony House.

During filming, all of adjacent Washington Square was transformed to resemble a street scene from the early nineteenth century. Street signs were removed, new facades were placed over the two movie theaters on the square, and dirt and sand were thrown down to cover the pavement. Making the work easier was the fact that many of the buildings on the square date from the 1840s or earlier. When actors in costume and horse-drawn carriages and wagons were added, the cameras began rolling.

Spielberg also constructed the colonial jail seen in the movie right in the middle of historic Queen Anne Square, but a week after filming wrapped, there was no hint that the seemingly formidable stone building was ever there. Other Newport locations included Clarke Street and St. John's Church.

for the *Saturday Evening Post?*—but the same can't be said for the **National Museum of American Illustration** (492 Bellevue Avenue, 851–8949; www .americanillustration.org). The museum, located in the Gilded Age mansion Vernon Court, is open only by appointment (no children under age twelve; individuals should call in advance to be placed with a scheduled group tour).

Still, art lovers may want to call ahead and fork over the $25 admission fee ($22 for seniors and military) to check out the museum's American Imagist collection, which features works by Rockwell, N. C. Wyeth, Maxfield Parrish, Howard Pyle, and others who achieved greatness through the relatively mundane media of advertisements, posters, and periodicals. In addition, the tour gives visitors an opportunity to take a look around Vernon Court, built in 1898 in the style of a seventeenth-century French chateau.

For a bargain, you can't beat nearby **Ochre Court** (100 Ochre Point Avenue, 847–6650; www.salve.edu), the first of the opulent Gilded Age mansions built by Richard Morris Hunt in Newport. Set on the center of the campus of Salve Regina University, Ochre Court now houses the school's administrative offices; admission is free (although donations are encouraged). There are no tours unless you are with a student who's thinking of attending the school, but visitors can admire the exterior details of this replica of a French medieval chateau, as well as the grand hall, with its carved stone walls and massive marble table. Ochre Court is

The Ghostly Images of Beatrice Turner

Art was Beatrice Turner's life, even if her subject matter was oddly limited. The only child of Adele and Andrew Turner, Beatrice spent her summers in Newport dreaming of becoming a painter. But her father, who wrote love poems to his beautiful daughter and turned away potential suitors, made Beatrice quit art school and stay home to paint self-portraits for his enjoyment.

When Andrew died in 1913, Beatrice refused to let officials take his body away until she painted his portrait. Her next work was an exterior one: She had her entire house painted black in tribute to her late father.

For years after, Beatrice and her mother were instantly recognizable denizens of Newport, decked out in full Victorian costume even as the nineteenth century became a distant memory. When Beatrice died a spinster in 1959, workers found more than 1,000 self-portraits in her house.

Today the ghost of Beatrice Turner is said to inhabit her old home, now Newport's elegant Cliffside Inn bed-and-breakfast. Even if you don't find Beatrice's luminescent visage hanging over your bed some night, however, you can find many reminders of this sad, eccentric lady. Most of Beatrice's artwork was destroyed after she died, but the owners of Cliffside have managed to acquire about one hundred of her self-portraits and other works, which now adorn the walls of the inn.

The Cliffside Inn (2 Seaview Avenue, 847–1811; www.cliffsideinn.com) has thirteen rooms in the main house—an 1880 Victorian mansion—plus three luxury suites in the nearby Seaview Cottage. Room rates range from $155 to $645. For information or reservations call (800) 845–1811.

open Monday through Friday 10:00 A.M. to 4:00 P.M. The public is also welcome to attend the daily mass held in the Ochre Point Chapel. The Salve Regina campus can also be accessed through a gate on the Newport Cliff Walk.

Short of risking a broken neck and imprisonment for trespassing, there's only one way to climb up onto the roof of one of Newport's Gilded Age mansions: the ***Rooftop and Behind-the-Scenes Tour*** at The Elms mansion.

Rather than spending a lot of time talking about how much time and money coal magnate Edwin Berwind spent to re-create a 1750s French chateau in 1901 Newport, this tour burrows down into the bowels of the elaborate mansion to show you how the other half lived—namely, the staff of forty people needed to maintain the property in its heyday. You'll see the coal tunnel where a special rail car brought unsightly deliveries into the house (away from the eyes of the Berwinds and their guests); the tour also visits the boiler room and explains some of the mansion's high-tech amenities, such as a mammoth, electric-powered ice maker, considered a marvel of its day.

After a stroll through the third-floor servants' quarters—modest compared to the rest of the house, though the staff did have its own maid service—it's time for the highlight of the tour, a sortie out onto the roof, where a viewing platform offers a fine view of the bay and the ocean.

The Rooftop tour costs $15.00 per person ($5.00 for children ages six to seventeen), lasts about an hour, and is offered hourly when The Elms is open for tours (10:00 A.M. to 5:00 P.M. daily); reservations are recommended. Call 847–0478 for more information or check its Web site at www.newport mansions.org.

The **Newport Casino** (194 Bellevue Avenue, 849–3990; www.tennisfame .com) is known as the host of an annual pro tour tennis tournament and as the home of the International Tennis Hall of Fame, where Chris Evert (1995), Jimmy Conners (1998), and John McEnroe (1999) have joined the ranks of the illustrious. More recent inductees include Martina Navratilova (2000), Ivan Lendl (2001), Boris Becker (2003), and Steffi Graf (2004). The Hall of Fame exhibits— greatly expanded in the past few years—are well worth a visit for any tennis buff, and the sprawling 1880 casino itself is a treat for the eyes, an excellent example of the shingle style pioneered by the famed architectural firm of McKim, Mead, & White.

One of the ways the Hall of Fame preserves the history of the game of tennis is by maintaining the casino's original court tennis court. Court tennis, also known as royal tennis, is the ancestor of modern tennis, dating back to the sixteenth century. Players use a curved racquet, and the ball can be played off the walls of the court as well as the surface, a la racquetball.

The court tennis court in Newport is one of only thirty left in the world. To get a real feel for the history of tennis, catch a match by members of the National Tennis Club, who occasionally don old-fashioned tennis whites and play the ancient game. In 1998 the U.S. Court Tennis Professional Singles Championships were held at the casino.

Although it is known today as a tennis mecca, the casino actually was built with a whole range of sports in mind. One of these was croquet, that favorite pastime of backyard cookouts. Croquet is taken seriously here, though, with regular tournaments and regional championships on the schedule. For $30 per person (doubles) or $40 per person (singles), you can break out your own mallets and give the old place a whirl.

Four dollars will get you onto the grounds of the casino and thus into the stands for any court tennis or croquet matches that are going on. Call ahead for schedule information. The casino's historic grass tennis courts also are available for rental ($35 per person for one hour, or $45 per person for 1½ hours) if you want to play where the stars have competed. Call 849–0642 to reserve.

For $9.00 per adult ($7.00 for seniors, members of the military, and students; $6.00 for children sixteen and under; $23.00 maximum per family), you get access to the grounds plus admission to the Hall of Fame's museum, where you can test your stroke on a simulated tennis court and learn about the sport and its stars through a series of interactive exhibits. Open 9:30 A.M. to 5:00 P.M. daily.

Another Bellevue Avenue landmark is the **Redwood Library and Athenaeum** (50 Bellevue Avenue, 847–0292; www.redwood1747.org). The oldest library building in America, the Redwood Library was built in 1750 and features a handsome, classic portico that—like the rest of the building, and outward appearance to the contrary—is constructed entirely of wood. Inside, the library's book collection includes almost all of the original volumes it opened with more than 250 years ago (members of the occupying British army are thought to have swiped the rest while they used the library as an officers' club during the Revolution). Many of these ancient tomes, purchased in England in 1749, can normally be seen in barred cases in the library's quiet Harrison Room, which is the original library building.

Only museum members may take out books, but visitors can check out the library's history on a short tour offered by the staff on weekdays at 10:30 A.M. or by appointment; ask at the main desk for information. Highlights include a copy of Gilbert Stuart's famous painting of George Washington and fine furniture by Newport's own Goddard and Townsend families. Open Tuesday to Thursday 9:30 A.M. to 8:00 P.M., Monday, Friday, and Saturday 9:30 A.M. to 5:30 P.M.; and Sunday 1:00 to 5:00 P.M.

Touro Synagogue (85 Touro Street, 847–4794; www.tourosynagogue.org) is the oldest Jewish house of worship in America, built in 1763. But the Jewish population in Newport predates the structure by a century, attracted by the gospel of religious tolerance preached by state founder Roger Williams.

The magnificent but unrevealing Georgian exterior of the synagogue gives way to a rich interior, featuring a dozen Ionic columns representing the twelve tribes of Israel. The synagogue features separate galleries for men and women, and a painting of the Ten Commandments by Newport artist Benjamin Howland provides a backdrop to the Holy Ark, where the congregation's Torahs are kept. Contrary to legend, there's no evidence that a trapdoor in the synagogue ever led to an underground passage out of the building—supposedly so that congregants could escape anti-Semitic oppressors. But the room below was used as a stop on the Underground Railroad to hide escaped slaves.

Free tours of Touro Synagogue are conducted every half hour, Sunday through Friday 10:00 A.M. to 5:00 P.M. in July and August; 1:00 to 3:00 P.M. Monday through Friday and 11:00 A.M. to 3:00 P.M. Sunday in September and October; Sunday 1:00 to 3:00 P.M. from November to April, with 1:00 P.M. tours only on Friday; and Monday through Friday 1:00 to 3:00 P.M. and Sunday 11:00 A.M. to 3:00 P.M. from May through June. Tours are also offered by appointment, but never on the Sabbath (Saturday) or on Jewish holidays. For an interesting sidelight, you can also peer into the nearby Jewish cemetery, which dates from the seventeenth century.

The massive stone walls of **Fort Adams** (841–0707; www.fortadams.org) never were needed to repel the enemy, but for years they presented an effective barrier to visitors. Although it is the centerpiece of well-traveled **Fort Adams State Park** (perhaps best known as the home of the Newport Jazz Festival), the 1825 fort itself was closed from 1983 to 1995 because of deteriorating and dangerous conditions. However, a subsequent restoration effort led the state to reopen the fort.

Some areas still are undergoing reconstruction but visitors can explore the walls, gun emplacements, and parade grounds of the fort, one of a series of fortifications built after the War of 1812 to protect East Coast harbors. Guides explain not only the fort's architectural nuances but also the military tactics and weaponry that made it an effective deterrent to sea attacks on Narragansett Bay.

Admission to Fort Adams is $10.00 for adults, $5.00 for seniors and youths ages six to seventeen (free for children under age five). Family admission is $25.00. Proceeds benefit the Fort Adams Trust, which conducts the tours from mid-May to October and is restoring the fort. Open daily; tours are conducted regularly 10:00 A.M. to 4:00 P.M. (Note: There's also a per-car admission fee to enter Fort Adams State Park.)

If Fort Adams sparks an interest in learning more about Newport's military history, shoot on over to the **Artillery Company of Newport Museum,** located at 23 Clarke Street (846–8488; www.newportartillery.org) just off Washington Square in the heart of downtown. Chartered in 1741 by King George II, the unit served in the French and Indian War, the American Revolution, the War of 1812, the Civil War, and the Spanish-American War. The company's circa 1836 armory houses a collection of military uniforms from around the world, artifacts representing the unit's colorful history, and a number of historic artillery pieces, including four brass cannons cast by Paul Revere in 1798. Admission is free, but donations are encouraged; open May to October on Saturday from 10:00 A.M. to 4:00 P.M. and by appointment year-round.

The popular **Apple & Eve Newport Folk Festival** and **JVC Jazz Festival** (847–3700; www.festivalproductions.net), both held each August and featuring a who's-who lineup of artists, are just two of many special events held in

A Fortress Never Tested

There's an old saying that generals are always fighting the previous war, and it holds true for Fort Adams. Built over the course of thirty-three years at the then-astronomical cost of $3 million, when completed in 1857 Fort Adams provided a formidable defense against wooden sailing ships armed with cannons. The problem was that by the time it was completed, advances in artillery made the fort's granite walls vulnerable.

Happily, Fort Adams was never put to the test. Without a significant navy, the Confederacy had no way of attacking Newport or Narragansett Bay. In fact, the Union considered Fort Adams so safe that it relocated the U.S. Naval Academy here during the Civil War. The fort also served for a time as home base for the aging USS *Constitution*—the fabled "Old Ironsides" of the Revolutionary War.

Defenses at Fort Adams were upgraded during the Spanish-American War around the turn of the century, but the fort's military usefulness continued to fade until, finally, it was decommissioned in the 1950s. Today, however, the imposing fortress has reclaimed a place of prominence, not only as a fascinating site to explore but also as an excellent example of military architecture and evolution.

Newport each year. Perhaps the most interesting is the annual **Black Ships Festival,** held in July to commemorate the opening of Japan by favorite Rhode Island son Commodore Matthew Perry in 1854.

Each year hefty sumo wrestlers descend on Newport, while delicate kites fill the air at Brenton Point State Park and the pounding of taiko drums shakes the walls of the Newport Casino. Local restaurants host sushi demonstrations, Japanese beer tastings, and elaborate tea ceremonies, while the Newport Art Museum presents origami (paper folding), bonsai (tiny tree pruning), and ikebana (flower arranging) exhibitions. You can even learn some conversational Japanese and get your face painted like a Kabuki dancer.

Most events are free, although admission fees are required for some of the more popular events, including the drum exhibition and the craft workshops. For tickets or information contact the Black Ships Festival Office (28 Pelham Street, 846–2720; www.blackshipsfestival.com).

Looming over lower Thames Street is the imposing brick facade of the **Samuel Whitehorne House** (416 Thames Street, 849–7300), a circa 1811 Federal-style mansion preserved by the Newport Restoration Foundation. Once the home of a shipping merchant, the house has been grandly restored and filled with elegant furnishings from the period, including many pieces by Newport craftsmen. Highlights include the Pilgrim period furniture in the brick-floored summer kitchen, the large fireplace and side-bake oven in the winter kitchen, and an herb and fruit garden typical of fine homes of the Federal period.

The Newport Restoration Foundation (www.newportrestoration.org) opens the house to visitors from May through October, on Saturday and Sunday 10:00 A.M. to 4:00 P.M. and Monday, Thursday, and Friday 11:00 A.M. to 4:00 P.M. Winter tours also are available with twenty-four-hours' notice. Admission is $10.00 for adults, $4.00 for children ages six to sixteen.

Shipbuilding may not quite be a lost art, but it's safe to say that there are far fewer young shipwrights learning the trade today than, say, a century ago. Newport's *International Yacht Restoration School* (449 Thames Street, 848–5777; www.iyrs.org) is a throwback to a simpler time, when boats were handcrafted from wood and canvas, as much works of art as working vessels.

The school is tucked away behind the shops of Thames Street, with its main classroom located in a spacious, turn-of-the-century power plant that once served the Newport Street Railway Company. A self-guided tour takes you onto a balcony where you can watch earnest young men and women planing, sanding, and painting vintage catboats, yachts, and motor launches, honing their skills with an eye on a career as marine craftspeople.

A number of the boats being restored were built by legendary Bristol yacht designer Nathaniel Herreshoff. Many of the students also help out on IYRS's long-term project to restore the 1885 schooner *Coronet,* now housed for public viewing in a new building on the school's broad stone quay. Called the oldest surviving grand American yacht in the world, the *Coronet* is 167 feet long and carries 8,500 square feet of sail when fully rigged. A veteran of two around-the-world cruises, the ship later was converted from sail to steam power, but IYRS is working to turn back the hands of time and return the *Coronet* to its original condition.

The school is open to visitors from 9:00 A.M. to 5:00 P.M. Monday to Friday and on summer weekends. Free; donations suggested.

What is it about firehouses and pizza that seems to go together? Is it the hot red tomato sauce hidden under a layer of smoldering cheese? The fireman's legendary appetite for junk food? Whatever the reason, Newport's *Firehouse Pizza* (595 Thames Street, 846–1199) stands out as a beacon to hungry strollers wandering the lower end of Thames Street.

If you're feeling a bit burnt out on colonial mansion tours and Victorian linen shops, the funky decor and Italian comfort food at Firehouse Pizza are the perfect antidote. Inside, the old firehouse practically screams college cool, with reggae posters, graffiti, and bright designs covering every conceivable surface, including the napkin dispensers on the tables. Open daily during the summer from 11:00 A.M. to 11:00 P.M.; closes 9:00 P.M. weekdays from September to May (open 11:00 A.M. to 3:00 P.M. only on Monday and Tuesday in the off-season).

On an otherwise quiet corner of Lower Thames Street, at the edge of New-port's Fifth Ward, the sound of amplified rock and techno music draws you to the open doors of **Thames Glass** (688 Lower Thames Street, 846–0576; www.thamesglass.com). The double doors are usually open—even in winter—to provide some respite to head glassmaker Matthew Buechner and his crew as they sweat over a bank of four kilns, which heat glass to 2000 degrees so it can be bent, blown, and molded into vases, bowls, perfume bottles, and Christmas ornaments.

Befitting its location, the adjoining Thames Glass showroom features a variety of nautical designs, including glass fish and shells; hand-blown glass fruit and vegetables are also part of the milieu. The small showroom on Lower Thames Street features slightly imperfect items at discount prices; the top-of-the-line handicrafts are for sale. Open Monday to Saturday from 10:00 A.M. to 6:00 P.M. and Sunday noon to 5:00 P.M.

Overexuberant sailors and seamen in Newport's bygone days sometimes found themselves guests at the Newport County Jail, located at 13 Marlborough Street. Since 1987 the former jail has been operating as the **Jailhouse Inn** (847–4638; www.historicinnsofnewport.com), with twenty-three "cells" adorned with striped bedsheets and a lobby that retains the feel of an old police station—a function the circa 1772 building had until 1986. Huge iron gates frame the entry to the inn's common room, which is adorned with photos of intimidating-looking police officers.

The inn doesn't go overboard with the jail theme, however. Rooms are air-conditioned and pleasantly furnished and have refrigerators, private baths, and televisions; a complimentary continental breakfast is served. Room rates range from $45 off-season to $275 in high season.

The east end of Marlborough Street terminates at Broadway, which in recent years has become Newport's hot spot for new restaurants. None is cooler than the **Salvation Cafe** (140 Broadway, 847–2620; www.salvation cafe.com), which unfolds as distinct spaces as you walk from front to back. From Broadway you enter a pastel bar with sky-blue barstools and animal-print couches, which gives way to a tropical tiki hut.

Executive chef Pat Lowney's menu is equally adventurous, globetrotting from Asia to New Zealand with dishes like teriyaki salmon and pad thai. The Salvation Cafe is open daily from 5:00 to 11:00 P.M. during the summer; it closes an hour earlier Sunday through Thursday in the winter.

Rocco's Little Italy (124 Broadway, 848–4556) is Broadway's classic corner restaurant, with checkered tablecloths and twinkling holiday lights providing the simple atmosphere to go along with Newport's best pizza, calzones, and classic Italian grinders. Open daily 11:00 A.M. to 10:00 P.M.

The eclecticism of the Broadway dining scene continues with two of the Salvation Cafe's closest neighbors, ***Tucker's Bistro*** (150 Broadway, 846–3449; www.tuckersbistro.com) and ***Pop*** (162 Broadway, 846–8456; www.popkitchenandcocktails.com). Tucker Harris has transformed a former storefront into a French-inspired fantasy of red lacquered walls, heavy drapes, and delicate table lamps—a loving re-creation of a Paris bistro of the 1930s. Classic jazz and blues music plays softly in the background as you are led to one of the Bistro's intimate dining spaces; Tucker himself is almost always on hand to offer a warm greeting along with stylish entrees like roast Statler breast of chicken served with smoked Gouda mashed potatoes, and a crab-encrusted salmon pan-roasted to perfection. Open nightly 6:00 to 10:00 P.M.

Decor-wise, Pop is the polar opposite of Tucker's, all sleek lines and urban hip; among the design flourishes is a painted antique refrigerator door hung on a wall. Patrons tend to flock to the rich couches in front of the fireplace in back, but despite its cool attitude Pop manages a warm welcome thanks to its friendly staff.

Pop specializes in well-stirred cocktails, from classics like the Bloody Mary to trendy pomegranate champagne mixes. But it's also one of the few places in Newport to get a late-night bite that won't give you heartburn later; the kitchen stays open to midnight serving a variety of pizzas and tapas, including their famous Yukon Gold mashed potato cocktail, blended with fontinella cheese and topped with sirloin tips. The dance floor opens up on the weekends, with a live DJ spinning; Wednesday is karaoke night. Open nightly 5:00 P.M. to 1:00 A.M.

Tucked around the corner from Broadway is Newport's only permanent live stage, ***The Firehouse Theater*** (4 Equality Park Place, 849–4373; www.firehousetheater.org). As you might have guessed, the forty-nine-seat performance space is located in a former firehouse; both in-house productions and shows by other troupes are featured on Friday and Saturday nights at 8:00 P.M. as well as on an occasional Sunday and Thursday. A wide variety of works is produced, from classics by Shakespeare and Eugene O'Neill to more obscure dramas.

Ducking down a side street off downtown's popular Brick Market Place brings you to Goddard Row, home of the inspired ***Sushi Go!*** (215 Goddard Row, 849–5155; www.sushi-go.com). Owner Jefferson Dube has a passion for sushi (he eats it every day), and it shows in his delicate preparation of raw and cooked sushi, including vegetable rolls and a Philadelphia roll that incorporates smoked salmon and cream cheese. A do-it-yourself menu lets you choose from a variety of seafood and veggies for made-to-order creations.

Decorated in simple, traditional Japanese style, Sushi Go! is open Monday to Saturday 11:00 A.M. to 9:00 P.M., and Sunday 11:00 A.M. to 7:00 P.M. Don't be surprised if there's a flood of fellow customers toward closing time: During the last hour of business each day, Jefferson puts all of the day's prepared sushi on sale for half price. The sale stock is usually snapped up quickly by savvy locals, so get there early if you want a piece of the action.

Some people may be born to be sailors, but admirals are made. Many of America's greatest naval leaders were shaped at Newport's Naval War College, located on Coasters Harbor Island. Founded in 1884, the college is the Navy's top school on the art of naval warfare, and it is the oldest school of its type in the world.

Housed in the college's Founder's Hall, the former Newport Asylum for the Poor (1820), is the ***Naval War College Museum,*** which provides a fascinating look at the history of the U.S. Navy in Narragansett Bay, as well as exhibits on the history of naval warfare. Torpedoes on display are a reminder that thousands of these explosives were manufactured and stored on tiny Goat Island, just off-shore downtown Newport, during World War II. Models and pictures depict the clash between the sloop *Katy* of the Rhode Island Navy and the sloop *Diana* of the Royal Navy in 1775, the first naval battle of the Revolutionary War. (The *Katy* was later rechristened the *Providence* and joined the Continental Navy; you can visit a replica of the *Providence* at Fort Adams State Park.) The exploits of Naval War College graduates like World War II Admiral Chester W. Nimitz are detailed in a special gallery.

On your way in or out of the museum, take a moment to appreciate the beauty of Founder's Hall, a white-painted fieldstone masterpiece that sits on a grassy hillside with a commanding view of the bay. Set on a small stone on the lawn is a plaque noting that Coasters Island was the site where European settlers first landed on Aquidneck Island in 1639.

Admission to the museum is free, and the exhibits are open year-round Monday through Friday 10:00 A.M. to 4:00 P.M., plus Saturday and Sunday noon to 4:00 P.M. from June to September. Follow the signs from the Newport Bridge to the Admiral Kalbfus exit; enter the Naval Education and Training Center through Gate 1 to get to the museum. Call 841–4052 or 841–1317 for information or visit the Web site at www.nwc.navy.mil/museum. (Note: Security at the Naval War College has increased since 9/11. To avoid hassles, it is strongly advised that you call the museum a day in advance if you plan to visit.)

The problem with most aquariums is that the fish are in there, but you're out here. Not so at the ***Save the Bay's Newport Exploration Center,*** located at Easton's (First) Beach in Newport (849–8430 or 617–877–5753; www.savebay.org/education_aquarium.asp). This hands-on aquarium aims to be as user-friendly and as kid-friendly as possible, a place where you can pick up a fiddler crab or sea urchin. The aquarium's educational mission is to teach visitors about the creatures that inhabit the waters of Narragansett Bay, and staff troll the local seashore and pick through fishing boat nets searching for interesting specimens.

Besides eels, horseshoe crabs, and other familiar creatures, each summer the waters of the bay also are home to an interesting variety of tropical fish carried north from the West Indies by the Gulf Stream. As a result, the aquarium tanks may hold such colorful species as damsel fish and butterfly fish.

The Newport Exploration Center is located downstairs from the ***Easton Beach Carousel***, which is another attraction worth a visit. The aquarium is open daily May to September 10:00 A.M. to 4:00 P.M. Admission is $4.00. There also is a fee for parking at the beach, but if you tell the lot attendant you're going to the aquarium, you'll get all but $2.00 back when you leave (on weekdays you'll get a full refund). Carousel rides are $1.00.

The ***Seamen's Church Institute*** (847–4260; http://members.cox.net/seamensnewport) at 18 Market Square on Bowen's Wharf houses the Chapel of the Sea, a small room with a tile floor inlaid with seashells, seascape murals on the walls, and a holy water font shaped like a clam shell, as well as a second-floor library with views of Newport Harbor. If you enjoy the sights, be sure to drop some coins in the donation box in the lobby. The downstairs Aloha Cafe serves an inexpensive breakfast and lunch (open 7:30 A.M. to 2:30 P.M.).

A Haven for Men of the Sea

The Seamen's Church Institute is one of Newport's most interesting—some might even say incongruous—institutions. Located smack-dab in the middle of tourist land, the institute is a throwback to a time when Newport's economy was driven by fishing, not summer rentals. The nonprofit group provides housing and emergency financial help to fishermen who have hit rough waters, giving them money to pay for health care, fishing gear and supplies, and other necessities.

Rooms at the institute building on Bowen's Wharf are $135 per week—a price that might make high-season visitors green with envy, until they ponder the true cost of seeking shelter here: Tenants are fishermen beset by declining fish stocks, closed fisheries, and industry downsizing.

Still, it's not all bad news: The Seamen's Church Institute helps fishermen find new jobs and deal with addiction and other problems. If you want to get away from your touristy surroundings for a few minutes and learn a little about Newport's seafaring economy, stop in at the institute's Aloha Cafe lunch counter and meet some of the men and women who still go down to the sea in ships.

Newport's scenic **Ocean Avenue** starts near the end of the cliff walk in the mansion district and runs along the ocean for 10 miles, passing some breath-taking scenery and eye-popping homes—stately old mansions and angular contemporary designs alike—along the way. After crossing over Goose Neck Cove and passing the Newport Country Club, Ocean Drive enters **Brenton Point State Park,** famous for spectacular views and constant sea breezes that make the park a mecca for kite enthusiasts. Although some drivers simply turn around at this point and head back to town, Ocean Avenue actually continues past the park before ending at Castle Hill.

Near the end of Ocean Avenue you'll see a sign for the **Castle Hill Inn and Resort** (849–3800 or 888–466–1355; www.castlehillinn.com) at 590 Ocean Avenue. Turn off here and follow the long driveway to this popular but out-of-the-way restaurant and inn. Once the home of naturalist Alexander Agassiz, this impeccable 1874 Victorian has a commanding view of Newport Harbor and the ocean, with a broad expanse of grassy lawn that runs to the edge of some impressive cliffs. Some of the guest rooms share similar views, including the magical suite in the turret described by Thornton Wilder in *Theophilus North.* Room rates range from $229 to $1,459 per night seasonally.

The lobby of the inn is dark and woody, in sharp contrast to the sunny, brightly decorated dining room overlooking the lawn. Dinner here is formal by Newport standards: Jackets are suggested for men, and jeans are forbidden. But you can dress down for the inn's popular Sunday brunch, which you can enjoy in the dining room or outside from 11:30 A.M. to 3:30 P.M. From the inn you can take a short walk east along the water to the **Castle Hill Light,** a small light-house perched precariously on the edge of a cliff.

One of the things that lure hordes of tourists to Newport each year is its scads of shops selling antiques, fine clothing, jewelry, and home furnishings. Everyone, it seems, wants to come away from the City by the Sea with a little piece of the Gilded Age. With so many retail shops, it stands to reason that Newport would have a fair number of unusual specialty shops as well.

Aardvark Antiques (9 Connell Highway, 849–7233; www.aardvark antiques.com) is a veritable jungle of stone creatures, statues, and fountains. "Urban archaeologist" Arthur Grover scours local estates and backyards looking for unique outdoor statuary, carousel horses, stained glass, antique furniture, bronze animals, and gates plucked from the driveways of old Newport mansions. In one of the more bizarre business pairings you will find, Grover also manufactures and sells bumper boats to amusement parks and for backyard use; you can see them on display at the Aardvark store or online at www.kiddiebumperboats.com. The warehouse is open Monday to Saturday 9:00 A.M. to 5:00 P.M. and Sunday 11:00 A.M. to 5:00 P.M.

Submarine Graveyard

One of the last battles between German and American forces in World War II took place in Narragansett Bay in May 1945. The German submarine *U-853* was operating off Rhode Island's Point Judith when the head of the U-boat fleet officially ended hostilities with the Allies. But the commander of the *U-853* didn't get the message, and on May 5, 1945, the U-boat torpedoed and sunk the USS *Black Point*. It proved a fatal decision; the U-boat was quickly detected and sunk by a pair of American sub hunters, the USS *Moberly* and the USS *Atherton*.

Today the wreck of the *U-853*, which went down with all hands, sits upright at the sandy bottom, her conning tower still pointed at the surface more than 100 feet above. The only thing missing from the sub are the propellors, which you can see in the driveway of the Castle Hill Inn and Resort. Certified scuba divers can view the *U-853* on a guided tour conducted by Newport Diving Center (call 847–9293 or e-mail stephen@newportdiving.com; www.newportdiving.com).

If you're heading back to the visitor center parking lot after spending a day seeing the sights, consider a short detour to the **Newport Dinner Train** (841–8700 or 800–398–7427; write P.O. Box 1081, Newport 02840 or visit www.newportdinnertrain.com). You can meet the train at 19 America's Cup Avenue (near the visitor center).

Departing from a small station on America's Cup Avenue, the dinner train takes a leisurely two-and-a-half-hour tour of the Newport, Middletown, and Portsmouth shoreline. As the train slowly moves along, guests are served drinks, appetizers, and dinner at neatly trimmed tables in the dining cars, while outside the windows there are views of U.S. Navy ships docked at Coddington Cove, quiet country streets and woods, Narragansett Bay, and the Mount Hope Bridge in the distance. Dinner choices include baby back ribs, ginger and sesame-crusted salmon, and Chicken Vanderbilt.

As well as the dinner-only excursions, the Dinner Train has murder mystery dinners, a cabaret evening excursion, and a kids' program narrated by Engineer Annie. A rail-to-sail luncheon excursion features a train ride followed by a cruise of Newport harbor aboard the *Spirit of Newport*. The dinner train operates Thursday to Saturday from March 31 through the end of December. Dinner and an approximately three-hour excursion (7:00 to 10:00 P.M.) will run you $54.95 plus tax and tip. Prices vary for other excursions.

If you want the train ride but not the meal, the **Old Colony & Newport Scenic Railway** (624–6951; www.ocnrr.com) offers eighty-minute excursions along the same route, with both coach and parlor seating available. You can meet this train at the same place as the Dinner Train. Regular excursions are

$11.00 for parlor-car seating, $7.50 for adult coach seating, $6.00 for seniors, and $5.00 for children under fourteen. The train operates on Sunday only from mid-January to late November, with departures at 11:45 A.M. and 1:45 P.M.

Places to Stay in Newport

(All Area Codes 401)

Castle Hill Inn & Resort
590 Ocean Avenue
849–3800

The Cliffside Inn
2 Seaview Avenue
847–1811 or (800) 845–1811

Elm Tree Cottage
336 Gibbs Avenue
849–1610 or (800) 882–3356

Hotel Viking
One Bellevue Avenue
847–3300

Hyatt Regency Newport
1 Goat Island
851–1234

The Ivy Lodge
12 Clay Street
849–6865

The Jailhouse Inn
13 Marlborough Street
847–4638

Murray House B&B
1 Murray Place
846–3337

Newport Harbor Hotel and Marina
49 America's Cup Avenue
847–9000

Newport Marriott
25 America's Cup Avenue
849–1000

Ocean Cliff
65 Ridge Road
841–8868

Stella Maris Inn
91 Washington Street
849–2862

Places to Eat in Newport

(All Area Codes 401)

Black Pearl
West Pelham Street
846–5264

Brick Alley Pub & Restaurant
140 Thames Street
849–6334

The Cheeky Monkey
Perry Mill Wharf
845–9494

Franklin Spa
229 Spring Street
847–3540

OTHER NOTEWORTHY ATTRACTIONS AND EVENTS IN NEWPORT

The Astors' Beechwood Mansion

The Breakers

Chateau Sur Mer

The Elms

Kingscote

Marble House

The Old Colony House

Rosecliff

Winterfest
February

Schweppes Great Chowder Cook-off
June

New York Yacht Club Regatta
June

Newport International Boat Show
September

Oktoberfest
October

Handy Lunch
462 Thames Street
847–9480

La Petite Auberge
19 Charles Street
849–6669

The Mooring
Sayer's Wharf
846–2260

Mudville's Pub
8 West Marlborough Street
849–1408

Sala's Dining Room
345 Thames Street
846–8772

Sardella's Italian
Restaurant
30 Memorial Boulevard West
849–6312

Scales & Shells
527 Thames Street
846–FISH or 846–3474

White Horse Tavern
Marlborough Street
849–3600

HELPFUL WEB SITES ABOUT NEWPORT

Best Read Guide to Newport
www.newportri.com

Newport Chamber of Commerce
www.newportchamber.com

Newport County Convention
and Visitors Bureau
www.gonewport.com

Newport Historical Society
www.newporthistorical.org

Newport This Week
www.newportthisweek.com

Visit Newport
www.visitnewport.com

SELECTED CHAMBERS OF COMMERCE IN NEWPORT

Newport County
Chamber of Commerce
45 Valley Road
Middletown 02842
847–1600

Newport County Convention
and Visitors Bureau
23 America's Cup Avenue
Newport 02840
(800) 976–5122

Newport County

Jamestown

Just as Rhode Island sometimes is overlooked by people speeding on the interstate between Boston and New York, Jamestown is perhaps best known to travelers for its bridge leading to and from Newport. That's a shame, because this Conanicut Island town is full of surprises for the informed visitor to discover.

After reaching the island either from the Pell Bridge to the west or the Newport Bridge to the east, take the North Road exit from either direction on Route 138, then head south toward the village of Jamestown. Looking carefully, the first thing you will see on your right (about 1⁹⁄₁₀ miles) is a small sign for **Watson Farm** (455 North Road, 423–0005; www.historicnewengland .org/visit/homes/watson.htm).

Beginning in 1796, Watson Farm was continually operated by the same family for 183 years. Today the 285-acre property is owned by Historic New England and still run as a family farm, raising cows, sheep, and lambs and working the earth to yield hay and vegetables. Visitors are free to explore the farm on their own or to hike the nature trails that offer good views of the bay. The farm managers are usually working around the fields and

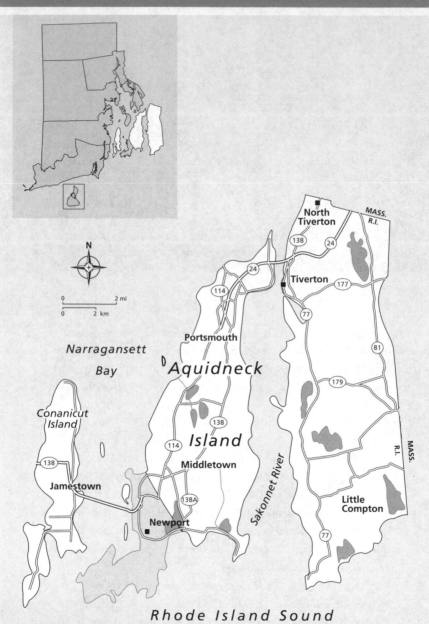

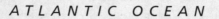

livestock and are happy to answer your questions. There also is a beautiful old farmhouse on the property; it is not open to the public, though, as it's where the farmers live. In addition to fresh produce, you can buy beef and lamb raised on the farm at the *Coastal Growers Farmers' Market,* held Saturdays from 9:00 A.M. to noon, May to October at Casey Farm in Saunderstown.

Visitors are welcome on Tuesday, Thursday, and Sunday, June 1 to October 15, from 1:00 to 5:00 P.M. Admission is $4.00 for adults, $2.50 for seniors, and $1.50 for children ages six to twelve. Children under six are admitted free.

The rich Native American heritage of Jamestown is evident in the *Sydney L. Wright Museum* (26 North Road, 423–7280; www.jamestownri.com/library), which is maintained by the Jamestown Philomenian Library. The small museum features artifacts from the West Ferry archaeological dig, which unearthed both pottery and items received in trade with the English in the mid-seventeenth century. A cemetery cremation site yielded stone bowls thought to be 3,400 years old, and these are on display along with a variety of arrowheads found around the island. Open Monday 10:00 A.M. to 9:00 P.M., Tuesday noon to 9:00 P.M., Wednesday 10:00 A.M. to 5:00 P.M. and 7:00 to 9:00 P.M., Thursday noon to 5:00 P.M. and 7:00 to 9:00 P.M., and Friday and Saturday 10:00 A.M. to 5:00 P.M. (Saturday 10:00 A.M. to 2:00 P.M., June 15 to September 15, and Sunday 1:00 to 5:00 P.M., mid-October to early May.) Admission is free.

Before construction of the Newport Bridge in 1969, the ferry was the only link Jamestown had to its sister island and the rest of Newport County. The old auto ferry service closed after the bridge was built, and though the glory days are gone forever, the memory lives on in the tiny, passengers-only *Jamestown & Newport Ferry Company* (423–9900; www.conanicutmarina.com/ferry.html), which is based at the East Ferry Wharf in downtown Jamestown.

For Newport visitors, the ferry provides a pleasant way to explore the quiet streets of Jamestown and its growing array of interesting restaurants. For those on the Jamestown side, the ferry presents a good alternative to dealing with the Newport traffic. Either way, you get a scenic ride on the bay. The $15 all-day pass is a bargain when you consider that you don't have to worry about the

AUTHOR'S FAVORITES IN NEWPORT COUNTY

Prescott Farm

Purgatory Chasm

International Polo Series
Portsmouth; June through September

Flo's Clam Shack

Tiverton Four Corners

Sakonnet Vineyards

bridge toll or pay for parking in Newport. Plus, your ferry ticket is good for $1.00 off admission to Rose Island, Fort Adams, and the Museum of Yachting. The ferry operates daily between June and mid-September and weekends through Columbus Day. The ferry makes stops at Bowen's Wharf, Perrotti Park, Fort Adams, and Rose Island.

Jamestown at night is a pretty place, with streets that grow quieter with each passing hour and lights that twinkle from the restaurants that have set up tables for outside dining. Two notable eateries that offer alfresco dining are **Trisha's TropiGrille** (14 Narragansett Avenue, 423–1490) and **Trattoria Simpatico** (13 Narragansett Avenue, 423–3731; www.trattoriasimpatico.com).

The spirit of island life is alive at Trisha's TropiGrille, though the vibe is more Key West than Jamestown. Decked out in glorious fiesta colors, the TropiGrille channels Jimmy Buffett to provide a sunny welcome any time of the year. But summer is best, when the outdoor patio and tiki bar open and diners are serenaded with laid-back beach tunes on the weekends.

The menu is as imaginative as the decor, providing a party-boat tour of Caribbean cuisine like Bahamian conch fritters, Cuban sandwiches, and Jamaican jerk chicken. After dinner, indulge on the Islander Key Lime Pie or head to the cozy upstairs bar for a strawberry or banana colada nightcap. Open daily 11:30 A.M. to 10:00 P.M. during the summer; check for winter hours.

For sophisticated dining in a small-town setting, Trattoria Simpatico can't be beat. Owner Phyllis Bedard and executive chef Chris Carruba have successfully wedded an imaginative menu to a setting that captures Jamestown's quiet charms. Located on Narragansett Avenue in the heart of town, Trattoria Simpatico has a small dining room inside a converted village home, but a screened-in porch and alfresco dining on the lawn are the main draw in the warmer months. There is live jazz in the delicately lit garden room in the winter and in the garden during the summer.

At Trattoria Simpatico, the setting makes for a casual, relaxed atmosphere. The food, on the other hand, is elegant and excellent. Meals start with fresh bread served with rosemary olive oil, then perhaps some calamari as an indulgence. Entrees represent both land and sea, including a juniper- and coffee-rubbed pork tenderloin, pan-seared salmon topped with an almond crust, and a tomato-saffron bouillabaisse. The soups and salads are also very good, and the restaurant has an extensive wine list. Entrees range from about $13 to $35. After dinner you can take the short walk down to the marina, where a small park overlooks the bay, Newport Bridge, and the lights of downtown Newport.

If you want to party in raucous Newport in the summer but still have a quiet place to lay your head when the day is over, then Jamestown's small group of inns is the perfect solution.

What's in a name? For **The Bay Voyage** (150 Conanicus Avenue, 423–2100; www.bayvoyageinn.com), quite a lot. The large Victorian house that comprises the inn and restaurant was moved in two pieces across Narragansett Bay in 1889, its owner fleeing Newport for the "more prosperous shores" of Jamestown. The inn was renamed to commemorate the successful transit.

Luckily for latter-day guests, the house did not move too far inland once it reached Jamestown: The Bay Voyage has a great view of the bay, the Newport Bridge, and, across the water, downtown Newport. Many of the rooms and suites have water views, some have private patios, and all inn guests can enjoy the scenery from the pool and patio area.

Overlooking the pool and the bay is one of the inn's two elegant dining rooms, where guests and the general public are welcome to sample the signature pan-seared jumbo scallops or a selection of entrees served tableside (lighter fare is served in the tavern). The restaurant also is acclaimed for serving Rhode Island's best Sunday brunch, which features breakfast fare like eggs Benedict as well as carving stations and seafood dishes.

Rates for the thirty-two one-bedroom suites range from $85 to $320 depending on season, view, and day of the week. Open for dinner Tuesday to Saturday (also open for dinner on Monday in the summer, plus lunch daily from 11:00 A.M. to 2:00 P.M.) from 6:00 to 9:00 P.M. (last reservation); entrees range from $21 to $30. Sunday brunch, served 10:00 A.M. to 2:00 P.M., is $29.95 for adults and $12.95 for children age ten and younger.

Lodging is otherwise pretty scarce on Conanicut Island, but there are a couple of bed-and-breakfasts that might catch your eye. **The East Bay B&B** (14 Union Street, 423–0330 or 800–243–1107; www.eastbaybnb.com) is a hundred-year-old Queen Anne Victorian with four guest rooms. Innkeepers Greg and Donna Kohler put out a generous continental breakfast to start your day; then it's just a quick walk to the shops and restaurants downtown. Room rates are $90 to $150. Nearby is the **Jamestown B&B** (59 Walcott Avenue, 423–1338), a simple but comfortable three-room affair highlighted by Mary Murphy's full breakfasts. For just $80 to $90 nightly, you get a great view of the bay; a spacious room with hardwood floors, lace curtains, and colonial furnishings; and an eye-opening morning spread that may feature Rhode Island jonnycakes, French toast, apple pancakes, or Mary's top-secret "Dutch babies."

Beavertail State Park (www.riparks.com/beaverta1.htm) is simply one of the most beautiful places in Rhode Island. Located at the southern tip of Jamestown, the park is centered on the 1856 **Beavertail Lighthouse,** the third beacon that has shone from this spot since 1749.

Set on a rocky prominence facing the open sea, the park is famous for its pounding surf. From the parking lot you can clamber down a short hillside to a

Captain Kidd's Booty

While strolling the shores of Jamestown, it might be wise to bring along a metal detector. Who knows—you could be the one to find the long-lost buried treasure of Captain Kidd.

Captain William Kidd shared a pirate's life with fellow brigand Thomas Paine during the 1690s, but by 1699 Paine had retired to Conanicut Island (Jamestown) and Kidd was on the run from the British. That spring, Kidd anchored a vessel full of loot off Jamestown and went ashore to visit his old friend.

After his stay with Paine, Kidd reportedly sailed to Gardiner's Island and then on to Boston, where he was arrested, taken to England, tried, and later hanged for piracy. During Kidd's trial, Paine told officials that Kidd had asked him to hold his gold for him, but that he had refused.

One theory holds that Kidd buried his treasure somewhere on Gardiner's Island. Yet local lore claims that Kidd really did give Paine his fortune, and that it may have been buried in Paine's yard in Jamestown. While she was in jail, for example, Kidd's wife instructed Paine to bring her a large amount of gold. And when Paine's house was renovated many years later, workers found an ivory tusk and a gold coin.

What really happened to the rest of the treasure? Your guess is as good as anyone's.

series of huge boulders, a great spot to sunbathe and picnic while the roaring breakers blast spray and foam below. Surf casters love Beavertail for its excellent fishing.

Beavertail also is the place to come to enjoy fantastic sunsets over an expansive ocean horizon. Officially, Beavertail is closed from sunset to sunrise; however, the gates to the park are often left open at night so that you can at least drive the road that loops around the lighthouse and admire the powerful, rotating beacon as it shines its warning out to ships in the East Passage.

The lighthouse itself is closed to the public, but you can get an up-close look at the mechanics of the light at the ***Beavertail Lighthouse Museum*** (423–3270; www.beavertaillight.org), which has on display the huge French glass lens used at Beavertail until 1991. Located in the old assistant keeper's quarters, the museum also includes exhibits detailing the lives of the men and women who had the vital, if sometimes perilous, job of maintaining Rhode Island's lighthouses. Eerie before-and-after photos of the ***Whale Rock Lighthouse*** tell the story of the hurricane of 1938, which ripped the top of the lighthouse off and killed the keeper. From Beavertail Point, the foundation of the Whale Rock light is plainly visible at low tide. (Look west toward the Narragansett shoreline for something that looks like the conning tower of a submarine.)

The museum, which also contains models and descriptions of every light-house in Rhode Island, is open weekends only from late May to mid-June, noon to 3:00 P.M.; daily from mid-June to Labor Day, 10:00 A.M. to 4:00 P.M.; and on weekends from Labor Day to Columbus Day, noon to 3:00 P.M. Admission is free. The park and museum are located at the southern end of Beavertail Road; from downtown Jamestown take Southwest Avenue south, then make a right turn onto Beavertail Road.

If you're traveling with a teenager, chances are a favorite part of Jamestown will be exploring the old gun emplacements and watchtowers at **Fort Wetherill State Park** (423–1771; www.riparks.com/fortweth.htm).

Perched atop a rocky hillside, the fort was built to guard the entrance to Narragansett Bay during World Wars I and II. The fort's guns, never fired in anger, are long gone, but you can still see the rotating platforms where they once rested and the rails that were used to transport ammunition from the bunkers below.

Save for a handful of picnic tables, the park is undeveloped, and the crumbling fortifications, with their warren of rubble-strewn underground chambers, are no place for unsupervised children or for folks who have trouble getting around. But the public is welcome to walk around the fort, and the view from the top is nothing short of spectacular. Fort Wetherill is located near the end of Highland Drive, south of downtown Jamestown.

More user-friendly is Fort Wetherill's cousin, **Fort Getty** (off Beavertail Road), which has some old fortifications but also a picnic area, campground, trailer hookups, a beach volleyball setup, and a panoramic view of small, undeveloped **Dutch Island** and the new **Jamestown Bridge.** There also is a small lighthouse at the tip of the park.

Middletown

It was a hot summer night in 1777 when a raiding party of American soldiers caught a British general with his pants down, literally. General Richard Prescott, commander of British forces occupying Aquidneck Island, was having an affair with the wife of Henry Overing, whose estate was situated north of Newport in the Middletown countryside. As often happens with such things, word soon got out that Prescott was spending his evenings at Overing's house. Acting on this information, a small band of colonial militiamen based in Tiverton made a daring nighttime raid across the Sakonnet River and through enemy territory to capture Prescott, who was hauled away in his nightshirt.

Although the daring of Colonel William Barton, leader of the raid, was recognized with the naming of Tiverton's Fort Barton, General Prescott's ignominious foray into Middletown has been memorialized with the naming of

Prescott Farm (2009 West Main Road/Route 114, 849–7300 or 847–6230; www.newportrestoration.com/prescott/prescott.html). A project of the Newport Restoration Foundation, Prescott Farm is a collection of historic Newport County buildings on the site of the former Overing estate. The property includes General Prescott's guardhouse, a fascinating windmill (circa 1812), and a former ferry-master's home (circa 1715), which was moved here from Portsmouth and restored as an old country store. (The 1730 Prescott [Nichols-Overing] House is not open to the public.)

The guardhouse, which once sat next to the Prescott House up the hill, includes old muskets and a remarkably well-preserved drum from a Massachusetts militia corps that fought against the British. In the loft upstairs are two tiny beds, proving that the visitors of Prescott's day were frequently small of stature, if not of rank.

The windmill, moved to this site from Warren, was restored in 1971 and remains in working order. Occasionally, the cotton sails are reattached to their wooden frames, and the gears and stones inside begin to turn as they have for almost 200 years.

Even when the windmill's mechanism is at rest, however, the docent-led tour is captivating. The entire grinding process is explained, and you can marvel at the ingenuity of the eighteenth-century technology that allowed the miller to lift a three-ton millstone with one hand on a lever. In the top level of the mill is the bonnet, a huge central gear powered by the wind-turned sails outside.

The Prescott Farm Windmill

The general store features herbs grown in a small, traditional garden behind the building, as well as honey from the beehives located on the Prescott property. Also take a few minutes to look over the eclectic collection of farm implements and children's toys gathered by the Restoration Foundation from the attics and barns of Newport County. Tours are $3.00 for adults and $1.00 for children; tickets can be purchased at the general store. Open Monday to Friday, 10:00 A.M. to 4:00 P.M., May to October.

If a tree falls in the forest when nobody's around, would it make a sound? Ponder that and similar thoughts as you follow the signs to ***Whitehall*** (311

St. George's School

One of Middletown's most prominent landmarks is the Gothic Revival steeple of the chapel at St. George's School (847–7565; www.stgeorges.edu), located on a hilltop off Purgatory Road. Built in 1901, St. George's is one of the best private boarding schools in the country, counting legendary Rhode Island Senator Claiborne Pell among its alumni.

You can see St. George's steeple from much of Middletown, and a drive up to the school's campus is rewarded by spectacular views of Second Beach and the Atlantic Ocean. Visitors are welcome to visit the chapel and the Hunter Art Gallery when school is in session. The gallery, which features the work of emerging artists, is located in the William H. Drury and Richard Grosvenor Center for the Arts and is open Monday to Saturday from 9:00 A.M. to 5:00 P.M.

Berkeley Avenue off Green End Avenue, 849–3672 or 846–3116; www.george berkeley.org.uk/whitehall.htm or www.nscda.org/museums/rhodeisland.htm), the American home of noted philosopher George Berkeley.

Berkeley, an Anglican clergyman who postulated that nothing can exist unless it is or can be seen, heard, or otherwise perceived, came to Newport in 1729 and stayed two years in an effort to build an Anglican school in America. The school never was built, but Berkeley did leave behind his fine country home, which is maintained as a museum by the National Society of the Colonial Dames of Rhode Island.

By 1897, when three ladies from Newport rediscovered it, Berkeley's home had fallen into such a state of disrepair that it was used as a hay barn. But the home has been fully restored and furnished to represent the fine residence of Berkeley's day. Each summer Berkeley scholars from around the world are invited to stay at Whitehall and act as tour guides, so you can spend your visit discussing *Alciphron*—which Berkeley wrote here—and admiring the rooms and herb garden.

Whitehall is open daily, except Monday, July 1 through the end of August 10:00 A.M. to 4:00 P.M. and other times by appointment; the house also is open for special events such as Colonial Day in May, Apple Day in September, and Christmas at Whitehall. Admission is $5.00 for adults and free for children.

A peaceful place to stop for a picnic lunch is the nearby *Paradise Valley Park,* located at the corner of Paradise Avenue and Prospect Avenue. (From Whitehall, proceed south on Berkeley Avenue until it becomes Paradise Avenue south of Green End Avenue.) Located at a quiet country corner, the park has blue-gravel walking paths that meander through a lush meadow, with the spire of St. George's School ever present in the distance. A pretty gazebo seems the ideal spot for a travel break.

Paradise Park also is home to **Boyd's Windmill,** the only surviving eight-vaned windmill in the United States. Built in 1810 and moved here from the Boyd family farm in Portsmouth, the windmill has been restored to full working order. The Middletown Historical Society (849–1870; www.middletown history.org/pages/boyd_mill.htm) gives tours on Sunday from July to September from 2:00 to 4:00 P.M.

A corner of the park is occupied by the **1875 Paradise School** (www .middletownhistory.org/pages/paradise_school.htm), listed on the National Register and home to the historical society, which operates a seasonal museum on educational history on the site.

This quiet corner of Middletown is 3 miles from the summer madness in downtown Newport and just a mile from the beach, making it a fine location for a bed-and-breakfast. Sharon and Rick Gallipeau have converted the barn behind their Victorian cottage on Prospect Avenue into two spacious luxury suites with views of the windmill, the old schoolhouse, and Sachuest Point in the distance. The **Windmill View Cottage** (98 Prospect Avenue, 846–6393; www.windmill viewcottage.com) suites are available for $225 to $275 nightly, depending upon the season, and include balconies, gas fireplaces, wet bars, and private baths.

Prepare to be awed by the **Inn at Villalon** (120 Miantonomi Avenue, 847–0902 or 800–352–3750; www.villaloninn.com). This magnificent mansion of

Far from a Teacher's Paradise

The next time someone bemoans the current state of public education, point him or her to the Paradise School for some perspective. Beautiful and quaint, this one-room schoolhouse nonetheless provides a sharp rap on the knuckles to nostalgia about the "good old days" of reading, writing, and 'rithmetic.

Typical of nineteenth-century Middletown schools, in the Paradise School a single teacher was responsible for presenting all subjects, at all grade levels, to a class of fifty or more. Students ranged in age from seven to sixteen, and school days stretched from 9:00 A.M. to 4:00 P.M., with an hour off for lunch.

Heat was provided by a wood- or coal-burning stove that needed to be stoked frequently. An outhouse served as the bathroom, and water had to be pumped from a well. The school's large windows provided the primary source of illumination: natural light.

For a tour of the Paradise School, call the Middletown Historical Society at 849–1870 or go to www.middletownhistory.org.

Inn at Villalon

Italianate Stick design, unlike those Newport "cottages" along the cliff walk, welcomes guests to stay for the night.

You approach the grand white building from a curved drive that edges the shady green lawn. Once inside, your eyes will feast on the wealth of detail that Richard Upjohn lavished on his home when he built it in 1853. Step into the grand entryway onto mahogany floors laid in a basket-weave pattern, and take a moment to admire the fine staircase in front of you and the French crystal chandelier hanging from the 14-foot ceiling overhead. To your left is the parlor with its stained-glass windows, huge, arched mahogany doors, and hand-painted, stenciled walls.

Upstairs, the eight guest rooms—each named for a nineteenth-century female author—are decorated with a Victorian flair and scented with potpourri. The spacious Elizabeth Barrett Browning room, the honeymoon suite, includes a copy of Browning's famous love poem, "How Do I Love Thee," which guests can take home.

Inkeepers Stefan and Claudia Wessel welcome arriving guests by flying the flag of their native country at the front of the house. Room rates range from $99 per night for an off-season weeknight stay to $350 on a summer weekend and include a full breakfast.

The smallness of Rhode Island makes for wonderful contrasts. For example, just minutes from the hustle and bustle of downtown Newport—and just a short walk from the crowds at Third Beach—is the tranquillity of the ***Norman Bird Sanctuary*** (583 Third Beach Road, 846–2577; www.normanbirdsanctuary .org), a remarkably varied nature preserve covering 400 acres just over the Newport town line in Middletown.

An ornithologist's paradise, the Norman Bird Sanctuary attracts more than 250 species of birds, including waterfowl, nesting songbirds, and pheasants. What attracts winged and two-legged visitors alike is the sanctuary's diverse topography, which runs the gamut from open fields and dense woodland to marshes and beaches.

Seven miles of hiking trails make the changing terrain easily accessible to visitors of all ages, and children will especially enjoy the trailside museum at the Paradise Barn, which includes history and science exhibits and a display on the epochal geographic changes that have created the preserve's unique landscape. Be sure to follow the trail to *Hanging Rock,* part of the series of rocky ridges that bracket the isolated wooded valley at the heart of the sanctuary. For centuries artists have sought to capture the beauty of Hanging Rock, and philosopher George Berkeley sought out a shady spot underneath the formation while writing one of his famous tracts. It's a serene place to contemplate the meaning of life—or just to stop for a breather.

The preserve is open daily 9:00 A.M. to 5:00 P.M. and until dusk on Wednesday evening during the summer. Admission is $4.00 for adults, and $2.00 for children ages four to thirteen. For early risers, there's a free Sunday morning bird walk that starts at 8:00 A.M., spring through fall (and on alternating Sundays in the winter).

In the same area as the Norman Bird Sanctuary are two other excellent natural sites worth investigating. Just a short jog south at the end of Sachuest Point Road is *Sachuest Point National Wildlife Refuge* (847–5511; www.fws.gov/northeast/sachuestpoint), 242 acres of grasslands, marsh, and beaches on a peninsula that juts out into Narragansett Bay between Second Beach and Third Beach. Here you can spy a variety of ducks, birds, foxes, and butterflies along the trails, which are open from dawn to dusk, and then check out the displays and information at the new visitor center.

Closest to Newport is *Purgatory Chasm,* a gaping fissure cut into the cliffs overlooking Second Beach. Legend has it that Purgatory Chasm was made by the Devil, chopping with an ax at the head of an Indian maiden. More likely, the 160-foot-deep crack was the result of centuries of waves battering against the rock.

Some daredevils and lovers (and aren't they the same thing?) have foolishly leaped across the chasm, but you don't have to: A wooden bridge spanning the cleft provides an excellent view of the chasm and the waves crashing into the opening far below. Braver souls can walk out to the edge of the chasm and peer down at the cave that the sea has hollowed out of the base of the cliff and that fills with water at high tide. From this spot you also have a great view of the bay meeting the ocean to the south, while the drifting sounds from Second Beach far below will draw your attention to the north.

A small parking area, located on the east side of Purgatory Road just south of the intersection of Hanging Rock Road and Paradise Avenue at Second Beach, serves visitors to Purgatory Chasm. There is no admission fee.

A shopping center is probably the last place where you would expect to find a winery, but then you would miss the tastings and tours offered by ***Newport Vineyards,*** located in the Eastgate Mall at 909 East Main Road/Route 138 (848–5161; www.newportvineyards.com). Founded by a former U.S. Navy captain in 1977, Newport Vineyards makes up in quality and variety (more than twenty vintages are available) what it lacks in setting. The Great White, a sweet blend of Cayuga and Vidal Blanc grapes, is the best seller, and the Riesling is excellent, as is the Vidal Ice wine, which has won national acclaim.

Actually, the inside of the winery is quite pleasant, and tours describing the wine-making process are conducted daily at 1:00 and 3:00 P.M.; $5.00 will get you a tour and tastings from a five-wine flight. Hours are Monday to Saturday 10:00 A.M. to 5:00 P.M.; noon to 5:00 P.M. Sunday.

Sharing the same shopping center with Newport Vineyards is the celebrated ***Glass Onion*** (909 East Main Road, 848–5153), one of the rare restaurants that succeeds with a huge menu (more than forty entrees, plus specials) of creative gourmet offerings. Mad Maggie's chili, named for owner Maggie Wiggins, is a big lunchtime crowd-pleaser, and the dinner menu runs the gamut from burgers to a sinful lobster and scallop pie and linguine Napoleon, topped with lobster meat and veal sautéed in a brandy cream sauce—mmm! Open for lunch Monday to Saturday from 11:30 A.M. to 3:00 P.M. and for dinner on weekdays from 4:30 to 9:00 P.M. and Friday and Saturday from 5:00 to 10:00 P.M.; open Sunday 11:00 A.M. to 9:00 P.M.

The neon- and chrome-clad ***Blue Plate Diner*** (665 West Main Road, 848–9500; www.seafareinn.com/blueplate.htm) is a throwback to a bygone era in many ways but doesn't go overboard with its Fifties decor or attitude. Alongside the cheeseburgers and shakes you might expect is a growing selection of New American entrees such as an Asian-inspired broiled salmon. The waiters, nattily attired in white shirts and bow ties, are one hint that, despite the name on the door and the folksy wisdom posted on the walls, the Blue Plate is no greasy spoon. This recent addition to Middletown's culinary landscape brought back memories of the great diners I grew up with on Long Island, and if it's not open twenty-four hours like a "real" diner should be, at least the Blue Plate has the good sense to serve breakfast all day. Open 7:00 A.M. to 11:00 P.M. daily.

Launched from a Middletown industrial park in 1999, Newport Storm Hurricane Amber ale has quickly become a sudsy staple at bars and restaurants throughout Rhode Island, including the Glass Onion and 15 Point Road in Portsmouth, where they pour the local brew fresh from the tap. The ale is by far the biggest seller, but you'll also find the Newport Storm label on the new Blizzard Porter and some limited-edition heavy ales.

Founded by a quartet of college buddies, the **Coastal Extreme Brewing Company** (307 Oliphant Lane, 849–5232; www.newportstorm.com) knows how to make a good time: After the work week is done, friends like you are invited over for a tour of the brewery and free samples of the wares. Tours are free and begin at 6:00 P.M. on Friday at the brewery, which is located in the Middletown Tradesman Center on Oliphant Lane (near the Newport State Airport) between West Main Road (Route 114) and East Main Road (Route 138). Note: Get there early because only the first seventy-five people will be admitted.

Come at lunchtime, and you're likely to find a crowd at **Becky's Real BBQ** (82 East Main Road, 841–9909), but the slow-cooked, pit-smoked barbecue is well worth the wait. Located in one of the few old homes on this stretch of Route 138 that hasn't been demolished to make way for a shopping center, Becky's has a small but comfortable six-table dining room and does a booming take-out business.

The hickory-smoked pork, beef brisket, ribs, and chicken have a subtly sweet taste, which you may or may not choose to accentuate with barbecue sauce. Dinner plates come with a choice of sides, and they're no mere afterthought: The moist corn bread is shot through with real chunks of sweet corn, and the cole slaw is made with a creative hint of honey. For a meal on the go, Becky's slaps together some barbecued pork and cole slaw to form the Elvis Sandwich—purportedly the King's favorite meal (besides peanut butter and marshmallow Fluff sandwiches, of course). Open Monday to Saturday 11:00 A.M. to 8:00 P.M. and Sunday noon to 8:00 P.M.

I'm always delighted when seemingly ordinary restaurants have special rooms that are hidden from general view unless you are "in the know," and there are a handful of great examples along the beach end of Aquidneck Avenue in Middletown. The downstairs of **Aquidneck Restaurant & Pizza** (27 Aquidneck Avenue, 849–3356), for example, is nothing special: a pizza counter and a few random tables. Upstairs, however, is a beautiful dining room and bar with huge arched windows overlooking Easton's Beach and the Atlantic Ocean. Similarly, the **Easton's Point Pub & Restaurant** (116 Aquidneck Avenue, 847–0001) enjoys water views from its second-floor lounge and dining room.

But the best of all is **KJ's Pub and Restaurant** (61 Aquidneck Avenue, 848–9991). A typical neighborhood bar downstairs, KJ's goes upscale upstairs, with a bright open dining room adorned with fanciful aeroplanes and balloons (again, those water views!) and a bar area meticulously decorated with Roaring Twenties murals, Tiffany lamps, giant fish tanks, and an impressive false balcony that would make Disney proud.

The Middletown location of **Flo's Clam Shack** (see page 159) also is in this neighborhood, which can get pretty busy during beach season but is otherwise rather quiet. For a room with a view within easy walking distance of the shore, the aptly named *Seabreeze Inn* (147 Aquidneck Avenue, 849–1211; www.theseabreezeinn.com) has some nice accommodations in a villa-like building, with spacious upstairs balconies for taking in the sunsets. A fresh, full breakfast is included in the room rates, which run from $75 to $245, and the downstairs cafe and ice-cream parlor draw big crowds in the summer.

Portsmouth

If you're playing tourist in Newport, chances are you'll hear or read about *Green Animals Topiary Gardens* (847–1000; www.newportmansions.org). Still, this country estate merits a mention, despite being relatively well known. Unlike the other properties maintained by the Preservation Society of Newport County (Kingscote, Chateau-sur-Mer, the Breakers, and other Newport mansions; www.newportmansions.org), Green Animals is located way off in the countryside of northern Portsmouth. And it is so very odd that it demands inclusion in any collection of offbeat attractions.

Those of us whose exposure to topiary animals is limited to a view from the monorail at Walt Disney World may find the idea of carving shrubs into amusing creature-shapes rather, well, silly. But Green Animals was serious business for gardener Joseph Carriero and his successor, George Mendonca, who created and maintained for eighty years the topiary gardens at the former estate of Thomas E. Brayton. Today there are about seventy green animals throughout the property, including camels, pigs, birds, and giraffes. The kids will love it.

The formal gardens overlook Narragansett Bay, and the estate house includes a Victorian toy exhibit and a gift shop. Admission to Green Animals is $10.00 for adults and $4.00 for children ages six to seventeen; you can also buy a variety of combination tickets that allow you to visit Green Animals and some or all of the other Preservation Society properties.

Open April to November daily from 10:00 A.M. to 6:00 P.M. (last tour is at 5:00 P.M.). Green Animals is located on Cory's Lane off West Main Road/Route 114 just south of the intersection with Route 24 and about 3 miles south of the Mount Hope Bridge.

Sleepy *Escobar's Highland Farm* (133 and 251 Middle Road, 683–1444; www.escobarshighlandfarm.com) comes to life each fall with Rhode Island's best corn maze, professionally designed on eight acres of cornfields with a different theme each year (past incarnations have included a U.S. flag, a cow, a pig, and a Rhode Island Red rooster). These mazes are truly challenging, with about 2 miles of winding trails, so expect to spend an hour or so figuring your way out. Escobar's also has pumpkin picking around Halloween, a Christmas tree farm, and hayride tours of its dairy farm.

Admission to the corn maze, located at 251 Middle Road, is $7.00 for adults and $5.00 for children ages five to eleven. The maze generally opens in mid-August and can be visited through early November. Open Monday to Saturday from 10:00 A.M. to dusk and Sunday 11:00 A.M. to dusk from mid-August to Labor Day, then Friday from 3:00 P.M. to dusk, Saturday from 10:00 A.M. to dusk, and Sunday 11:00 A.M. to 7:00 P.M. into November.

Island Park reminds you of those towns out west that used to sit on Route 66, the main drag before the era of interstate highways. At one time, Point Road led to a stone bridge that crossed the Sakonnet River to downtown Tiverton. But in 1954 Hurricane Carol washed out the center span of the bridge and it was never rebuilt, taking Island Park off the beaten path. (Today, the Sakonnet Bridge to the north makes Route 138/Route 24 Portsmouth's main link to the eastern mainland.)

Still, this is no ghost town, and the chance to view the remains of the old bridge (from the Stonebridge Marina) is worth the detour off Route 138 (if head-

Portsmouth Polo

When polo was introduced to America in nearby Newport in 1876, it was strictly a rich man's game. But while owning a "string of poloponies" (pronounced puh-LOP-puh-nies, to quote *The Honeymooners'* Ed Norton's famous malapropism) may still be a measure of wealth, anyone with ten bucks burning a hole in their pocket can attend a polo match at *Portsmouth's Glen Farm* (www.glenfarm.com).

Every summer Saturday at 5:00 P.M., teams from England, India, Spain, and even farther afield saddle up for a few chukkers of world-class polo, part of the annual Newport International Polo Series. Along with the hoi polloi, you may rub shoulders with nobility, actors, and other tony Newport visitors. Well-heeled fans tailgate as if at a football game but with Bentleys and Jaguars standing in for trailers, and spectators scarfing wine and cheese rather than wings and beer.

Despite polo's country-club image, the sport is fast-paced and occasionally dangerous (to players, not spectators). The version of the game you'll see at Glen Farm is nearly identical to that played more than a century ago.

Glen Farm, a hundred-acre park that features a grand old manor house, is located on Route 138 in Portsmouth. Tickets for polo are sold at the Glen Farm gate on match days. Polo tickets are $10.00 for adults and free for children, and tailgaters are welcome.

For more information call the polo hotline at 846–0200 or visit www.newport internationalpolo.com.

ing north, take a right onto Park Avenue; use Boyd's Lane if traveling south). Also, Island Park has built a solid reputation for its variety of seafood restaurants, including the waterfront **15 Point Road** (15 Point Road, 683–3138; www.15pointroadrestaurant.com).

This small bistro has a 180-degree view of the river and an ambitious menu that has won raves from readers of *Newport Life* magazine, who vote 15 Point Road the best restaurant in Portsmouth just about every year. Signature dishes include the Mount Hope Lobster Casserole baked with sherry and cream, and Chicken Nanaquaket, sautéed with apples, celery, lingonberries, walnuts, and brandy. Open Wednesday and Thursday (plus Tuesdays June to October) 5:00 to 9:00 P.M., Friday and Saturday 5:00 to 10:00 P.M., and Sunday 4:00 to 9:00 P.M.

It might be a stretch to call **Flo's Clam Shack** a restaurant, but Flo's is a must-see if you want a taste of what living in a seaside New England community is all about. They mean it when they say "shack": Flo's is a rough-hewn drive-in adorned with fishing nets and weather-beaten buoys, with a porch supported by old telephone poles and a parking lot of crushed shells. After you order, the person at the window will give you a small beach stone painted with a pick-up number, and a couple of picnic tables make up the dining area. You get the idea.

But the fried clams and fish are fantastic, and Flo's has been here forever. (A sign noting that the place is closed during hurricanes is only half in jest: Flo's has weathered uncounted storms since it opened more than sixty years ago, and a previous shack was washed out to sea in the 1938 hurricane.) Many folks take their orders across the street and sit on the seawall or go down to the small beach. Flo's is located at Park Avenue in Island Park.

A second, newer location at 4 Wave Avenue (847–8141; www.flosclam shack.com) in Middletown offers similar fare and caters to the Easton's Beach crowd. It has a great upstairs deck with ocean-view dining and drinking, as well as a lush patio filled with nautical detritus. Flo's in Portsmouth is open April to October; hours are 11:00 A.M. to 8:00 P.M. daily during summer (weather permitting) and weekends in the spring and fall. The Middletown location stays open till 9:00 P.M. on weekdays and 10:00 P.M. on weekends.

Island Park Beach, by the way, is open to the public and parking along the seawall is free, if limited.

For a completely different dining experience, it's well worth the drive down Portsmouth's East Main Road to the **Sea Fare Inn** (3352 East Main Road/Route 138, 683–0577; www.seafareinn.com). Those in the know have been traveling up from Newport or down from Providence for twenty-five years to indulge in chef George Karousos's Greek-inspired cookery. An herb garden on the restaurant grounds is the source for many of the fresh ingredients that are the key to the Sea Fare Inn's success. How fresh, you say? Well, consider that the Sea Fare Inn doesn't even have a freezer on the premises.

Dishes like steak au poivre complement an array of seafood entrees and have helped Karousos earn high praise both locally and nationally. The grilled swordfish is served in a nice sherry sauce and is topped with lobster, accompanied by julienned carrots and zucchini. The signature Lobster Gourmet is served with a Mornay sauce and surrounded by shrimp, scallops, and crabmeat. Service is professional, attentive, and unhurried. Wednesday-night guests are treated to a free cooking demonstration along with dinner.

Thanks to its reputation and popularity, the restaurant has grown to take over most of the 1887 colonial-style estate house that once belonged to the Webb family. Speaking of family, that's how you'll be treated by the Karousoses, who also operate *Sea Fare's American Cafe* in downtown Newport (151 Swinburne Row, 849–9188; www.seafarecafe.com). The Portsmouth restaurant is open Tuesday to Thursday 5:00 to 8:30 P.M., Friday and Saturday 5:00 to 10:00 P.M. and Sunday for brunch from 10:30 A.M. to 2:00 P.M. The Newport location is open Monday to Thursday from 11:00 A.M. to 9:00 P.M. and Friday to Sunday 11:00 A.M. to 10:00 P.M.

Rhode Island's youngest winery, *Greenvale Vineyards* (582 Wapping Road, 847–3777; www.greenvale.com) is also located off East Main Road/Route 138 in Portsmouth. The vineyard, within hailing distance of the Sakonnet River,

A Farm with a Berry Nice View

There are plenty of pick-your-own farms in Cranston, Foster, Johnston, North Smithfield, and throughout the West Bay half of Rhode Island. But my friend's father—who lives in Cranston and seeks out only the best berries for making pancakes, muffins, and jam—insists on making the long drive out to Portsmouth to pick strawberries at *Quonset View Farm* (895 Middle Road, 683–1254).

Not only are the berries here bigger, better, and cheaper, but the beautiful views of Narragansett Bay and Quonset Point are well worth the trip. Plus, the steady breeze off the water keeps amateur pickers cool, even during the height of the summer harvest season. Strawberry-picking is in June; you also can pick your own pumpkins in October and tag Christmas trees in November and December.

To get to Quonset View Farm, take Union Street from either Route 114 or Route 138 to Middle Road, then head north. For brochures listing Rhode Island's pick-your-own farms and roadside farm stands, contact the state Department of Environmental Management's Division of Agriculture, 22 Hayes Street, Providence 02908; 222–2781.

takes advantage of the moderating effect of the ocean and the rich soil of Aquidneck Island to produce complex vintages from young vines. Greenvale only began producing its Chardonnays, Cabernets, Francs, and Vidal Blancs in 1993, yet its wines have appeared on the lists of such upscale eateries as the Pot au Feu restaurant in Providence. For a simple table wine, try the Skipping Stone White.

The vineyards surround an 1860s Victorian Gothic house and stable, the latter of which has been refurbished into a tasting room. Greenvale Vineyards is open Monday to Saturday 10:00 A.M. to 5:00 P.M. and Sunday noon to 5:00 P.M. Tours are daily at 2:00 P.M., and a flight of five tasting wines and a souvenir glass will cost you $3.00. To get there, take East Main Road to Sandy Point Avenue, then turn right onto Wapping Road. The winery is about ½ mile down on your left.

Tiverton

Although officially part of Newport County, Tiverton and Little Compton share Bristol County's geographic isolation from the rest of Rhode Island. Like their neighbors to the north, the two towns are located on a small peninsula jutting into Narragansett Bay, with far more secure land links to Massachusetts than to the Ocean State.

What's especially engaging about Tiverton is the way the town quickly gives way to country as you head south. One minute, you're passing between the rows of homes that make up the modest seaside village; the next, you're driving through a pastoral landscape where glimpses of the water are an ever-present companion.

Rising above the village of Tiverton is **Fort Barton,** the launching point for one of the most heralded military exploits in American history. Built in 1777 to prevent the British occupiers of Newport from attacking Boston or Providence, the redoubt known as the Tiverton Heights Fort was the base for Colonel William Barton. Just a week after the fort was commissioned, Barton led a party of soldiers on a daring raid to British-held Aquidneck Island and captured General William Prescott, commander of the Newport garrison. The mission was such a morale boost to the beleaguered Continental Army that the fort was renamed in Barton's honor.

Two centuries later, Fort Barton is a tranquil plateau crisscrossed with nature trails that lead through a narrow right-of-way to a larger preserve known as the Fort Barton Woods. There's not much left of the fort itself besides some earthen walls, but a modern observation tower provides a nice view of Narragansett Bay and the Mount Hope Bridge. Birdsong and children's laughter drifting upward

vineyardvictuals

Sakonnet Vineyards produces some of the East Coast's best wines, and Rhode Island is home to some of New England's best restaurants and one of the nation's top culinary schools, Johnson and Wales University. At the Sakonnet Master Chefs series, you can learn how to put fine wine and great food together to create memorable meals.

Held each spring and fall, the day-long cooking classes at Sakonnet Vineyards feature guest chefs from around the region. The hands-on instruction includes basic cooking techniques and meal preparation, with a big banquet to end the day. Visiting chefs also share their favorite recipes with students.

The one-day classes typically cost about $125 (plus $50 for a dinner guest) and include lunch, dinner, and wine. For more information contact Sakonnet Vineyards at 635–8486 or visit www.sakonnetwine.com.

from a nearby school serve as accompaniment to this otherwise quiet spot. The main Red Trail leads you to a pond and four bridges crossing the **Sin and Flesh Brook,** whose grisly name recalls the murder of a white settler during King Philip's War in 1676.

Parking for the fort is located on Highland Road. There's no office on the park grounds, but **Tiverton Town Hall** is across the street and the folks there are very helpful in answering questions.

Continue south on Highland Road and you will intersect with Main Road (Route 77). Make a left turn, and you almost immediately will be greeted by **Evelyn's Drive-In** (2335 Main Road, 624–3100; www.evelynsdrivein.com). A stop at Evelyn's is a great topper to a hot summer day spent at the beach or driving around Bristol County. You could take your meal inside the small dining room, but in nice weather the best idea is to order from the outside window and dine alfresco on the canopied picnic tables or patio. Nothing fancy about this busy roadside seafood shack, just great fried fish, shrimp, and clams. Open from April to November, Monday to Thursday 11:00 A.M. to 8:00 P.M. and Friday to Sunday 11:00 A.M. to 8:30 P.M.

Tiverton is home to one of the strangest "zoos" you will ever see. The **Newport Butterfly Farm** (409 Bulgarmarsh Road, Route 177, left turn just south of Evelyn's, 849–9519; www.butterflyzoo.com) includes more than thirty species of butterflies, which are raised by owner Marc Schenck in a large Quonset greenhouse that has had many of its glass panes replaced by screens, allowing a nice breeze to blow through. Visitors are guided on a tour that includes a look at a (dead, but preserved) Goliath birdwing butterfly. With a wingspan of more than a foot, it is the largest butterfly in the world.

You also get to walk through the screen houses, which are full of fluttering butterflies and the tropical plants and weeds they need for food and reproduction. Thanks to a strict "no touch" rule, the butterflies are so tame that you can get up close and personal with them while they eat, mate, and lay eggs. In addition to the mature butterflies, the plants are home to the caterpillars that one day will turn into a chrysalis and later sprout wings. (Come between 11:00 A.M. and 1:00 P.M. for the best chance to witness this metamorphosis.) Schenck also grows butterfly-attracting plants outside the greenhouse to lure wild butterflies like red admirals, question marks, and tortoise shells to the property.

Any long-term resident of New England can tell you that there are not as many butterflies around as there once were; in fact, Schenck says that some native species are extinct and many others are threatened. On the bright side, he says, by growing the right kinds of flowers and plants you can easily attract butterflies to your own yard; the farm sells kits to help you out. The Newport Butterfly Farm is open late May to Labor Day, Monday to Saturday 11:00 A.M. to 4:00 P.M., Sunday noon to 4:00 P.M., weather permitting (sunny days are best; closed rainy days). Admission on weekdays is $6.00 for adults and $4.00 for children ages three to twelve.

Route 77 continues south, hugging the shore of the pond and affording a nice view of a small peninsula and the Sakonnet River beyond. At this point you are truly in the country, as evidenced by the abundance of nature preserves in the area. The first one you can visit is the *Emile Ruecker Wildlife Refuge,* located about ⅛ mile west on Seapowet Road. (It's a right turn at the next crossroads you will come to on Route 77.) This Audubon Society of Rhode Island (949–5454; www.asri.org/ruecker.htm) property features short, easy-to-walk trails along the salt marshes to *Jack's Island Beach.* Fiddler crabs patrol the beach and herons and ducks ply the waters of the marsh and river, while a feeding station attracts a variety of birds in the winter.

If you exit the parking lot and turn right, Seapowet Road ends almost immediately at Seapowet Avenue. Head south (left turn) and you will soon come to a small bridge that crosses Seapowet Creek, which leads into the undeveloped *Seapowet Marsh Wildlife Refuge.* Slow down for a view of the river (which looks more like a bay) on one side and the creek on the other.

Seapowet Avenue ends at a bend in Puncatest Neck Road; bear left, and a short drive past pretty Nanquit Pond will bring you to *Tiverton Four Corners* (crossroads of Main Road/Route 77 and East Road/Route 179; www.tiverton fourcorners.com).

Locals boast of Tiverton's rural character by pointing out that this intersection has the only traffic signal in town, but there's more reason than a red light to stop at Four Corners. This crossroads has always been a prominent part of Tiverton: A sawmill and gristmill were erected here in the late 1600s, and Robert Grey—the explorer who discovered the Columbia River and established the United States' claim to modern-day Idaho, Oregon, and Washington—made his home here.

In more modern times, many Providence families have taken a ride in the country as an excuse to stop at **Gray's Ice Cream** (624–4500; www.graysice cream.com), at 16 East Road, often called the best in the state. Dozens of ice-cream flavors are offered, including seasonal oddities like pumpkin and eggnog, and there's also a decent selection of sherbet and frozen yogurt varieties. Order from the outside window or go inside the shop, which doubles as a convenience store and cafe. Open year-round from 6:30 A.M. to 8:00 P.M. and until 10:00 P.M. in July and August.

For a picnic lunch, you can't do much better than the deli sandwiches served at the **Provender** (3883 Main Road, 624–8084). Typical is the Mamma Mia, with sliced turkey topped with roasted garlic basil mayo, provolone cheese, and marinated peppers. The Provender's fresh soups lean heavily on the veggies, including broths flavored with Brazilian black beans and a carrot-and-tomato soup with fresh dill. And don't forget to throw in some of the Provender's award-winning cookies—favorites like chocolate chip and oatmeal raisin, plus such novelties as chocolate orange, espresso, and vegan cookies made with peanut butter.

Located in a three-story Victorian, which for years was the local general store (evidenced by the high ceilings and squeaky wooden floors), the Provender also serves muffins and coffee for breakfast. Call ahead and they'll pack you a box lunch tied up with a pretty bow, or you can settle into one of the benches on the wraparound porch and watch the world (slowly) go by. Open daily 9:00 A.M. to 5:00 P.M. in summer; winter weekdays 9:00 A.M. to 3:00 P.M. (closed Monday; closed Tuesday after Christmas through March 1); and winter weekends 9:00 A.M. to 5:00 P.M. The Provender also closes for the months of January and February.

The **Donovan Gallery** (3895 Main Road, 624–4000; www.donovangallery .com), features the original work of more than twenty-five contemporary New England artists. It's open Monday to Saturday 10:00 A.M. to 5:00 P.M. and Sunday noon to 5:00 P.M. in summer. Weekday hours are trimmed to 11:00 A.M. to 5:00 P.M. in spring and fall, and the shop is closed Monday and Tuesday from January through March. Also at the crossroads is the **Cottage at Four Corners** (3847 Main Road, 625–5814; www.thecottageri.com), which sells Maine Cottage and Mitchell Gold/Bob Williams maple furniture, home accessories, pottery, and handblown glass. The Cottage is open Tuesday through Saturday 10:00 A.M. to 5:00 P.M. (plus Monday in the summer) and Sunday noon to 5:00 P.M.

Next door is **Abigail and Magnolia's** (3851 Main Road, 624–2636), a funky, eclectic shop that mixes upscale women's clothing with an assortment of architectural garden pieces—go figure. Open 10:30 A.M. to 5:00 P.M. weekdays and 1:00 to 5:00 P.M. Saturday and Sunday in summer; the same hours from Wednesday to Sunday in the winter.

The *Four Corners Grille* (3841 Main Road, 624–1510), with its pine floors, wooden booths, and small dining room, has a colonial, almost rustic feel. It's got a great selection of sandwiches, from chicken cordon bleu served on a French roll ($7.95) to mixed vegetables on grilled rosemary focaccia bread ($6.95), all served with excellent, beer-battered fries on the side. Dinner entrees focus on comfort foods, such as shepherd's pie and meat loaf, and seafood. Salads and soups—including a creamy lobster bisque full of bits of lobster meat—are also served. Open daily 8:00 A.M. to 8:00 P.M. during winter and till 9:00 P.M. during summer.

Just down the road—a few hundred feet south on Route 77—are the charming *Mill Pond Shops,* located in a converted mill complex connected by a wooden bridge that spans a stream-fed raceway. The specialty shops include *Little Purls,* a children's clothing store (3952 Main Road, 625–5990; open Monday to Saturday noon to 5:00 P.M., and Sunday noon to 5:00 P.M.; closed on winter Mondays except between Thanksgiving and Christmas); *Amy's Armoire,* a women's clothing and accessories shop (3964 Main Road, 624–2594; open Monday to Saturday 10:00 A.M. to 5:00 P.M. and noon to 5:00 P.M. on Sundays in July and August and around Christmas; generally open Saturdays 10:00 A.M. to 4:00 P.M. and noon to 4:00 P.M. the rest of the week, but call ahead for seasonal hours); and *Courtyards,* which specializes in garden statuary, decorative fountains, fine crafts, and "eccentricities" selected by owners Sharon and Wendy Prazak (3980 Main Road, 624–8682; www.courtyardsltd.com; open Monday to Saturday 10:00 A.M. to 5:00 P.M., Sunday noon to 5:00 P.M., closed Monday January through April).

The *Magic Garden of Tiverton* (3988 Main Road, 625–1344), located just a few steps from the Mill Pond Shops, is a showcase for the genius of environmental artist Michael Higgins, who uses a chainsaw to create whimsical and unique wooden figures. Higgins has turned tree stumps into noble eagles, provided schools with painted mascots, carved a nativity scene for the nearby Amicable Church, and even sculpted an entire Wizard of Oz troupe for a home-owner's backyard. Populated by wacky birch "bugs," dragons, and other products of Higgins's imagination, the Magic Garden serves both as a studio for custom jobs and a retail stop. Carvings range in price from $10 to thousands. Open daily 8:00 A.M. to 6:00 P.M.

Finally, the *Tiverton Historical Society* operates a small museum at the *Chase Cory House*, located a few steps south of Four Corners at 3908 Main Road (624–4013). A typical colonial-era home (listed as built in 1730, although local historians think it might actually date from 1690), complete with a tremendous fireplace and tiny doorways, the Chase Cory House is open to visitors on Sunday from 2:00 to 4:30 P.M., May to September, or by appointment.

After this brief stop in civilization, our journey takes us back to nature again. About a half mile east of Four Corners on East Road (Route 179) is the entrance to secluded *Weetamoo Woods,* a sweetheart of a nature park that boasts some great natural and artificial attractions.

Named after the queen of the Pocasset Indians (the name translates as "sweetheart"), Weetamoo Woods consists of 450 acres of oak and holly woodland, swamp, and rocky prominences surrounding the remains of an old mill and mill village. Along with the adjoining *Pardon Gray Preserve,* it makes up the largest swath of unfragmented forest in the East Bay. When you first enter the property, you will be standing on the remains of *Eight Rod Way,* a seventeenth-century cobbled road lined with stone walls. A large cedar swamp feeds the streams that cross the property, and hikers will cross a number of ancient slab bridges as they follow the paths to the old *Borden Mill.* Here you can see the overgrown remains of an eighteenth-century sawmill, including the dam and raceway that once fed water to the wheel that powered the mill. There is also a pretty arched bridge, and the remnants of the homes of mill workers also are visible. Weetamoo Woods is open sunrise to sunset. Call the Town of Tiverton, which owns the property, for more information at 625–6700.

If you've seen enough forest and crave the sounds and sights of the sea instead, head south from Four Corners on Route 77 for about 1½ miles and look for Pond Bridge Road on your right. Take this road, past the small dam that gives it its name, until you reach Fogland Road. Make a left and look for the sign for *Fogland Beach* on your right.

The rocky beach itself is nice enough, with a small picnic area and playground located along the bay. The lack of any significant waves makes this a great spot to take the little ones. Kids of all ages, however, will enjoy looking for Tiverton's *Speaking Rocks.* Since they were discovered in the mid-1700s, the hieroglyphs carved in a set of boulders along the beach here have mystified local residents and scholars. Various theories have attributed the carvings to Norsemen, Native Americans, or other early explorers, but to this day there is no consensus as to their origin. At one time there were six carved rocks, but some were hauled away and others claimed by the sea, so today there remains only one. The carvings have faded over time, but to see if you can find the last of the speaking rocks, walk along the shore about ½ mile south of Fogland Beach.

Little Compton

Nothing much has changed in Little Compton over the past couple of centuries, which suits locals just fine. From the time the area was settled in 1674 until well into the twentieth century, Little Compton's residents primarily were farmers, both working the land and raising livestock, including the famous Rhode Island Red rooster. Gentrification has come in the form of fine homes for some of the state's wealthier residents, but Little Compton still retains most of its rural charm and Yankee character.

If you do happen to find the Speaking Rocks, you may be in the mood to celebrate (especially if you've figured out what they mean). If so, you're in luck, because just over the Tiverton/Little Compton border are the cool cellars of *Sakonnet Vineyards* (left turn off Route 77/West Main Road, 635–8486; www.sakonnetwine.com).

Sakonnet's hospitality center lies at the end of a winding, rutted dirt road, and the abstract sculptures on the lawn lend a modern touch to an otherwise rustic setting. Inside the cool, dark center you can sample any of a dozen or so vintages available—$5.00 for six sample wines and a souvenir glass. The tasting room is open 11:00 A.M. to 5:00 P.M. daily October 1 to Memorial Day, 10:00 A.M. to 6:00 P.M. in summer. Tours of the winery are given at noon and 2:00 P.M., plus 4:00 P.M. during the summer; you can also pick up a map and take a self-guided tour of the vineyards themselves.

Sakonnet's Chardonnays and Gewürztraminers have received rave reviews, and the signature wine is a dry Vidal Blanc that is a great accompaniment to

Disturbing the Peace

How did the town of Little Compton come to possess such a prize piece of real estate for its Town Landing—almost five acres of beautiful waterfront property on the Sakonnet River?

Some locals say that two neighbors in the area had a long-running spat about access to the property. No sooner would one of the feuding ladies open the gate on the road, then the other would shut it.

The story goes that the fight carried over into the hereafter: When one of the women died, she left the waterfront property to the town, hoping to annoy the surviving neighbor by allowing other residents to come down and launch boats, fish, play, and picnic—presumably creating a lot of noise and traffic in the process.

If so, the strategy was not especially successful. Like most of Little Compton, the Town Landing is still a pretty sleepy place—by outsiders' standards, anyway.

Rhode Island's fresh seafood. Sakonnet also released its first sparkling wine, the 1995 vintage Samson Brut, named after the winery owners, and has won accolades for its Vidal Blanc estate wine. The most popular seller, however, is the Eye of the Storm, a fruity blush wine so named because it was created when white and red grapes accidentally were mixed during a hurricane. It's a great wine for a picnic, and Sakonnet is happy to oblige. You can buy snacks at the hospitality center or pack a picnic lunch, pick up a bottle of chilled wine, and sit outside to admire the rows of grapes destined to become this year's vintage.

It's no surprise that Sakonnet Vineyards chose a rooster as its logo; the world-famous Rhode Island Red breed was developed here, and there's even a monument to the plucky little bird in the nearby village of Adamsville. Perhaps the most out-of-the-way town in Rhode Island, **Adamsville** is located in the far northeastern corner of Little Compton and has firmer ties to Westport, Massachusetts, than to any community in Rhode Island. To get there, either follow Route 179 east from Tiverton Four Corners or make a left onto Peckham Road just south of Sakonnet Vineyards. At the end of Peckham Road, make a left onto Long Highway, then a quick right onto Colebrook Road, which will take you right into Adamsville.

For such a small town, Adamsville has a decent number of attractions for back-roads explorers.

The aforementioned **Rhode Island Red Monument,** located on Main Road in downtown Adamsville, is no big deal, just an inscribed plaque, really. Then again, how many towns can claim they have a monument to a chicken?

Across the street is **The Barn** (11 Main Road, 635–2985), which readers of *Rhode Island Monthly* say serves the best breakfast in the state. This is no greasy-spoon; gourmet breakfasts served inside or on the patio out back include eggs Benedict topped with a homemade pesto hollandaise sauce, eggs Sakonnet topped with lobster and asparagus, traditional Rhode Island jonny-cakes, and fresh-squeezed orange juice. Open 6:30 A.M. to noon weekdays and 7:00 A.M. to 1:00 P.M. weekends.

Gray's Store (4 Main Street, 635–4566) is an Adamsville institution. Built in 1788, the store is one of the oldest in America, and it has been in the Gray family since 1879. Gray's still serves a vital function as Adamsville's sundries and grocery store, and its long history is reflected in the old soda fountain (order a malted or a frappé), antique penny-candy and tobacco cases, and freestanding ice chest. Current owner Grayton Waite (his grandmother was a Gray) keeps the store shelves filled with jonnycake meal, penny candy, cigars, and pancake mixes; Hannah's gifts and collectibles round out the inventory.

For many years Gray's and the former Manchester's Restaurant across the street took turns housing the local post office, until a separate post office building finally was built to serve the town. The old post office, circa 1935, is still preserved in one corner of Gray's Store, including the original blotters and clerk's station.

Gray's is open 9:00 A.M. to 5:00 P.M. from Monday to Saturday and noon to 4:00 P.M. on Sunday and holidays; closed Monday, Tuesday, and Wednesday during the winter.

A hundred feet over the state line in Massachusetts sits **Gray's Grist Mill** (638 Adamsville Road, 508–636–6075; www.graysgristmill.com), a working seventeenth-century mill that still produces cornmeal for jonnycakes and pancakes from rare whitecap flint corn. The mill's gift shop is open Tuesday to Sunday noon to 4:00 P.M., and visitors are encouraged to tour the mill and its grounds, including the race that channels water from the Westport River to turn the millstones. Weekends are your best bet for seeing the mill in action, grinding corn to meal the same way it has for the last 300 years.

From Adamsville, you need to double back on Colebrook Road to Long Highway (left) and then Peckham Road (right) to reach the next destination. After turning onto Peckham Road, take the second left onto Willow Avenue, which soon delivers you to the **Commons.**

Most people's vision of the classic New England town would fit neatly into the narrow rectangle known as the Commons, although such a setting is a rarity in Rhode Island. In fact, Little Compton owes its village structure to Massachusetts, which at one time laid claim to the town and where setting important public buildings around an open patch of land accessible to all residents was, if you'll pardon the pun, common practice.

At the green center of the Commons is the 1832 Georgian-style **United Congregational Church** (635–8472; http://ucclcri.org) and its old graveyard. Take a few moments to walk the rows of headstones in a setting that is remarkably tranquil considering that it is in the heart of town. This is where Benjamin Church, who defeated King Philip, is laid to rest. Also buried here is Elizabeth Padobie, daughter of John and Priscilla Alden and the first white girl born in New England. Look for the grave of Elizabeth Palmer, whose headstone notes that she "should have been" the wife of the man she married but refused to live with.

Surrounding the refreshingly untouristy village green are all the municipal buildings that make up the infrastructure of a prosperous New England farming community. Individual buildings house the Wilbur School, Grange Hall, Legion Hall, police station, library, post office, and Town Hall. At the east end of the square is the **Commons Restaurant,** also known as the Commons Lunch (635–4388), which offers seafood platters at reasonable prices. The quahog chowder (New England–style, of course) is excellent, lobster rolls and boiled lobsters are a specialty, and the restaurant is known for serving the East Bay's best jonnycakes.

The restaurant—which burned down in 2004 but was quickly reopened—draws a crowd of locals as well as tourists, and you can sit at the dinerlike counter in front, the dining room in back, or out on the patio in warmer weather. Open Sunday to Thursday 5:00 A.M. to 7:00 P.M. and Friday and Saturday 5:00 A.M. to 8:00 P.M.

Next door to the restaurant is the *C. R. Wilbur General Store* (635–2356), which remains essentially unchanged since it opened more than one hundred years ago. Staying true to its name, you can find almost anything you need for sale at Wilbur's—it's bigger than it looks. In addition to hardware and housewares, the store includes a popular gift shop and deli. Open Monday to Saturday 7:00 A.M. to 6:00 P.M. and 7:00 A.M. to 1:00 P.M. Sunday.

On Long Highway, about a mile or so from the water in the quietest corner of Little Compton (and that's pretty quiet!), the *Harmony Home B&B* (456 Long Highway, 635–2283) is located on an eighteenth-century farm, the house surrounded by stone walls and gardens. Guests can choose from three rooms decorated with antiques or a cottage that's available for weekly rental. Open May through the end of October. Rates are $100 to $150; cottage is $850 per week.

Doubling back to Route 77, our next stop is the 1690 *Wilbor House* (548 West Main Road, 635–4035; www.littlecompton.org), currently operated as a museum by the *Little Compton Historical Society.* Visitors may tour the house, with its period furniture, as well as an 1860 barn that houses a collec-

HELPFUL WEB SITES ABOUT NEWPORT COUNTY

Discover the Coastal Villages
www.coastalvillages.com

Jamestown Community Homepage
www.jamestownri.com

Little Compton Historical Society
www.littlecompton.org

Newport CVB
www.gonewport.com

Newport County
Chamber of Commerce
www.newportchamber.com

Tiverton Guide
www.tiverton.org

Town of Middletown
www.middletownri.com

Town of Portsmouth
www.portsmouthri.com

tion of horse-drawn carriages and sleighs. There also is an old one-room schoolhouse on the property. The museum is open Thursday to Sunday from late June to Labor Day and weekends in September and October from 1:00 to 5:00 P.M.; also open by appointment. Admission is $5.00 for adults and $1.00 for children under twelve.

Not quite as old as the Wilbor House, but with perhaps a more colorful history, is the **Stone House Club,** located at the bend in the road where West Main Road becomes Sakonnet Point Road (122 Sakonnet Point Road, 635-2222; www.stonehouseclub.com). Built in 1836 by David Sisson, an engineer who built Sakonnet Point's first breakwater, the Stone House was a popular speakeasy during Prohibition and currently operates as a membership club, inn, tavern, and restaurant.

Given his experience with seaside construction, it's not surprising that Sisson built a house that has weathered more than a century of hurricanes and nor'easters, despite an exposed hillside location overlooking a freshwater pond and the ocean beyond. The exterior of the aptly named Stone House Club is somewhat forbidding—the house is constructed of 2-foot-thick granite walls—but the inn is bright and inviting inside, with a parlor and common areas on the first floor and eleven guest rooms (including two suites) on the second and third floors.

The basement Tap Room, with a fireplace that's in use during cooler months, serves both as a cozy tavern and restaurant. True to its English pub flavor, the tavern offers a wide selection of brews, while the restaurant pays homage to the sea nightly with fresh seafood specials. Saturday is soup and sandwich night, and several interesting pasta dishes are the feature on Sunday night.

Since the Stone House is a membership club, overnight stays and use of the restaurant are limited to members and their guests. Membership fees are $25 annually per person and $40 per couple; nonmembers who want to eat at the restaurant pay a $5.00 per table fee. Excluding membership fees, the inn's room rates range from $70 to $250 per night. In addition to the rooms in the Stone House Club, there is a loft in a converted barn on the property. Room rates include continental breakfast.

From this point, Route 77 continues south for a couple of miles and ends at **Sakonnet Point.** If you take the road to the end, you may see local fishermen pulling in their catch at the **Town Landing,** and you also can get a look at the offshore **Sakonnet Light.**

Places to Stay in Newport County

(All Area Codes 401)

JAMESTOWN

Bay Voyage Inn
150 Conanicus Avenue
423–2100 or
(800) 225–3522

The East Bay B&B
14 Union Street
423–0330

Jamestown B&B
59 Walcott Avenue
423–1338

MIDDLETOWN

Atlantic House B&B
37 Shore Drive
847–7259

Bartram's B&B
94 Kane Avenue
846–2259

Courtyard by Marriott
9 Commerce Drive
849–8000 or
(800) 321–2211

The Inn at Villalon
120 Miantonomi Avenue
847–0902 or
(800) 352–3750

Sea Breeze B&B
36 Kane Avenue
847–5626

PORTSMOUTH

Bestemor's House B&B
31 West Main Road
683–1176

**Founder's Brook
Motel & Suites**
314 Boyd Lane
683–1244

Holiday's B&B
20 Silva Lane
683–2416

LITTLE COMPTON

Harmony Home B&B
456 Long Highway
635–2283

Places to Eat in Newport County

(All Area Codes 401)

JAMESTOWN

The Bay Voyage Inn
150 Conanicus Avenue
423–2100

Chopmist Charlie's
40 Narragansett Avenue
423–1020

Jamestown Oyster Bar
22 Narragansett Avenue
423–3380

Schoolhouse Cafe
14 Narragansett Avenue
423–1490

Trattoria Simpatico
13 Narragansett Avenue
423–3731

Tricia's TropiGrille
14 Narragansett Avenue
423–1490

OTHER NOTEWORTHY ATTRACTIONS AND EVENTS IN NEWPORT COUNTY

Butts Hill Fort
Portsmouth

**Jamestown Fire Department
Memorial and Museum**
Jamestown

Memorial to Black Soldiers
Portsmouth

Fool's Rules Regatta
Jamestown; August

SELECTED CHAMBER OF COMMERCE IN NEWPORT COUNTY

Newport County Chamber of Commerce
45 Valley Road
Middletown 02842
847–1600
www.newportchamber.com

MIDDLETOWN

Sea Shai
747 Aquidneck Avenue
849–5180

PORTSMOUTH

15 Point Road Restaurant
15 Point Road
683–3138

Flo's Clam Shack
Island Park
(847–8141)

Sea Fare Inn
3352 East Main Road
683–0577

TIVERTON

Evelyn's Drive-In
2335 Main Road
624–3100

Gray's Ice Cream
16 East Road
624–4500

The Provender.
3883 Main Road
624–8084

Stone Bridge Restaurant
1848 Main Road
625–5780

LITTLE COMPTON

The Barn
Main Road, Adamsville
635–2985

Commons Lunch
The Commons
635–4388

Crowther's
90 Pottersville Road
635–8367

The Stone House Club
122 Sakonnet Point Road
635–2222

South County— North Kingstown and Inland

People talk a lot about how small Rhode Island is, yet more diversity is packed into South County than is found in some whole states. Here you run the gamut from the genteel resort ambience of Watch Hill to the honky-tonk of nearby Misquamicut, from dense wilderness to waves crashing onto pristine beaches. There are the subdivisions of North Kingstown and the country lanes of Exeter, surfing in Narragansett and skiing at Yawgoo Valley. And there is the otherworldly atmosphere of secluded Block Island, with its mix of Victorian hotels and natural wonders that led the Nature Conservancy to name the island one of the last great habitats left on earth.

If South County lacks anything, it's a big city, but that's fine with folks around here, who have fought casinos and giant retailers alike to preserve the rural character of their home. By the way, if you look at a map, you'll see that the region is called Washington County. Don't call it that, though, because no one will know what you're talking about. South County is not only a name, it's a state of mind.

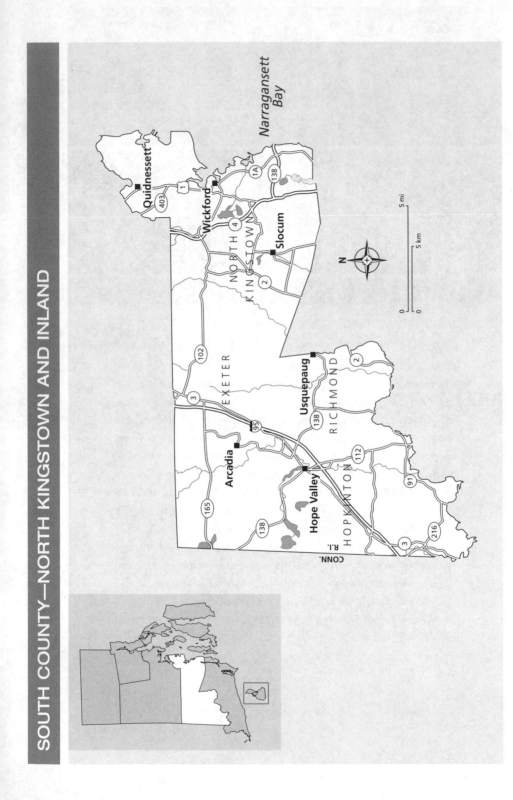

North Kingstown

One of the oldest highways in America, **Post Road** follows the course of the old Pequot Trail, a main thoroughfare for native tribes even before Europeans settled the shores of Narragansett Bay in the seventeenth century. Later, Post Road became the major mail and stagecoach route between New York and Boston (in fact, in many stretches it still is known as the Boston Post Road) and remained a major artery until the advent of the national highway system and the construction of I–95 some fifty years ago.

In Rhode Island, much of the northern part of Post Road remains a well-traveled byway, while in the southern part of the state a large stretch of lmited-access highway was built between North Kingstown and Westerly. This is the express route to South County's beautiful ocean beaches, although on beach mornings and evenings it can sometimes resemble a very long parking lot. This part of Route 1 actually bypasses much of Old Post Road, which still exists in many places as Scenic Route 1A.

A great way to sample many of North Kingstown's hidden treasures is to take a drive on one of the older stretches of Route 1/Post Road, starting at the intersection of Route 1/Post Road and Route 403/Devil's Foot Road. (Route 403 is the second exit off Route 4 south; bear left off the ramp.)

Quonset Point lent its name to the famous domed huts created here by the Seabees during World War II, and the mascot of the Naval Construction

The Devil's Footprints

Local legend has it that the Devil, old Satan himself, once stomped his way across North Kingstown, leaving his cloven hoofprints on a spot known since at least 1671 as Devil's Foot Rock.

There are a number of stories about the strange markings on **Devil's Foot Rock,** located just off Post Road (Route 1) near the intersection with Devil's Foot Road (Route 403) near Quonset Point. The most interesting tale involves a local Indian woman who supposedly sold her soul to the Devil and would brew up potions and spells on the rock ledge. When the Devil came to claim her soul, the story goes, the woman ran off, and the Devil left his footprints as he chased her.

Although parts of Devil's Foot Rock (also known as Devil's Foot Ledge, the Devil's Footprint, and the Devil's Tracks) have been lost to road construction and quarrying, two of the "footprints" remain visible. Park on the west side of Post Road just south of the railroad bridge near Quonset Point, and from there it's a quick scramble up the rock formation that overlooks the railroad tracks, to the footprints themselves.

Battalion ("CBs," get it?)—a giant, wrench-carrying honeybee—guarded the entrance to the military base. (The Seabee was restored and returned to public display.) During the war, just about every American naval fighter, dive-bomber, and torpedo-bomber pilot was trained at the former Quonset Point Naval Air Station or one of its satellite bases.

This remarkable period of Rhode Island history is preserved at the **Quonset Air Museum** (488 Eccleston Avenue, 294–9540; www.theqam.org), located at Quonset Point State Airport. Route 403/Devil's Foot Road ends at the base, and to get to the museum you make a right turn at the traffic signal onto Quonset Road, then drive approximately 2 miles and make a left onto Eccleston Avenue. Look for the Quonset Air Museum hangar on your right.

Described by the late curator Howard Weekley Jr. as a "working museum in progress," the Quonset Air Museum will not be mistaken for the Smithsonian. However, located in the air base's old, brick Hangar 488, the museum now contains an impressive collection of vintage and unusual aircraft. Staff are constantly working to restore the decades-old planes and repair the aging hangar.

Awesome Air Show

My family and I moved a few years ago to a beautiful new home, but the one thing we really miss about our modest ranch house in North Kingstown is being within biking distance of the annual Rhode Island National Guard Air Show, held in early June at Quonset State Airport (275–4110; www.riairshow.com).

The week before the air show was always full of great anticipation, especially with the Blue Angels' FA-18s skating across the sky at treetop height as they rehearsed their incredible precision-flying routine. On the weekend of the big two-day show, we would jump on our bicycles and pedal over to the sprawling Quonset Point base. The first time, the longish ride provoked some protests from the children, but all that was cured when a giant C5-A Galaxy transport flew directly over us on the way to the show, barely 200 feet up. The kids weren't scared—they were hooked.

The Quonset air show is one of the nation's best and features some of the most interesting aircraft in the world. In past years we've seen a Russian MIG-29 demonstrate high-performance turns over the airfield and marveled as a Harrier jet showed off its vertical-takeoff capabilities. An F-117 stealth fighter also has made a few visits to the tarmac, guarded by serious-looking soldiers carrying assault weapons (the unspoken but clear message: Look, but don't touch!).

If you can bicycle in, you'll save the parking fee (donated to charity) and a lot of time waiting in traffic at the end of the day. Either way, though, the show is highly recommended.

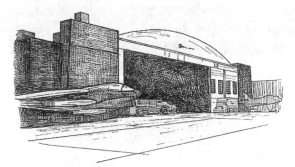

Quonset Air Museum

It is fascinating to watch the restoration process and realize the amount of work it takes to bring an old aircraft back into presentable shape after decades of neglect, as is the case with the museum's Grumman F6F Hellcat. Salvaged from the bottom of the ocean off Martha's Vineyard, the World War II fighter is undergoing a restoration expected to take nearly another decade to complete.

The Hellcat is just one example of the aircraft at Quonset Point; others include a Grumman AGE Intruder and a Sikorsky SH3 Sea King helicopter. In all, the Quonset Air Museum has more than twenty aircraft on permanent display, including a Polish Air Force MiG-17F, a pair of Douglas A-4 Skyhawks, and a "Top Gun" F-14A Tomcat. More unusual displays include the world's only sur- viving Curtis X-15C jet and a Grumman C-1A Trader. Other assorted military equipment and memorabilia also are on display, including a 1940s-vintage U.S Army half-track.

The Quonset Air Museum is open 10:00 A.M. to 4:00 P.M. daily from July to September, Saturday and Sunday only October to June. Admission is $7.00 for adults and $3.00 for children under age twelve.

A welcome addition to Quonset is the ***Vineyard Fast Ferry*** (295–4040; www.vineyardfastferry.com), a high-speed catamaran that whisks passengers from the state pier on Narragansett Bay to Martha's Vineyard in about ninety minutes. For $46 one-way/$69 round-trip for adults, $40/$64 for seniors, and $34/$45 for children ages four to twelve), you'll get a brief passage through lower Narragansett Bay followed by a breezy 30-knot journey to the historic and natural wonders of the Vineyard. The ferry is located at the end of Roger Williams Way within Quonset Point.

Smith's Castle at Cocumscussoc (55 Richard Smith Drive, 294–3521; www.smithscastle.org) frequently surprises visitors, who turn onto the access road off Route 1/Post Road looking for some sort of medieval fortress and find only a simple wooden house. When first raised around 1638, the original

AUTHOR'S FAVORITES IN SOUTH COUNTY— NORTH KINGSTOWN AND INLAND

Rhode Island National Guard
Air Show
North Kingstown; June

Wickford

Wickford Art Festival
North Kingstown; July

Wickford Festival of Lights
North Kingstown; December

Casey Farm

Allie's Donuts

Yawgoo Valley Ski Area and
Water Park

Step Stone Falls

Washington County Fair
Richmond; August

structure on this site was a fortress, a blockhouse that could be used by early settlers to defend against attack from the native tribes in the area.

Thanks to the efforts of Roger Williams, for more than half a century no such defense was needed against the local inhabitants. Williams lived and preached at Cocumscussoc for many years and established peaceful relations with Conanicus and Miantinomi, the chiefs of the Narragansetts. It was not until 1675 that hostilities broke out between the white settlers and the native tribes, resulting in the 1676 burning of Smith's Castle and ending with the Great Swamp Massacre, where the Narragansetts were nearly annihilated by armies from Massachusetts and Connecticut. Rebuilt in 1678, Smith's Castle later became a prosperous plantation and political center for the former Narragansett territory.

Presently maintained by the Cocumscussoc Association, the house and grounds are open to visitors from May through October. Not only are the historic house and its eighteenth-century garden worth a visit but the plantation also sits on a lovely cove facing a small island, deeded by the wife of Conanicus to Roger Williams so that he could graze his goats.

House tours are conducted at noon, 1:00 P.M., 2:00 P.M., and 3:00 P.M. Thursday through Sunday from June through August and Friday through Sunday in May, September, and October. Tours also can be arranged by appointment in the off-season. You can visit the grounds any time of year. Admission to the house and tour is $5.00 for adults, $1.00 for children ages six to twelve. The turnoff for Smith's Castle is located on the east side of Route 1/Post Road, approximately 1½ miles south of Quonset Point.

Just south of Smith's Castle, on the right side of the road past the state police barracks, is a small wooded spot called **Richard Smith's Grove.** This is a nice place to stop for a picnic lunch, and it also offers access (but no trail) to undeveloped Cocumscussoc State Park, a dense, stream-fed woodland.

The next intersection you will come to is the turnoff for Route 1A, which leads south through the village of Wickford and into Narragansett. If you keep going straight on Route 1, you'll soon come to **Duffy's Tavern** (235 Tower Hill Road, 295–0073), the place to stop for good, inexpensive seafood right off the boat. Open Monday through Thursday 11:30 A.M. to 9:00 P.M., Friday and Saturday 11:30 A.M. to 10:00 P.M., and Sunday noon to 9:00 P.M.

Crossing over Route 102 (Ten Rod Road) and continuing south, look for **Oak Hill Tavern** on your right (565 Tower Hill Road, 294–3282; www.oakhill tavern.com). My family used to avoid this place because the dining room was always wreathed in a cloud of cigarette smoke, but thanks to Rhode Island's 2005 smoking ban, we felt safe to try again. Like us, you'll be pleasantly surprised to find that this rather ramshackle-looking place is not only family friendly (free, fresh-popped popcorn, and peanuts from a giant barrel) but boasts some of the state's best, slow-smoked barbecue. There's also live rock or country music, or karaoke, most nights of the week. Open Monday to Saturday, 11:00 A.M. to 1:00 A.M., Sunday noon to 1:00 A.M. (kitchen closes at 9:30 P.M.). If you make this pit stop, though, be sure to double back and pick up the road to Wickford.

The seaside village of **Wickford** (www.wickfordvillage.org) gets a lot of attention for its distinctive, upscale specialty shops and its annual art festival, one of the largest on the East Coast. But this charming little town also has a sometimes overlooked series of quiet residential streets dating from the eighteenth and nineteenth centuries. On Church Lane, accessible via a narrow footpath off Main Street, sits the **Old Narragansett Church** (294–4357; www.episcopalri.org/org_onc.cfm), built in 1707 and one of the oldest Episcopal churches in America. The church was originally built on Shermantown Road and stood there for nearly a hundred years. But around the turn of the nineteenth century, as the story goes, residents of the north and south ends of town began arguing over possession of the old church. On a cold, clear night in January 1800, a group of residents from the north part of town gathered twenty-four teams of cattle, slid the church onto wooden runners, and pulled the structure across the ice and snow to Wickford, where it remains to this day.

The Old Narragansett Church has a fine collection of Queen Anne communion silver (used in services the first Sunday of August) and houses the oldest church organ in North America, manufactured in 1680 and still played during services and recitals. Famous portrait artist Gilbert Stuart was baptized

The Navy's Fightin' Engineers

File clerk Frank Iafrate was working at the massive Quonset Point Naval Air Station in January 1942 when a Navy lieutenant approached him with a strange request: Could he design an insignia for a new unit of construction engineers, one that would reflect both their building and fighting prowess?

Iafrate, an amateur artist, agreed. His first choice for a mascot was a beaver, praised for its industriousness. But research showed that beavers usually run away when confronted with danger—not exactly the image the Navy wanted for its fightin' engineers.

Instead, Iafrate settled upon the bee—another hard worker that has a nasty sting when provoked. Asked to draw a Disneyesque character, Iafrate sketched a honeybee wearing a sailor's cap and holding a machine gun, wrench, and hammer in his white-gloved (a la Mickey Mouse) hands. It was a fitting mascot for men who built airfields on islands across the Pacific, driving payloaders with a gun at their side—which they often were forced to use.

When Iafrate took his bee and stuck a naval reference in front of it, the famous nickname for the Construction Battalions was born: the Seabees.

here, and there's an old cemetery across the quiet, shady street. Open 11:00 A.M. to 4:00 P.M. Thursday to Monday in July and August.

Perhaps the town's most intriguing (and mouthwatering) shop is *Wickford Gourmet Foods* (21 West Main Street, 295–8190 or 800–286–8190; www.wickfordgourmet.com), a two-story building stuffed with exotic pasta, canned fruits and vegetables, cheeses, fabulous homemade cookies, spices, teas, cookware, and dishes, not to mention a gourmet deli counter, a coffee bar, and a small cafe (with free wireless Internet) upstairs. "Rhode Island elves" are credited with creating the Rhode Island Gift Basket, full of such goodies as Kenyon's jonnycake and pancake mixes, Eclipse coffee syrup, and jam from a Little Compton berry farm. A light dinner, accompanied by live music, is served on Friday nights. Open daily 7:00 A.M. to 9:00 P.M.

Not only is the *Tavern by the Sea* (16 West Main Street, 294–5771) the only restaurant with a liquor license in the village of Wickford, it's the only one that's open for dinner. But those are far from the only reasons to check out this charming little eatery. The Tavern by the Sea offers a remarkably large menu of hot and cold appetizers, gourmet pizzas, soups, salads, sandwiches, and a variety of seafood, steaks, pasta, and other entrees. Standards include a Tavern Pasta with sausage and sirloin in a sweet plum tomato sauce over penne, and a portofino pork tenderloin with a port-wine demi-glace.

The dining room is tiny, so it's best to come when the weather is favorable and you can relax under an umbrella on the restaurant's two-level deck, which looks out over the tidal channel and pond that bisect the village. The Tavern is open 11:00 A.M. to 10:00 P.M. every day during the summer; on winter Mondays, only lunch is served (11:00 A.M. to 4:30 P.M.).

For an even closer look at Wickford Harbor, your group can charter the yacht **Brandaris,** which you'll find anchored across the street from the Tavern by the Sea. This beautiful wooden sailing vessel, which rescued 330 troops during the evacuation of Dunkirk during World War II, is available for nature excursions and sightseeing tours (rates are $30 to $70 per person for two- or four-hour cruises); call 294–1481 or visit www.yachtbrandaris.com for information.

The annual **Wickford Art Festival** is held on the second weekend in July and attracts more than 200 artists, who display their work up and down Brown Street. The festival always is a lot of fun, although the crowds may have you wishing the town fathers had installed wider sidewalks. If you can't make the festival, you can visit the Wickford Art Association's permanent gallery at 39 Beach Street, at the North Kingstown Town Beach. Open Tuesday to Saturday 11:00 A.M. to 3:00 P.M., Sunday noon to 3:00 P.M. (For more information call the Wickford Art Association at 294–6840 or see www.wickfordart.org.)

An equally pleasant time to visit Wickford, but with a much more local flavor, is during the village's annual **Festival of Lights,** held in early December to herald the arrival of the Christmas season. The town Christmas tree is lit, as are festive lights all along the business district; the streets come alive with the sounds of carolers; and horses drawing hay wagons clip-clop around town. The lights stay on throughout the holiday season. For information contact the North Kingstown Chamber of Commerce at 295–5566 or see www.wickfordvillage.com.

Other than during the annual art festival—when the town fairly bustles—Wickford is a pretty quiet place year-round, making it a nice setting for a cluster of bed-and-breakfasts, most located in historic homes in or near downtown. In the heart of the village is the **Haddie Pierce House** (146 Boston Neck Road, 294–7674; www.haddiepierce.com), a three-story Victorian topped by a widow's walk—a standard feature for almost every seaport home built in the seventeenth and eighteenth centuries. Innkeepers Darya and John Prassl's B&B is within easy walking distance of downtown Wickford and has five guest rooms with private baths, including rooms populated with stuffed bears and vintage dolls. Rates range from $115 to $150 nightly and include a full breakfast.

A bit farther away from "town," you can immerse yourself in Victoriana at **Mount Maple of Wickford** (730 Annaquatucket Road, 295–4373; www

.virtualcities.com/ri/mountmaple.htm), a B&B in an 1869 former millworkers rooming house that's surrounded by a huge veranda. Mount Maple has three rooms with private baths, ranging in price from $90 to $130 nightly and including blue-corn pancakes and other breakfast treats prepared by innkeeper Nancy Dooley.

Leaving Wickford, you must make a left at the end of Brown Street and cross a small bridge to continue on Route 1A. As you drive south of the village, keep your eyes open for a small parking lot located in the middle of a wooded stretch of road on the left (east) side of the road (approximately 2⁵⁄₁₀ miles south of the Wickford bridge). This unpretentious spot is the access point to one of North Kingstown's true hidden treasures: *Rome Point.*

Once upon a time, the Narragansett Electric Company dreamed of building a nuclear power plant at Rome Point. But the Three Mile Island disaster and staunch opposition from North Kingstown residents cooled the utility's ardor for the plan. Through the years, the electric company continued to hold title to the undeveloped, 250-acre spit of land jutting into Narragansett Bay. But Narragansett Electric wisely deeded the property to the town, which turned Rome Point into an official park, the John H. Chafee Nature Preserve.

Hikers, surfcasters, and nature lovers have enjoyed Rome Point for years. Visitors typically hike the straight path from the parking lot down to the rocky bayfront. Emerging from the quiet woods to a pristine stretch of beach, you may be rewarded with a unique opportunity to view harbor seals—winter visitors to the bay—soaking up the warmth of the sun on the rocks a few hundred feet offshore.

Just north of the access path for Rome Point is Gilbert Stuart Road; turn here and follow the signs to the *Gilbert Stuart Birthplace and Museum* (815 Gilbert Stuart Road in Saunderstown, 294–3001; www.gilbertstuartmuseum.com).

Whether you know it or not, a little bit of Gilbert Stuart likely passes through your hands each day. Stuart, born in 1755, is the portraitist who painted the most famous likeness of George Washington, which appears on the face of the dollar bill. Fittingly, the museum includes reproductions of Stuart's greatest works, including portraits of the first five presidents of the United States.

Stuart's family home, one of several structures on the museum site, is an interesting combination of dwelling and workplace. The upper floors of the two-and-a-half-story, gambrel-roofed home (circa 1750) are where the family ate and slept, warmed by corner fireplaces in each room. But in the basement, in the same room as the kitchen, stands a water-powered snuff mill, the source of the Stuart family's prosperity. The mill, powered by a waterwheel under the house, has been fully restored, and tour guides show how the mill was used to grind tobacco into snuff.

The museum grounds are especially lovely, located in a remote spot next to a rushing stream fed by an impressive waterfall. Each spring, hundreds of thousands of herring and eels use the fish ladder here to return to their spawning grounds. Behind the house is tranquil Carr Pond, and nearby bubbles the Eye Spring, which local legend says has curative powers for ocular conditions. The other major structure on the site is a wooden gristmill filled with old grindstones.

Gilbert Stuart Birthplace and Museum

The Gilbert Stuart Birthplace and Museum is open May through October, Thursday through Monday 11:00 A.M. to 4:00 P.M. Admission is $6.00 for adults and $3.00 for children ages six to twelve.

Return to Route 1A and proceed south for another half mile. Watch for a farm surrounded by an old stone wall on your right side. At the light blue sign, turn right into the driveway.

You are drawn to **Casey Farm** (2325 Boston Neck Road/Route 1A; 295–1030; www.historicnewengland.org/visit/homes/casey.htm) by the circa 1750 farmhouse and the promise of fresh eggs and produce, but even better are the parts of the farm you don't immediately notice.

The farmers who still live and work at Casey Farm raise a variety of crops and livestock, much as farmers here have done for generations. Tours of the farmhouse are conducted regularly when the farm is open to the public, but Casey Farm also functions as a working museum, where visitors can explore the fields, barns, and pens while they actually are being used. The farm also hosts a seasonal farmers' market.

Situated between Narragansett Bay and the Pettaquamscutt (Narrow) River, Casey Farm flourished because goods could be moved easily to either waterway for transportation. Fortunately, Historic New England, which manages the farm, was able to obtain the property intact, so visitors can follow trails well beyond the cultivated fields. One such trail leads past the overgrown stone walls that mark the path of an old road to the riverbank, while another (across Route 1A) leads down to the rocky shoreline of the bay. In all, there are 300 acres of Casey Farm to enjoy.

Beware the Quahog

Glance at the menu in a Rhode Island restaurant, and chances are you'll find an exotic-sounding dish alongside the more familiar scrod, shrimp, and lobster: the quahog, or quahaug. But don't go asking the waiter why there's some kind of pork dish listed with the seafood: Quahog is the fancy name for a native Rhode Island clam.

Officially *Artica islandia,* the ocean quahog is a bivalve mollusk that populates the waters off Rhode Island as well as Narragansett Bay. Locally, it's used to make quahog chowder, quahog cakes, stuffed quahogs—even quahog chili. Local cartoonist and humorist Don Bousquet has even made a tidy living playing off Rhode Islanders' fondness for this funny-sounding clam. (For the record, Webster's says it's pronounced "KWA-hog," but if you want to sound like a local, you should say "KO-hog.")

There's a lot of history to this old farm, as well: Silas Casey was a general during the Civil War, and Thomas Lincoln Casey was an architect who helped design the Washington Monument and Grant's Tomb. Casey Farm is located on Route 1A in Saunderstown, 1 mile south of the intersection with Route 138. The farm is open to visitors from June 1 to October 15 on Saturday 11:00 A.M. to 5:00 P.M. Admission is $4.00 for adults.

A detour is necessary in order to see some of North Kingstown's other points of interest. Route 102, known locally as Ten Rod Road, connects with both Route 1A (at the southern end of Brown Street in Wickford village) and Route 1/Post Road (south of the Route 1A turnoff). Taking Route 102 west from Wickford, you'll pass though the old village of **Lafayette,** with its restored brick mill (now used for offices) and fine old homes. If you make the left turn onto Lafayette Road, you'll be rewarded by a fine view of the old mill pond; pause for a breath of fresh air or a photo before continuing to the entrance to **Ryan Park,** which includes a hiking trail that follows the railbed of the old New York, New Haven, and Hartford Railroad line into Wickford.

Park in the lot on the left side of the road, and walk or bike east on one of two trails. Closer to the Lafayette mill and mill pond is the graded railbed, where you will still find the occasional arched stone bridge, old ties, and spikes in the woods. If you walk directly east from the parking lot, there's a sunnier dirt path that meanders over open fields and into the woods. Both pass by secluded **Belleville Pond** and are ideal for hiking or mountain biking.

Returning to Route 102, continue west and pass under the railroad tunnel that marks Wickford Junction. On your right you'll see a shopping center with a string of stores on the west side of a roundabout. This is the home of **Junction Pizzeria** (1051 Ten Rod Road, #7; 294–4400), one of the best places to get thin-crust, brick-oven-baked New York–style pizza in South County. The storefront locale is belied by a spacious, bistrolike dining room adorned with frescoes that look good enough to eat. A full menu of pasta dishes and other Italian specialties also is served. Open Sunday to Thursday 11:30 A.M. to 9:00 P.M., Friday and Saturday 11:30 A.M. to 10:00 P.M.

Another half-mile drive will bring you to the intersection with Route 2 north, known here as Quaker Lane. Make the right onto Route 2 and proceed for about a mile to our next stop, which is on your left.

Rhode Islanders love their donuts. In fact, the state seems to have a donut obsession, and it's hard to drive too far on any major road without passing a donut shop of one kind or another. But the undisputed champion of Rhode Island donutry is ***Allie's Donuts*** at 3661 Quaker Lane (295–8036).

Rhode Islanders, who as a rule don't like to drive anywhere, will make the trip from Providence and beyond to pick up donuts from Allie's. If you have never had anything other than franchise-type donuts, then you're in for a treat. Unlike those other shops, which tend to pile a lot of sugar onto rather light-weight donuts full of air pockets, Allie's donuts are dense and heavy, with less emphasis on the sweet and more on the cake. The effect is a much more subtle experience. Crunchy on the outside, soft on the inside, the donuts are like the ones your grandmother used to make. It says something about the quality of Allie's donuts when one of the most popular varieties is the plain, unglazed Old Fashioned.

Allie's is open Monday to Wednesday 5:00 A.M. to 3:00 P.M., Thursday and Friday 5:00 A.M. to 5:00 P.M., and Saturday and Sunday 6:00 A.M. to 1:00 P.M.

Doubling back to Route 102/Ten Rod Road, travel another mile west, passing the interchange for Route 4. Soon you'll reach the intersection with the continuation of Route 2, also known as the South County Trail. Make the left turn onto Route 2 south, and the first major landmark you'll come to is ***Schartner Farms*** (1 Arnold Place, Exeter, 885–5510), on your right. Schartner's is the place where many South County residents come for their fresh produce, and their fruit pies are also top-notch. Schartner's does it all: berry picking in the summer, pumpkin picking in the fall,

atrioofhatcheries

Besides the Lafayette Trout Hatchery, the state of Rhode Island maintains two other fish hatcheries that you can visit: the Perryville Trout Hatchery in South Kingstown, off Old Post Road just west of the terminus of Route 110/Ministerial Road (783–5358); and one in Richmond in the Arcadia Management Area (539–7333), off Arcadia Road, where salmon are raised.

All three hatcheries are open Monday to Friday 8:30 A.M. to 3:30 P.M., and admission is free.

and cut-your-own Christmas trees in the winter. They also have a large green-house and a stand out front selling fresh-cut and deep-fried french fries, made from red potatoes pulled from Schartner's own fields. Open daily 8:00 A.M. to 6:00 P.M. and till 7:00 P.M. in summer.

Just south of Schartner Farms is Hatchery Road (on your left), which twists through the woods for about a half-mile before reaching the access road for the *Lafayette Trout Hatchery* (424 Hatchery Road, 294–4662).

Established in the 1920s, the trout hatchery is the main supplier of brook, brown, and rainbow trout for local ponds and rivers, which are stocked each year for sport fishing and to try to repopulate the species. The hatchery includes pools and a mesh-covered raceway teeming with trout fry of varying sizes, more than 60,000 in all. (The enclosures keep raccoons and birds from eating the fish.) The kids will love this place, and the staff at the state-owned facility can explain how the hatchery works. Free; open Monday to Friday 8:30 A.M. to 3:30 P.M.

Exeter

Although the owners certainly would prefer otherwise, the *Yawgoo Valley Ski Area and Water Park* (294–3802 for ski info, 295–2276 for snow-tubing, and 295–5366 for the water park; www.yawgoo.com) remains one of Rhode Island's most overlooked attractions. Even many local skiers don't realize that there's a ski area right in their own backyard. With two chairlifts and a vertical drop of just a couple of hundred feet, Yawgoo won't be drawing any comparisons with Vail or Stowe. But as they like to say around here, it's not the height of the mountain, it's how many times you go up and down that counts.

The truth is that Yawgoo, with four main trails, makes a nice, affordable afternoon or evening of winter fun, either on its own merits or as a tune-up for a trip to the big mountains up north. It's also a good place to learn to ski, especially for kids. Yawgoo has a base lodge restaurant and bar—just like the big ski resorts—and has added snow-tubing to its winter-fun activities. Full-day lift tickets range from $25 to $37 for adults, $20 to $32 for children.

During the summer Yawgoo operates a twin-tube water slide that's a lot of fun on a hot day. There's also a kiddie pool, a climbing wall, a pitch-and-putt golf course, and a beach volleyball court. To get to Yawgoo Valley, take Route 2/South County Trail south of the intersection with Route 102/Ten Rod Road for approximately 4 miles, then make a left onto Yawgoo Valley Road; drive for 1 mile, and the park will be on your right.

As the population of South County has grown, development has picked up along the once-desolate South County Trail. In the Oak Harbor Village shopping center you'll find *Caspita* (567 South County Trail, #109, 295–2900), a clubby little Italian restaurant that, like its neighbor the **Celestial Cafe** (295–5559), has brought a touch of sophistication to rural Exeter. The menu isn't especially adventurous, but Caspita delivers expertly prepared pasta, fish, and chicken dishes and a delicately sweet marinara that's to die for. The warm interior decor is perfectly matched by the jazz music playing in the background and performed live on many evenings. Open Tuesday to Friday 11:00 A.M. to 3:00 P.M. for lunch and Tuesday to Saturday 5:00 to 9:00 P.M. for dinner.

A bit farther down the road you'll find another outpost of civilization, **Sophie's Coffee** (705 South County Trail, 294–8188), which has a nice selection of java, tea, smoothies, pastries, quiches, and sandwiches in a garden setting with an art gallery and free Internet access. Open daily 6:00 A.M. to 5:00 P.M.

Running from Voluntown, Connecticut, to Wickford, Rhode Island, **Ten Rod Road**'s name refers to its width. Constructed in the early eighteenth century, the road was built 10 rods (165 feet) wide to allow farmers to drive herds of cattle down to the seaport in Wickford. Exploring the rest of rural Exeter is relatively easy, since nearly everything is located on or near scenic Ten Rod Road.

As you head west from the intersection of Ten Rod Road/Route 102 and South County Trail/Route 2, you pass through some lovely countryside, especially where the road dips into a small valley that is partially filled by the golf course at the **Exeter Country Club.** After passing the town grange, look for Widow Sweets Road on your right. (The town clerk's office is on this corner.) Turn onto Widow Sweets Road, then make the right onto Pardon Joslin Road and follow the signs to the parking area of the **Fisherville Brook Wildlife Refuge** (949–5454; www.asri.org/fisherville.htm).

This 937-acre refuge has 5 miles of trails that cross bridges over the Fisherville Brook, cut through stands of white pine, and skirt a historic cemetery. There's also a small dam and waterfall from an artificial pond on the property. The refuge is maintained by the Audubon Society and is open daily from dawn to dusk.

As you continue west on Route 102 past Tripps Corner Road, the paved road suddenly veers off to the north, while a smaller, wooded road continues straight ahead in a westerly direction. This actually is the continuation of Ten Rod Road (hereafter known alternatively as Route 165), so make sure you get off the main road at this point.

Almost immediately you'll come to an intersection with Gardiner Road. Make the left turn here and proceed south to the **Spring Hill Sugar House** (522 Gardiner Road, 788–7431).

You'll see the sign for Spring Hill Sugar House on the right side of the road; pull in the driveway, and the combination shop and maple syrup factory is at the bottom of the hill. Maple syrup, tapped from trees on the farm, is available in sizes ranging from a tiny sampler ($3.00) to a half gallon ($23.00) for those Paul Bunyan types.

The back of the shop building is filled with the evaporators that are used to distill the raw syrup that comes out of the maple trees each spring. If you visit on weekends between March and mid-April, you can see a demonstration of the whole sap-boiling process, from tapping the trees to the finished product. In September and October, owners Gibby Fountain and Brian Tefft start pressing apples for cider, also for sale in the shop. Fall brings pumpkin picking and a free corn maze, as well. Fountain also breeds llamas and Sicilian donkeys, which the kids can visit in a pen just a few steps away. The shop is open 10:00 A.M. to 4:00 P.M. daily.

When you're writing a book about out-of-the-way places in Rhode Island, there's no way you can resist including the **Middle of Nowhere Diner** (222 Nooseneck Hill Road/Route 3, 397–8855). It's tiny, but the friendly staff will treat you like locals and serve up great diner burgers and yummy fish-and-chips and clam cakes daily. After returning to Ten Rod Road from the Sugar House, continue west to the intersection with Route 3. Make a right, and this short detour will bring you to the diner, which boasts some of the biggest portions in the state. The name says it all. Stop here if you're wandering the boondocks and need a bite to eat. Open daily 5:00 A.M. to 8:30 P.M. and till 9:00 P.M. in the summer.

Continuing west on Ten Rod Road, you'll soon enter the dense forest of the **Arcadia Management Area,** a 13,000-acre, state-managed wilderness of woodland, ponds, and trees with numerous hiking trails and places to swim. One of the park's best beaches is at Beach Pond, protected by lifeguards and located on Route 165 near the Connecticut state line.

toolingdown thebackroads ofexeter

If you've got one of those rugged-looking SUVs that's never left the comfort of pavement, here's your big chance to get some mud under the fenders. Rural Exeter has a great network of dirt roads to explore, cutting through thick forests, past colonial-style farmhouses, an old Quaker meeting-house, and up and down challenging hills.

Often rutted, always bumpy, and sometimes treacherous after a hard rain, graded dirt tracks like Frosty Hollow Road, Skunk Hill Road, and Plain Road can put your driving skills and dental work to the test. Exeter also is crossed by the New London Turnpike, perhaps the longest dirt road in southern New England. This dusty, ancient byway runs all the way from Richmond through Exeter and West Greenwich before reverting to blacktop in Coventry.

Biking Arcadia

One of the many ways that you can enjoy the Arcadia Management Area is on a mountain bike. The huge park has miles and miles of narrow trails (known to mountain bikers as singletrack), fire roads, and graded dirt roads for both hiking and biking, with tracks suitable for novice riders as well as those that should be tackled only by experts.

One of the things mountain bikers like best about Arcadia is that there are very few people crowding the trails; it's also something you need to be aware of if you decide to hike or bike in Arcadia. While it may not be comparable to the backcountry at Yellowstone, Arcadia is about as wild as Rhode Island gets. Bring plenty of water and a compass.

Many of the Arcadia trails can be accessed on the north and south sides of Ten Rod Road. You can simply park your car and go, but stopping beforehand for a trail map from the Arcadia park ranger's office—another significant trailhead, with ample parking—on Arcadia Road is highly recommended. For information call 539–2356 or go online to the New England Mountain Bike Association's Web site: www.nemba .org/ridingzone/arcadia.html.

Continuing a bit farther west on Ten Rod Road, take the left turn for Summit Road and proceed to the ***Tomaquag Indian Memorial Museum*** (390 Summit Road, 539–7213 or 491–9063 for appointments; www.tomaquag museum.org).

Part of the purpose of the Tomaquag Museum is to remind visitors that the local Native American tribes did not vanish in the seventeenth century, as some school textbooks assert, but remain a vital part of Rhode Island culture. Many Native Americans, including members of the Narragansett tribe, help to run the museum, which for fifty years has been collecting and displaying artifacts from New England tribes and others from as far away as Alaska.

Particularly significant are the museum's collection of handmade dolls and baskets, the latter woven by Northeastern tribes from birch bark and porcupine quills. There also are arrowheads, ax heads, and beadwork on display, as well as photos of Narragansett tribal leaders of the past. A new multimedia exhibit on "The Pursuit of Happiness" highlights the role of education, language, family, and sovereignty on Narragansett life.

The Tomaquag Indian Memorial Museum is open Monday to Friday 11:00 A.M. to 4:00 P.M. and by appointment, plus on weekends for seasonal events. Admission is $4.00 for adults and $2.00 for children ages five to twelve.

Step Stone Falls technically is just across the town line in **West Green-wich,** but the best way to get there is off Ten Rod Road. From the Tomaquag Museum, double back to Route 165, then make a left and head west to Escoheag Hill Road (approximately 2⅗ miles). Make a right and head north past **Stepping Stone Ranch** (201 Escoheag Hill Road, 397–3725; www.stepping stoneranch.com), an oddball mix of horse farm and concert venue in the tiny village of Escoheag.

The ranch offers horseback rides and there's a snack bar on the grounds, too. For a unique experience, saddle up for one of the ranch's overnight trail rides, which include a five-hour ride, dinner, breakfast, and a stay in a lakefront cabin or "roughing it" on a "posse ride" with a stay at a wooded campsite. Overnight rides are offered for groups of six to eight persons from May to October and cost $160 per person. Three-hour lunch rides ($90) also are available. (Overnight riders should have some riding experience.)

Leaving the few houses of Escoheag behind, continue north to Falls River Road and make a right. From here you'll have a slow (15 mph) half-mile drive over a bumpy dirt road to the parking lot for Step Stone Falls, located just before a small concrete bridge that spans the Falls River. (Look for a sign marking the nature trails.)

Not only is this one of Rhode Island's most obscure attractions, it is also one of the most lovely. The Step Stone Falls get their name from the series of rock ledges that the rushing water pours over on its way downhill; the ledges, only partially covered by water, make an excellent spot for sunbathing or picnicking. (Note: If you want to see the falls at their peak, come in the springtime; it's still a pretty spot in midsummer, but the water flow does tend to slacken during the dry part of the year.) On the west side of the falls is a nature trail that follows the river downstream, passing near an abandoned campground and the remains of an old sawmill and gristmill along the way.

Hopkinton

On Main Street (Route 138) in Hopkinton are a pair of local institutions that have recently received a welcome facelift: **Boucher's Wood River Inn** (1139 Main Street, 539–9800) and the **Stagecoach House Inn,** directly across the street at 1136 Main Street (539–9600; www.stagecoachhouse.com).

Built circa 1850 as a general store serving the thriving crossroads with Nooseneck Hill Road (present-day Route 3), and formerly a local tavern with the unflattering nickname of "The Zoo," the Wood River Inn has shaken off its rough-and-tumble image in recent years.

Hopkinton's Crooning Country Kid

To most Rhode Islanders, Hope Valley, located in the town of Hopkinton, is out in the country. For people in the rest of the nation, however, this small town—like the rest of Rhode Island—is strictly Yankee territory, the most unlikely of places for a preteen country singer to burst upon the scene.

Nonetheless, Hope Valley really is the home town of diminutive singing sensation Billy Gilman (www.billygilman.com), who grew up listening to country music at his grandparents' house, and got one of his first big breaks opening for the group Alabama at Rhode Island's former Warwick Musical Theater.

A sign on Main Street in Hopkinton proudly points out the local claim to fame, noting that Gilman is the youngest recording star ever to win platinum status for record sales (for his debut, *One Voice,* which has sold more than two million copies to date). *One Voice* also was nominated for a Grammy award, and Gilman subsequently released a Christmas record; and country albums, *Dare to Dream, Music through Heartsongs, Everything and More,* and the self-titled *Billy Gilman.*

The dark but friendly bar features a small stage for live music on the weekends (including bluegrass on Sunday nights); a former street-level storefront has been converted into a cozy billiards parlor. Adjoining the tavern are a pair of cheerful dining rooms, one with a fireplace and the other warmed by a woodstove; the menu features a variety of sandwiches and fresh seafood entrees. The unofficial town hall of the tiny village of Wyoming, the Wood River Inn opens for breakfast at 7:00 A.M. daily and serves dinner until 9:00 P.M.; the tavern stays open and serves hot appetizers until 11:00 P.M. Sunday to Wednesday and 1:00 A.M. Thursday to Saturday.

For many years, the Stagecoach House looked as if it might tumble into the very road that, for more than 200 years, has brought travelers to its doors. But the Boucher family, which also owns the Wood River Inn, renovated the historic old building, turning the lower level into shops and a bakery, and the second floor into a small inn.

Ranging in price from $100 to $199 nightly, some of the twelve cheerful rooms share access to a long, spacious deck that overlooks a beautiful stretch of the Wood River. Every room has a fireplace, Jacuzzi tub, and cable TV. In fact, the rooms are quite modern, which may explain why the resident ghost, nicknamed Oliver, prefers to haunt the hallways. Local legend explains that Oliver is the troubled spirit of a sailor, killed in a fight over a woman in the dance hall that once occupied the second floor of the building.

Richmond

Off Route 112 is the Washington County Fairgrounds, which is nothing more than a big field, unless you happen to come by in mid-August, when it comes to life with the opening of the annual *Washington County Fair.*

With its country music, livestock exhibits, truck pulls, and rodeo, the Washington County Fair may seem somewhat incongruous to visitors who think of New England in terms of colonial-era homes and lobster-in-the-rough. But the truth is that many parts of Rhode Island are fiercely proud of their agrarian past and present, and the forty-year-old fair fits right into the semirural, small-town patina evident in much of the state.

Even for city slickers, the Washington County Fair is a great time. Each year a giant midway with food booths, rides, and games is created, and contestants vie for prizes in tractor pulls, pie-eating contests, and, yes, a dung-throwing contest. Special events for children include a cow-milking contest, costume parade, three-legged race, and pedal tractor pull, though the kids will probably have as much fun walking around the fairgrounds meeting the cows, sheep, and pigs competing for the blue ribbons for best-of-show. Entertainment includes performances by country acts like Billy Gilman and Ricky Skaggs, and the crowning of the Washington County Fair Queen and Princess is always a highlight.

Every year the fair starts on a Wednesday in mid-August (it always ends the third Sunday of the month). Admission is a bargain at $8.00 for adults and free for children under twelve. For information call 783–2070 or visit www.washingtoncountyfair-ri.com.

For a glimpse of an authentic nineteenth-century mill village, make a turn off Route 2 onto Old Shannock Road, which leads to the small hamlet of *Shannock.* On the road into town, you'll cross a narrow white-fenced bridge next to an unusual horseshoe-shaped waterfall, the landmark for which the town is best known (to those few people who know about Shannock at all). You can stop here for a moment of peaceful relaxation or continue into town.

With ample waterpower and the railroad running right through town, it's not hard to imagine Shannock's past as a thriving mill town during the Industrial Revolution. Now the mill that once supported the town is in ruins, adding to the feeling that Shannock is the Place That Time Forgot.

Places to Stay in South County— North Kingstown and Inland

(All Area Codes 401)

NORTH KINGSTOWN

America's Best Value Inn
6481 Post Road
884–9153 or 884–9300

The Haddie Pierce House
146 Boston Neck Road
294–7674

The Kingstown Motel
6530 Post Road
884–1160

Mount Maple of Wickford
730 Annaquatucket Road
295–4373

Wickford Junction Inn
1266 Old Baptist Road
295–4434

HOPKINTON

The General Thurston House 1763 B&B
496 Main Street
377–9049

The Stagecoach House Inn
1136 Main Street
539–9600

RICHMOND

Country Acres B&B
176 Townhouse Road
Route 112
364–9134

Places to Eat in South County— North Kingstown and Inland

(All Area Codes 401)

NORTH KINGSTOWN

Allie's Donuts
3661 Quaker Lane
295–8036

The Breakfast Nook
6130 Post Road
884–6108

Duffy's Tavern
235 Tower Hill Road
295–0073

OTHER NOTEWORTHY ATTRACTIONS AND EVENTS IN SOUTH COUNTY— NORTH KINGSTOWN AND INLAND

Carolina Management Area
Richmond

Fiddlesticks Miniature Golf
North Kingstown

Locustville Pond Public Fishing Area
Hopkinton

Rhode Island Veteran's Cemetery
Exeter

Rockville Management and Public Fishing Area
Hopkinton

Strawberry Festival
Smith's Castle
North Kingstown; June

National Guard Leapfest
Richmond; July

Colonial Crafts Festival
Hopkinton; September

The Harborside Grill
68 Brown Street
295–0444

**Hoofinfeathers
Carriage Inn**
1065 Tower Hill Road
884–6242

Oak Hill Tavern
565 Tower Hill Road
294–3282

A Taste of China
6188 Post Road
885–2216

Wickford Gourmet Foods
21 West Main Street
295–8190

EXETER

Caspita
567 South County Trail
298–2900

Celestial Cafe
567 South County Trail
295–5559

**The Homestead
Restaurant**
750 South County Trail
294–7810

Middle of Nowhere Diner
222 Nooseneck Hill Road
397–8855

Sophie's Coffee
705 South County Trail
294–8188

HOPKINTON

The Wood River Inn
1139 Main Street
539–9800

HELPFUL WEB SITES ABOUT SOUTH COUNTY—NORTH KINGSTOWN AND INLAND

North Kingstown Chamber of Commerce
www.northkingstown.com

Town of Exeter
www.town.exeter.ri.us

Town of Hopkinton
http://hopkintonritownhall.com

Town of Richmond
www.richmondri.com

Village of Wickford
www.wickfordvillage.org

SELECTED CHAMBER OF COMMERCE IN SOUTH COUNTY—NORTH KINGSTOWN AND INLAND

Chamber of Commerce North Kingstown
245 Tower Hill Road
North Kingstown 02852–4811
295–5566

South County—
The Ocean Shore and
Block Island

Narragansett

Unnoticed by most tourists—who naturally are drawn to Narragansett's fine bay beaches—the **Narrow (Pettaquamscutt) River** flows quietly from a series of inland ponds down to Pettaquamscutt Cove and, eventually, Narragansett Bay. In doing so, the river passes through undeveloped watershed lands and past historic homes as well as a pond whose steep sides give the impression of a fjord.

One of the best ways to stir the secret waters of the Narrow River is to use a kayak or canoe. **Narrow River Kayaks,** located riverside next to the bridge on Middlebridge Road, rents boats and offers lessons to novice paddlers. For beginners they even have special, easy-to-handle "kiwi kayaks." With a guide or solo, you can paddle upriver or down to the bay beaches, and there are pleasant spots along the way to stop for lunch.

Narrow River Kayaks is located at 95 Middlebridge Road, which connects Route 4 to the west and Boston Neck Road/ Route 1A to the east. Prices start at $24 for two hours, or $38 for a half-day; for rates and information call Rob Ryder at 789–0334; www.narrowriverkayaks.com.

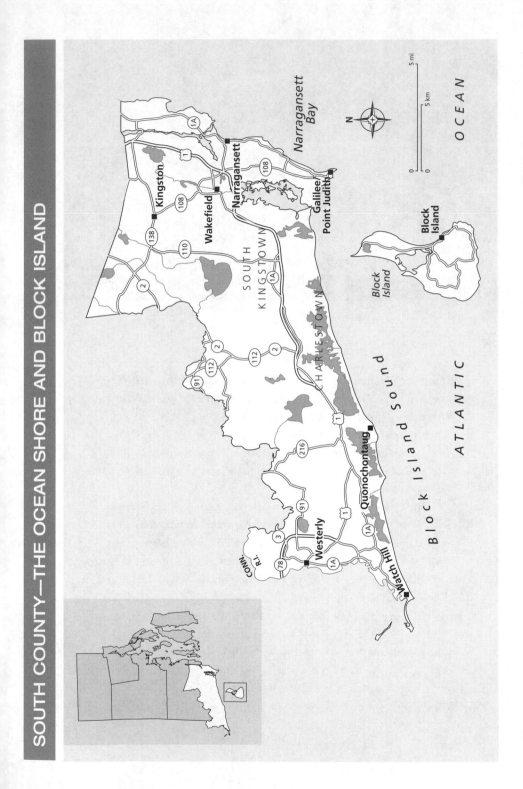

SOUTH COUNTY—THE OCEAN SHORE AND BLOCK ISLAND

The **South County Museum** (783–5400; www.southcountymuseum.org) is an excellent assemblage of artifacts and information on the history of this area and the lives of the people who have lived here. The exhibits are varied and imaginative and are presented in an airy, high-ceilinged wooden building. One display features items that might have appeared in an early twentieth-century country kitchen, while another reproduces an old country store. When we first visited, a collection of bathing costumes from Narragansett Pier's resort heyday were on display in a section reserved for revolving exhibits. Later, the museum added a collection representing the items sold at Kenyon's Department Store, a South County institution that closed down a few years back. The current standing exhibit focuses on coastal and village life over the past three-plus centuries.

Adjacent to the main museum building is a blacksmith's forge and barn that contains horse-drawn carriages, a hearse, a milk wagon, and a mail truck once used in the area; neighboring **Canonchet Farm** includes hiking trails. A living-history exhibit includes tours of a nineteenth-century farmhouse and an introduction to some of Rhode Island's "heritage breeds" of livestock, including Rhode Island Red hens and Romney sheep. The museum is open from May to June, September, and October Friday and Saturday 10:00 A.M. to 4:00 P.M. and Sunday noon to 4:00 P.M. In July and August, it's open Wednesday and Thursday as well. Admission is $5.00 for adults and $2.00 for children ages six to twelve.

Soon after you pass the Narragansett Town Beach, Route 1A becomes Kingstown Road and heads off to the west. The second right after you turn west (away from the beach) is Strathmore Street, which passes through a housing development before ending at the museum.

Doubling back to Beach Street and turning right, you'll see a pair of formidable stone towers in front of you. This is all that remains of the **Narragansett Casino** (782–2597; www.thetowersri.com), built by Stanford White (of the famed architectural firm McKim, Mead & White) in 1883 and destroyed by a fire in 1900. The Casino hosts periodic public events, including live musical performances and holiday gatherings. Just after you pass under the arch on Ocean Road, you'll see a stone building set beyond the breakwater. Once the headquarters of the Narragansett Pier Coast Guard Station, it now houses the **Coast Guard House** restaurant (40 Ocean Road, 789–0700; www.thecoastguardhouse.com).

The Coast Guard House was heavily damaged by Hurricane Bob in 1991—not surprising, given its exposed location—but was rebuilt and has come back strong as one of South County's best restaurants. Seafood, of course, is always on the menu, but steaks and other continental fare are also available; favorites include the seafood fettuccine and the surf and turf. Whether you choose to dine indoors or on the outside deck, awesome views of the pounding surf are

Victorian Vistas in Narragansett

In its Victorian heyday, Narragansett was one of the most popular resorts on the East Coast. Drawn by the beautiful beaches and cool ocean breezes, visitors flocked to Narragansett by rail from around New England and New York during the late nineteenth century. The prosperity of this time was reflected in the great Narragansett Casino, built in 1883 by the famous architectural firm of McKim, Mead & White.

The fire that swept through the casino in 1900 coincided with a decline in Narragansett's fortunes. But like the great stone casino towers on Ocean Road, Narragansett survived the fire and remains a popular summer destination. Although many of the grand Victorian hotels are gone, they have been replaced by an excellent selection of small inns and bed-and-breakfasts.

One B&B that is reminiscent of Narragansett's illustrious past is the **Richards B&B** (144 Gibson Avenue, 789–7746), an 1884 stone mansion with a distinctive front gable, which has four guest rooms with working fireplaces. The gardens and spacious grounds are reminders that this once was the centerpiece of a sprawling country estate. Rooms are $125 to $165 nightly.

For a completely different experience, try the **Pleasant Cottage B&B** (104 Robinson Street, 783–6895), hosted by Fred and Terry Sepp and within easy walking distance of Narragansett Pier and the beach, or the **Blueberry Cove Inn** (75 Kingstown Road, 800–478–1426 or 792–9865; www.blueberrycoveinn.com), an 1870 Victorian with nautically themed rooms and a whirlpool suite.

a constant dinner companion. Open Monday to Friday 11:30 A.M. to 3:00 P.M. for lunch and 5:00 to 10:00 P.M. for dinner Monday to Thursday, 5:00 to 11:00 P.M. for dinner Friday and Saturday, and 4:00 to 10:00 P.M. on Sunday. Sunday brunch is served 10:00 A.M. to 2:00 P.M.

From the pier it's a very pretty waterfront drive down Ocean Avenue to *Point Judith,* where you can walk around the *Point Judith Lighthouse* or catch the *ferry to Block Island* (Island High Speed Ferry: 877–733–9425; www.islandhighspeedferry.com or Block Island Ferry: 783–7996; www.block islandferry.com). First, though, consider a stop at *Aunt Carrie's Seafood Restaurant* (1240 Ocean Road, 783–7930; www.auntcarriesri.com), for more than seventy-five years a Rhode Island landmark at the corner of Ocean Road and Route 108.

Aunt Carrie's is one of those places that expends less effort on outward appearances than on delivering fresh, inexpensive seafood to its customers. Its many devotees will tell you that the best clams in the state can be found here. You can also enjoy traditional Rhode Island shore dinners and a hearty chowder; it's BYOB in the dining room, so bring along your favorite white wine or hearty brew to complement the fish. In Narragansett, Aunt Carrie's is what summer is all about. Open noon to 9:00 P.M. Memorial Day to Labor Day; closed Tuesday. Also open April 1 to Memorial Day and Labor Day through the end of September, 4:00 to 8:00 P.M. on Friday and noon to 8:00 P.M. on Saturday and Sunday.

A brief drive north on Route 108, followed by a left turn on Galilee Escape Road, will land you at the seaport of **Galilee,** Rhode Island's leading fishing port, both commercial and recreational, and home to a variety of fine seafood restaurants. Take a seat on the deck at **Champlin's** (256 Great Island Road, 783–3152; www.champlins.com) for fresh ocean breezes and great harbor views. Open daily 11:00 A.M. to 9:00 P.M. in the summer, 11:00 A.M. to 4:00 P.M. on Monday, and 11:00 A.M. to 6:00 P.M. Friday to Sunday during the winter. Or, drop in at **George's of Galilee** (250 Sand Hill Cove Road, 783–2306 or 800–399–8477; www.georgesofgalilee.com) and learn why Rhode Islanders have been coming here for lobster and fish since 1948. Among the boats in this busy harbor are those belonging to the **Frances Fleet,** including the 105-foot yacht *Lady Frances,* which departs daily for the open ocean on whale-watching tours.

Aided by state-of-the-art sonar equipment and reports from other boats, the *Lady Frances* cruises up to 35 miles out to sea to chase down humpback, finback, right, and minke whales. Among the most commonly spotted are the 80-foot-long finbacks, which are seen speeding around their summer feeding grounds off Block Island each year. Rarest are the right whales, which were hunted nearly to extinction during the latter half of the nineteenth century and the early part of the twentieth century.

You'll get to see whales on most days, but even when the whales are shy the *Lady Frances* gives you a bird's-eye view of fish, Portuguese man-of-wars, and an abundance of waterfowl. The ship has a large outdoor observation deck as well as an air-conditioned cabin and a galley stocked with food and beverages.

The *Lady Frances* departs on five-hour whale-watching cruises daily at 1:00 P.M., weather permitting, from July 1 to August 31. Tickets are $38 for adults,

The *Lady Frances*

$32 for seniors, and $25 for children. Tuesday and Friday are family days, when two adults and two children can cruise for $99. Reservations are recommended and can be made by calling 783–4988 or 800–662–2824, or by going to www.francesfleet.com. From Route 1 south, get off at the Point Judith/Galilee exit, then take Route 108/Point Judith Road south to Galilee, making a right onto Galilee Escape Road. At the end of the road make a right, then take the first left. The Frances Fleet ticket office is located at the Capt.'s Tackle store.

For a less ambitious but no less enjoyable boat ride, check out the *Southland Riverboat* (783–2954; www.southlandcruises.com), a sightseeing riverboat that cruises around Point Judith and the Great Salt Pond, offering a unique perspective on such landmarks as the Point Judith Lighthouse, sheltered Great Island and Harbor Island, and the tiny fishing hamlet of Jerusalem, not to mention numerous clammers and quahoggers at work. You'll also get a close-up look at the massive stone breakwaters that create the Point Judith Harbor of Refuge. One and three-quarter-hour narrated cruises are $14.00 for adults and $8.00 for children ages four to twelve. Sunset cruises cost $16.00 for adults and $10.00 for kids and include music spun by a live DJ. The boat sails Memorial Day to Columbus Day.

Human stewardship of Narragansett Bay has a long and checkered history. Slowly poisoned by pollution flowing from rivers that were harnessed for the Industrial Revolution, the bay has become a much cleaner, healthier place thanks in large part to conservation efforts by groups like Save the Bay. Yet many challenges remain, including storm runoff contaminated with fertilizer and pollution from failed septic systems.

The *Coastal Resource Center* at the University of Rhode Island's Narragansett Bay Campus (South Ferry Road, 874–6211; http://omp.gso.uri.edu/omp/mar-sci/coast-int-vis-center.htm) works to further understanding of the relationship between the coastal environment and human populations and promote better stewardship of coastal ecosystems worldwide. Located on a bluff overlooking Narragansett Bay, the ***Coastal Institute Visitor's Center*** features a bookstore and an interactive science exhibit called Living on the Edge.

The Living on the Edge exhibit includes a dune machine and stream table that help explain the mechanics of the coastal environment. Visitors can also learn a little about the science and technology used to study changes in the coastline, and can track the movement of the Gulf Stream, which has a tremendous impact on New England weather and commerce. The exhibit is free, kid-friendly, and takes about a half hour to visit.

The Coastal Institute Visitor's Center is open Monday and Wednesday from 11:00 A.M. to 1:00 P.M. (hours change periodically, so call first). The Coastal Resource Center is located on the URI Narragansett Bay Campus: To get there, turn onto Bridgetown Road where Route 1 intersects with Route 138, cross Route 1A onto South Ferry Road, and look for the campus entrance on your right after passing an industrial park and the South Ferry Church.

South Kingstown

Start your exploration of South Kingstown at the northeast corner of Route 1/Tower Hill Road and Route 138, where you will see a tall wooden observation tower. A popular misconception is that the tower was used to spot forest fires. Actually, it was built in 1937 as a military lookout to keep watch over the waters of the lower bay; frequent U-boat activity around this region a few years later justified the concerns of the builders.

Park in the small lot at the base of the 100 foot tower and make the climb to the top to enjoy a commanding view of the new ***Jamestown Bridge,*** as well as the western shoreline of Jamestown itself. In the foreground is the valley cut by the Pettaquamscutt (Narrow) River.

Beside the tower is ***Hannah Robinson's Rock.*** The stone recalls the classic South County romance about young Hannah and her lover, an older man who was her French tutor. Hannah's father disapproved of the romance, so the lovers would secretly meet at this rock. Later, Hannah ran off and got married, only to be abandoned by her husband. Sick and heartbroken, she eventually returned to her family, passing by the rock she had visited so many times in her younger days.

From this point, head west on Route 138, which takes you over a hilly, rather desolate landscape until you reach the village of ***Kingston.*** There is at least one good reason to stop along the way, however: the ***King's Rose*** bed-and-breakfast (1747 Mooresfield Road/Route 138, 783–5222; www.virtualcities .com/ons/ri/s/ris8701.htm). A country estate built in colonial style in 1933, the

National Register property is highlighted by lovely grounds that include a formal English garden, a goldfish pool and rose arbor, and a pair of tennis courts.

The gardens make a peaceful backdrop both for the seven guest bedrooms and for the full breakfast served in the sunroom, on the patio, or in the formal dining room. Known locally as the Tootell House, the King's Rose was once the house of Rhode Island State College (now the University of Rhode Island) hero Fred Tootell, who won the gold medal in the hammer throw at the 1924 Olympic Games in Paris. Innkeeper Perry Viles's Quaker family helped settle the area in the seventeenth century; Perry maintains the gardens, while wife Barbara, a retired nursing supervisor, does the cooking. Room rates in this pet-friendly inn range from $90 to $175.

Home to the main campus of the University of Rhode Island, Kingston also has a cluster of historic homes centered on the crossroads of Kingstown Road (Route 138) and the Old North and Old South Roads. The **Kingston Free Library** (2605 Kingstown Road) dates from 1775; the **First Congregational Church** (2601 Kingstown Road) was built in 1820.

Owing partly to its proximity to one of the state's centers for the arts and education, Kingston also is a center for South County's creative minds. The **Helme House Gallery,** located in another historic home at 2587 Kingstown Road (783–2195; www.southcountyart.org), is the headquarters of the South County Art Association, which holds regular exhibits of artwork by association members and local residents. The gallery also hosts art classes year-round, and an annual holiday pottery and art sale—beginning the day after Thanksgiving and continuing for two weeks—is quite popular. Open Wednesday to Sunday 1:00 to 5:00 P.M. The **Fayerweather Craft Center** (1859 Moorsefield Road/Route 138, 789–9072) occupies the 1820 home of the town blacksmith and holds workshops every second Saturday from May to September. Crafts by local artisans are on sale year-round. The center is open Tuesday through Saturday 10:00 A.M. to 4:00 P.M.

Idyllic as Kingston may sound, the community had its share of trouble-makers like any other town. For many years, running afoul of the law in this part of the state could land you in a dark cell at the **Old Washington County Jail** (2636 Kingstown Road, 783–1328; www.freewebs.com/pettaquamscutt). Built in 1858, the jail had separate but equal cells for men and women, and neither had windows. Visitors can see for themselves how nineteenth-century justice was meted out, thanks to the Pettaquamscutt Historical Society, which maintains the jail and opens the building for tours three days a week.

Besides the old jail cells, the historical society has created exhibits illustrating different aspects of the lives of South County residents during the past 300 years. Some rooms and former prison cells are furnished to represent a typical

Ride the South County Trail

Route 2, also known as the South County Trail, has an excellent bike route that officially begins at the intersection with Route 138 in South Kingstown. With wide shoulders and a moderate traffic flow, Route 2 gives riders a great opportunity to get a taste of rural Rhode Island without leaving civilization entirely.

The official bike trail stretches north from Route 138 to the intersection of Routes 2 and 102 in North Kingstown, a distance of about 6 miles that features a few challenging hills but also stretches of nice, flat cruising. Along the way, you'll pass such landmarks as the Rhode Island Veterans' Cemetery, Schartner's Farms, the Homestead Restaurant, and Barber's Pond—a beautiful spot to pull over and enjoy a picnic lunch. If you reach the halfway point and need some replenishment, Oatley's Junction at the intersection of Routes 2 and 102 has a convenience store and a restaurant.

Although Route 2 south of the Route 138 intersection is not officially marked as a bike route, the shoulders here are equally wide and inviting. The hills, however, are steeper and longer, but your exertion is rewarded by more beautiful countryside, as you cross over cold-running streams and pass by turf farms that look like the world's largest front lawn. If you're riding a mountain bike, you might want to pull off at Great Swamp Monument Road to visit the memorial to the Narragansett tribe.

For more information on organized rides and bicycling throughout Rhode Island, contact Narragansett Bay Wheelmen (www.nbwclub.org) or write NBW, P.O. Box 41177, Providence 02940-1177.

home in the area, and central to the collection is a large eighteenth-century clock that once belonged to John Raleigh Eldred, a Kingston artist who graduated from the College of Agriculture and Mechanical Arts (now URI) in 1900. Another room depicts a school classroom, and there also are displays of locally made textiles, tools used by local farmers and artisans, and antique toys. A famous mural, *The Economic Activities of the Narragansett Planters,* is on display. An extensive historical and genealogical library is housed in the building.

The Old Washington County Jail is open year-round on Tuesday, Thursday, and Saturday from 1:00 to 4:00 P.M. Suggested admission is $3.00.

The sheer size of the URI campus is not evident from a car window as you cruise down Route 138, but a turn onto any of the streets leading into the school grounds from downtown Kingston reveals blocks and blocks of college buildings, dorms, and other facilities, sometimes interspersed with old village homes.

Many of these facilities are for students only, but the ***Bradford Boss Ice Arena*** (turn at the URI Athletic Center marquee) offers year-round public ice skating on Sundays (2:00 to 3:50 P.M.) and Monday to Friday (10:00 A.M. to 11:50

P.M.); during the week, there's also an hour adults-only session starting at 9:00 A.M. and pickup hockey from noon to 1:50 P.M. The adult skate costs $3.00 per person, public skating is $5.00 per person and open to all ages, and hockey is also $5.00 per person. The neighboring **Ryan Center** (788–3200) is home to the URI basketball teams and also hosts occasional concerts and performances.

Kingston village appears bereft of places to eat, but the secret is that there are a cluster of restaurants catering to URI students centered on Fortin Road, just a couple of blocks up on your right when you take the left off 138 onto Upper College Road. Here you'll find outlets of **Spike's Junkyard Dogs** (gourmet hot dogs and chicken sandwiches; 789–1700; www.spikesjunkyarddogs .com), **Mamma Leone's** for Italian food (789–4350), the **Caliente Mexican Grill** (284–2816; www.calientemexicangrill.com), and the sprawling **International Cafe** (782–2720; www.theinternationalcafe.com), which has everything from Greek salads and gyros to chicken soup, calzones, and soft-serve ice cream. The profusion of deep-fried appetizers on the menu (mozzarella sticks, chicken fingers, and such) is a clue that the restaurant mainly caters to college students, but the food is pretty good nonetheless.

In an era when professional basketball teams recruit players right out of high school, and many college athletes are students in name only, the world has needed something like the **International Scholar-Athlete Hall of Fame and Museum** (3045 Kingstown Road/Route 138, 874–2405; www.international sport.com/sa_hof).

On the western edge of the URI campus, local philanthropist Alan Shawn Feinstein and the Institute for International Sport have erected a gleaming, classically inspired tribute to those students who excel at academics as well as sports. Visitors who pass under the colonnaded portico into the spacious exhibit hall may be struck more by the architectural beauty and potential of the facility than its actual contents. But reading the plaques dedicated to the twenty scholar-athletes elected to the hall of fame each year gives you a new appreciation of stars like Dallas Cowboys running back Calvin Hill, who excelled in academics at Yale, tennis star Althea Gibson, who graduated from Texas A & M at age twenty-one, and Montreal Canadiens goalie Ken Dryden, who earned his law degree at McGill University.

The museum collection includes a sports photography collection as well as Olympic flags, posters, sports art, and memorabilia, including the Olympic cap, jersey, and awards won by Brown University runner Norman Vincent Taber, who broke the world record in the mile in 1915. The Hall of Fame, which also serves as headquarters for the Institute for International Sport (www.international sport.com), is open year-round, Monday to Friday from 10:00 A.M. to 5:00 P.M., Saturday from 10:00 A.M. to 3:00 P.M., and Sunday by appointment. Admission is free, but donations are suggested.

Leaving Kingston and heading west, you travel only about a mile and a half on Route 138 before reaching the village of *West Kingston.* As you approach town, you cross a small bridge, and immediately there is a fork in the road. If you turn left off Route 138 into Liberty Lane, a short drive will bring you to Great Neck Road; a left turn here will bring you to the parking lot for the *Great Swamp Wildlife Management Area,* a huge nature park with a swamp that drains Wordens Pond. It was on an island fortress in the Great Swamp that the Narragansett Indians were attacked and defeated during King Philip's War. A memorial to the people who died in that 1675 battle stands in the swamp and is reached by the aptly named Great Swamp Monument Road, located on the left side of Route 2 about 1¼ miles south of the intersection with Route 138.

Just before the railroad bridge on Route 138 is the turnoff for the *Kingston Station* (http://kingstonstation.org) parking lot. This quiet Amtrak station, with its lovingly restored 1875 depot building and small museum on local railroad history, also serves as the northern terminus of the *William C. O'Neill Bike Path* (www.dot.state.ri.us/bikeri).

Just past the Route 2 intersection on Route 138 is the tiny *Queen's River Baptist Church,* a simple white building hugging a bend in the road. This is one of my favorite places in Rhode Island, a quintessential country church with an old cemetery, completely surrounded by open farmland. Pull over to the right just past the church to park, and take a few moments to walk through the rows of ancient headstones. Besides the occasional passing car, there is nothing to disturb your silent contemplation but the muted sounds of a tractor in the nearby fields, toiling at that endless cycle of sowing and harvesting that is a metaphor for life itself.

Back in the car, a short drive farther west on Route 138 brings you to Old Usquepaugh Road; turn right here, then right onto Glen Rock Road, and on your right you'll see *Kenyon's Grist Mill* (783–4054, 800–7–KENYON; www .kenyons gristmill.com).

For centuries, gristmills occupied an important place in New England village life. The grains harvested by local farmers were not of much use until they were taken to the miller, who would crack the grain with huge grindstones powered by wind or water and make flour and meal. In the modern age, most of these old mills have been demolished, abandoned, or turned into museums.

Part of what makes Kenyon's Grist Mill such an interesting place to visit is the fact that it remains a viable business. Built in 1886, the mill still produces a variety of products, including Kenyon's Jonny Cake Corn Meal and flours made of whole wheat, rye, and buckwheat. Sold in small, turn-of-the-century-style bags, Kenyon's products can be found in specialty stores throughout

Rhode Island, as well as in the Grist Mill Store located across the street from the mill.

Behind the mill you can walk out onto an old dam and see the millrace that carries water under the mill. The Queen's River no longer powers the mill, but the original grindstones are still in use, and the miller is always happy to show visitors how the raw grains are turned into edible products. Tours of the gristmill are by appointment and for groups only (no tours August to October). Mill owners Paul Drumm Jr. and Paul Drumm III, who also sell jams and jellies, relishes, mincemeat, syrup, pancake mix, and homemade soap, welcome visitors to stop by whenever the wheels are in motion. The mill is open Monday to Friday 10:00 A.M. to 4:30 P.M. (call ahead to confirm hours in the off-season).

Glen Rock Road leads north into one of the quietest, most scenic backroad areas in the state. In a scant 2½-mile loop from Glen Rock Road to Dugway Bridge Road back down to Route 138, you cross three bridges over Glen Rock Brook and other small streams, drive past a towering stand of pine trees, and see pastoral country homes.

One stop you definitely should make on Glen Rock Road is at **Peter Pots Pottery** (494 Glen Rock Road, 783–2350; www.peterpots.com). Peter Pots's fine stoneware pottery is produced at the historic 1779 Glen Rock Mill. Lamps, pitchers, vases, and tea sets are just some of the handcrafted items fired in the kilns of this old gristmill and offered for sale in the mill shop. By tradition, most of Peter Pots's pottery is glazed in either mahogany brown or seagull blue.

Besides pottery, the Peter Pots store has an assortment of antiques on display. It's a fun place to poke around in, and the view out the side window, where the river rushes under and past the mill's old waterwheel, is in itself worth the visit. Open Monday through Saturday from 10:00 A.M. to 4:00 P.M. and Sunday 1:00 to 4:00 P.M.

Peace Dale, located off Route 108 in the most populous part of South Kingstown, is one of Rhode Island's prettiest mill villages. (Route 108, also known as Ministerial Road, connects with Route 138 in Kingston to the north and with Route 1 in Wakefield to the south.) At the center of the village, on Kingstown Road (Route 108) next to the Saugatucket River, is the mill complex that formerly housed the **Peace Dale Manufacturing Company.** From 1802 on, the Hazard family built a succession of cotton and textile mills that were the lifeblood of Peace Dale. During the Civil War the Peace Dale mill made blankets for Union soldiers; during World War I khaki was woven for uniforms.

Today a group of smaller companies lease the mill buildings, but you can still walk around the courtyard and admire the mill's nineteenth-century architecture and gaze down upon the river waters rushing through the sunken, well-preserved raceways. Across the street from the mill is the 1856 Peace Dale Office

The Peace Dale Manufacturing Company

The history of the Peace Dale Manufacturing Company includes many of the touchstones of the American Industrial Revolution. The company founded by the Hazard family in 1802 began as a mixture of manufacturing mill and cottage industry: Rhode Island's first carding machine separated the tough cotton fibers at the mill, but the bundles of processed wool were then turned over to local families to spin on hand looms. Power looms were installed in 1814, and the company became known for its shawls and blankets.

Like mills all over the United States, the Peace Dale Manufacturing Company was built with the sweat of immigrant labor. More than a hundred Irish immigrants worked at the mill by 1857, driven out of their homeland by the great potato famine. The latter half of the nineteenth century saw improvements in work conditions and the rise of unionism: The workday was shortened in 1887, and a noon recess was established. In 1906 weavers at the mill went on strike, and a train full of Italian strikebreakers was brought in from Lowell, Massachusetts.

After World War II, the Peace Dale mill began to experience the same problems as many other New England textile firms: high labor costs and aging facilities. By 1947 the owners had shuttered the mill and moved the operation to North Carolina in search of cheap labor and lower transportation costs. The mill, which once employed 40 percent of Peace Dale's residents, was relegated to the shadows of its former importance, and the town gradually made the shift from mill village to suburb.

The Peace Dale Manufacturing Company is one of several Peace Dale sites on a historic driving tour created by the town of South Kingstown (www.southkingstownri .com/code/oth_020201 162627.cfm).

Building, home of the ***Museum of Primitive Art and Culture*** (1058 Kingstown Road, 783–5711; www.primitiveartmuseum.org), which houses a collection of tools, weapons, and artifacts of Native American tribes and other native cultures from around the world. The museum is open Labor Day through Memorial Day, Tuesday to Thursday 10:00 A.M. to 2:00 P.M.; Memorial Day to Labor Day, Wednesday noon to 2:00 P.M.; and by appointment; $2.00 donation suggested.

Behind the office building is a small park that runs along the riverbank, with a big playground and a pretty footbridge that spans the stream. Across Columbia Street is the ***Hazard Memorial Library,*** built in 1891 (1057 Kingstown Road, 783–4085; www.skpl.org/ski.html).

Just north on Route 108 (Kingstown Road) is an 1888 pumping station that provided water to Peace Dale until 1946, when it was abandoned. The fieldstone building was renovated in the 1960s, however, and once again is serving the res-

Perryville's Most Famous Son

"We have met the enemy, and he is ours."

The tiny South Kingstown community known as Perryville has one very big claim to fame: It's the birthplace of Commodore Oliver Hazard Perry, hero of the Battle of Lake Erie in the War of 1812.

Born here in 1785, Perry became a Navy midshipman at the tender age of fourteen and served in the West Indies and in the Tripoli wars in the Mediterranean. He received his first command in 1811, and in 1812 he was sent to Lake Erie to take on a large British fleet that threatened that critical waterway.

During the ensuing battle, Perry's flagship, the brig *Lawrence,* was battered by the British and nearly sunk. But Perry transferred his flag to the *Niagara,* and fifteen minutes of pounding cannon fire later he had defeated a squadron of British ships. Perry's victory and his famous message back to Washington—"We have met the enemy, and he is ours"—made national heroes of him and his crew, and the battle ultimately turned the tide of the war.

To learn more about Perry, see www.brigniagara.org/perry.htm or www.nps.gov/pevi/HTML/perry.html or http://en.wikipedia.org/wiki/oliver_hazard_perry.

idents of Peace Dale as the ***Pump House*** restaurant (1464 Kingstown Road, 789–4944). The towering, peaked ceiling in the dining room is one visible reminder of the building's history, and the restaurant is nicely decorated with plants and lots of polished wood. The fish-and-chips is a menu favorite, but the Pump House also serves a variety of fresh seafood dishes, chicken, and top cuts of steak. The price of your dinner includes unlimited trips to the salad bar. Open Monday to Saturday 4:00 to 10:00 P.M., and Sunday noon to 9:00 P.M.

If you're one of those people who believe that the best flavor enhancer for seafood is a mild salt breeze, proceed south on Route 108 to Route 1 south, then take the South County Hospital/Salt Pond Road exit to find ***J.G. Goff's Pub*** (210 Salt Pond Road, Wakefield, 782–0210). Located between a pair of picturesque marinas, the pub is small, local, and friendly, and both the indoor dining rooms and the outdoor deck offer great views of Salt Pond. The deck and outdoor bar are open in warm-weather months, and there's live music year-round on the weekends. Open March to October; call for hours.

The William C. O'Neill Bike Path, which starts at the old Kingston Train Station on Route 138, follows an old railroad spur into the Great Swamp Management Area and into Peace Dale and Wakefield, giving bikers and joggers an intimate look at South Kingstown's wild areas, village life, old mills, and more. A favorite spot along the 5.5-mile path comes just before Wakefield village, where the path skirts an old cemetery and then crosses a quiet stretch of the Saugatucket River.

If you take an early morning ride on the bike path, the shopping center at the southern end of the trail is home to the *Bluebird Cafe* (554 Kingstown Road, 792-8940), one of the best breakfast spots in the state (try the famous huevos rancheros). Owned by a Rhode Island native who previously ran a similar restaurant in New Orleans, the Bluebird Cafe also serves creole, southwestern, and southern dishes along with breakfast all day long. The catfish and jambalaya dishes come out on Friday night for dinner. Open Monday and Wednesday 7:00 A.M. to 2:00 P.M., Friday 7:00 A.M. to 2:00 P.M. and 5:00 to 9:00 P.M. for dinner, and Saturday and Sunday 8:00 A.M. to 2:00 P.M.

Rarely has a supermarket received as much local "buzz" as Wakefield's *Belmont Market;* everyone in town seems to love this store in the otherwise nondescript Belmont Shopping Mall (600 Kingstown Road, 783–4656). It's primarily a whole-foods market like the ones you now find popping up in health-conscious communities all over, but Belmont Market is unique in that it sublets space to other local vendors, such as Newport's Sushi-Go, reminding me of an old indoor farmers' market I loved visiting as a kid. Visitors to Wakefield can stop in for all the fixings of a picnic lunch, and Belmont also stocks a wide variety of local products that make great take-home souvenirs, such as Del's Lemonade mix and products from Kenyon's Grist Mill, including their famous white-corn jonnycake mix.

Standing atop a hill at the head of a fjordlike pond, *Silver Lake Cottage* (361 Woodruff Avenue, 782–3745; www.silverlakecottage.com) is a hidden gem in the heart of Wakefield. Located in a residential neighborhood, within easy walking distance to both downtown and the bike path, this colonial revival summer home has been transformed into an upscale bed-and-breakfast by owners Susan and Robert Clendenen.

The house is lovely enough, but walking around back is a revelation: Suddenly, you're no longer in the heart of suburbia but on the patio of a private estate, with well-tended gardens and a path leading down a steep hillside to waiting canoes on the pond. A fully enclosed porch, running the length of the back of the house and capped with skylights, has plenty of wicker chairs and couches for relaxing and enjoying the view.

A similar perch can be found in a guest room in the southeast corner of the inn, which has a king bed and a fainting couch by the corner window. The inn has five rooms in total, with rates ranging from $170 to $200 per night, including breakfast.

There are myriad summer rentals, motels, and small inns and bed-and-breakfasts to choose from around the Matunuck Beach area, but one of the best is the **Admiral Dewey Inn** (668 Matunuck Beach Road, 783–2090 or 800–457–2090; www.admiraldeweyinn.com). Named one of Rhode Island's top seashore inns by *Rhode Island Monthly* magazine, the Admiral Dewey is a National Register Victorian home with a big running porch and ten guest rooms, many with ocean views. Once a boardinghouse for beachgoers, the inn is now dressed in high Victorian style, with brass beds, big overstuffed chairs, and fine antiques collected by innkeeper Joan LeBel. Room rates are $110 to $160, year-round, including a "continental-plus" breakfast.

South County's best venue for live music is located right on the beach in Matunuck: the **Ocean Mist** (895 Matunuck Beach Road, 782–3740; www.oceanmist.net). More an oversize bar than a concert hall, the Ocean Mist gets you within arm's-length of local and nationally known reggae, rock, punk, ska, and hip-hop bands. Plus there's an amazing variety of drink and food specials, from taco night to wing night and $3.00 burgers on Sunday from 6:00 to 11:00 P.M. If you need a breath of fresh air, you can duck outside on the deck overlooking the ocean. Even when there's no band playing, the Ocean Mist can be a fun place to hang around with friends. The food is reasonably priced and good—even breakfast is served on the weekends—and on Tuesday there's free pool from 6:00 to 11:00 P.M. Open Monday to Thursday 4:30 P.M. to 1:00 A.M., Friday 11:30 A.M. to 1:00 A.M., and Saturday and Sunday 9:00 A.M. to 1:00 A.M.

Charlestown

You have to be hungry to find the **Nordic Lodge** (178 East Pasquiset Trail, 783–4515; www.nordiclodge.com): First because it probably is the most out-of-the-way restaurant in Rhode Island, and second because it serves an incredible all-you-can-eat buffet that includes unlimited lobster and filet mignon.

Getting to the Nordic Lodge is part of the fun: "If you find us, you'll like us" is the restaurant's motto. From Route 2 in Charlestown, turn onto Maple Lake Farm Road at the NORDIC LODGE sign, then proceed 1⁷⁄₁₀ miles to Old Coach Road. Make a right, then follow this twisting rural road until you start wondering why in the heck anyone would put a restaurant up here. About this time you'll see a sign for the Nordic Lodge entrance. A narrow road will eventually bring you to the restaurant parking lot.

The Nordic Lodge is set in a pretty location by the side of sparsely developed Pasquiset Pond. Operated by the Persson family since 1963, the restaurant's modest exterior and brick-lined dining room belie the fantastic spread laid out for the buffet. What sets the Nordic Lodge apart from your average buffet is not the *quantity* of food but its *quality*. There are trays full of oriental spare ribs, chicken cordon bleu, and baked mushrooms. Filet mignon, prime rib, and mar-

The Narragansetts

Central Charlestown is dominated by the 2,500-acre Narragansett Indian Reservation, home of the native people who once controlled the entire West Bay side of Rhode Island. Called "the people of the small point," about 10,000 Narragansett once lived here, but the plagues, wars, and enslavement associated with the arrival of European settlers in the seventeenth century reduced the population to about 500 by 1682.

The survivors settled on the Charlestown reservation, where they saw their land whittled down from 15,000 acres to just 2 acres in 1880; a 1978 court decision restored the current reservation land to the tribe. In recent years the tribe has been fighting to establish a gambling casino or high-stakes bingo operation on its reservation.

You can get a taste of Narragansett history by visiting the tribe's Royal Indian Burial Ground, located on Narrow Lane off Route 2/112 near Post Road, or by attending the annual Narragansett Indian Powwow, held on the reservation in August; call 364–1100 or see www.narragansett-tribe.org for information.

inated teriyaki steak tips are served from a charcoal grill. And there are mounds of jumbo shrimp and hot lobsters, fresh from a 200-gallon cooking pot. If somehow you make it to dessert, the Nordic Lodge has a Haagen Dazs ice-cream bar and a wide variety of cakes and pastries. If you want to at least make a nod to sensible eating, there's also a selection of fresh fruit and nuts.

Such wild indulgence does have its price, and at the Nordic Lodge that price is $70 per person for the unlimited buffet (sliding-scale discounts for children under age thirteen). The restaurant is open Friday 5:00 to 9:00 P.M., Saturday 4:00 to 9:00 P.M., and Sunday 2:00 to 7:00 P.M. Also open Thursday 5:00 to 9:00 P.M. during summer, and hours are sometimes extended to accommodate bus tours. Closed mid-December to mid-April.

The Nordic Lodge gets very busy on weekends, so come early. While you wait for your table, you can amuse yourself by visiting the Norwegian fjord horse, Australian emu, or other animals in the pens outside. Or prepare for the coming feast by reviewing the buffet map over a cold one at the Nordic Lodge's spacious bar.

Located at the junction of Route 2 and Route 112, the ***Gentleman Farmer Restaurant*** (4349 South County Trail, 364–6202) is a crossroads in more ways than one: Businesspeople on their way to work, families, and bikers cruising South County rub elbows in the tiny dining room and at the outdoor picnic tables when the weather warms up (there's also a take-out window if you want to grab a few sandwiches on the way to the beach).

For a small place, the Gentleman Farmer whips up an impressive range of victuals, including more than thirty breakfast entrees; burgers, club sandwiches, and grinders (subs) for lunch; and seafood, chicken, and pasta dishes for dinner. Open Sunday to Thursday 6:00 A.M. to 8:00 P.M. and 6:00 A.M. to 9:00 P.M. Friday and Saturday (open till 9:00 P.M. daily in the summer).

The **Fantastic Umbrella Factory** is like a time capsule from the 1960s, an artists' cooperative that over the years has transformed an abandoned eighteenth-century farm into a minivillage of small shops surrounding a wonderful wildflower garden.

What's nice about the Fantastic Umbrella Factory is its utter lack of pretense. Narrow dirt paths, sometimes covered by a tin-roofed arbor, lead from one shop to the next through overgrown gardens and past the rusted hulks of old cars. A sign by the garden notes, CLOTHING OPTIONAL; SHOES REQUIRED.

Vines and creepers hang from the ramshackle buildings, but inside the stores are surprisingly neat. The main building, known formally as the **International Bazaar** (364–6616), is filled with an eclectic array of unusual toys, windsocks, posters, bath accessories, jewelry, and, yes, umbrellas. Blown-glass and handmade pottery are the centerpieces at **Small Axe Gallery** (364–1060), where the artists often are working before your eyes.

The tie-dyed atmosphere continues at **New Beginnings** restaurant (364–9240), which offers a full plate of vegetarian dishes, as well as salads, Mexican dishes, sandwiches, paninis served on homemade focaccia, and a kids' menu. Open Monday, Thursday, and Friday noon to 3:00 P.M., Saturday and Sunday 11:00 A.M. to 4:00 P.M. in the winter, later in the summer. After lunch, why not take the children over to the barnyard, filled with sheep, hens, and crowing roosters.

If your lasting impressions of the Fantastic Umbrella Factory are images of those flower gardens, fear not. The **Greenhouse** (364–9166), open in the spring and early fall, sells a variety of traditional perennials and unusual daylilies like those found growing around the property.

The Fantastic Umbrella Factory is located on Scenic Route 1A; take the Ninigret Park/Tourist Information exit off Route 1 and proceed past the tourist information center and the entrance to Ninigret Park. Drive slowly or you'll miss the dirt road leading to the Umbrella Factory parking lot, which is a short distance farther on your right. Open daily 10:00 A.M. to 6:00 P.M. during the summer; 10:00 A.M. to 5:00 P.M. after Labor Day.

Returning to Route 1 south, you quickly will come to the turnoff for East Beach Road. Like all of South County's ocean beaches, **East Beach** (332–0450; www.riparks.com/eastbeach.htm) is popular with sun lovers from Connecticut, Massachusetts, and Rhode Island. What makes East Beach unique, however, is

Ninigret Park's Hidden Charms

The charms of Charlestown's *Ninigret Park* (364–1222) are not immediately apparent: At first glance, you're likely to notice grassy fields and long stretches of pavement (actually the remains of runways from the old Charlestown Naval Airfield), but little else.

But give the 1,172-acre park a chance, and you'll be rewarded. As you drive on the main access road, one of the first things you'll see is the Frosty Drew Observatory (596–7688; www.frostydrew.org), open to the public for stargazing at dusk every Friday night. With its lack of lights and distance from any major city, the park is an ideal place to explore the heavens, as our family found when we brought our telescope down to view the Hale-Bopp comet in 1997.

Push on, and you'll find a quiet, spring-fed swimming pond ("Little Nini Beach") that's great for families with small children, a bicycle racing course, playing fields, and walking trails. A nine-hole frisbee golf course is an interesting recent addition to the park; bring your own disk or borrow one from a ranger. Keep your eye out for herds of wild deer and the occasional vestiges of the old airfield, where future president George H. W. Bush and other naval aviators honed their skills during World War II.

Ninigret Park also hosts an annual visit by the Big Apple Circus (364–0890; www .bigapplecircus.org) in July and the taste-tempting Charlestown Seafood Festival (364–3878; www.charlestownchamber.com/seafoodfestival.html) each August.

the combination of a small parking lot (maximum capacity of ninety-six cars) and a 3-mile-long expanse of undeveloped beachfront.

If you crave solitude, this is your place. Down by the parking lot at the west end of the beach are lifeguards and crowds, but there are fewer and fewer people as you walk east along the shoreline until, in many places, you have the beach pretty much to yourself. In front of you are the ocean and the shadowy outline of Block Island; behind you are Ninigret Pond and the dunes of the Ninigret Conservation Area. If you keep walking east, you will eventually reach the Charlestown Breachway, marked by huge boulders piled on each side of the inlet.

Parking at East Beach is $14.00 on the weekend and $12.00 during the week for nonresidents ($7.00 and $6.00, respectively, for nonresident seniors); the lot fills up quickly during the summer, so get there early.

The *General Stanton Inn* (4115 Old Post Road, 364–8888; www.general stantoninn.com) has developed a long and rich history during 340 years of feeding and housing guests. The rambling yellow building on Old Post Road claims to be the oldest continually operating inn in America and remains a center of Charlestown life with its historic Night Watch Tavern, fine dining rooms, and a weekend flea market that attracts up to 200 vendors from May to October.

The restaurant at the inn took a giant leap forward when executive chef Jean Claude Bourlier took over the kitchen, adding a fine layer of polish to such traditional favorites as Black Angus Prime Rib and Scallops Nantucket. Suddenly, the General Stanton Inn was on the local culinary map again. Guests can start (or finish) their visit with a drink at the dark woody tavern, which has a locals' atmosphere and live music on the weekends.

The main dining room, a former gambling parlor, is bright and cheerful, with hanging plants and simple colonial decor. But informed dinner guests request a table in the Indian Room, an intimate space with its own fireplace located in one of the inn's oldest rooms. Once used as a classroom for local Indians and slaves, this room is great for romantic couples.

Dinner entrees at the General Stanton Inn range from about $10 to $26; room rates vary seasonally from $76 to $300 a night. To get to the inn, take the Charlestown Beach exit off Route 1.

Westerly

The town of **Westerly** has two main communities, and neither should be missed. First is the village of Westerly itself, an early center of commerce on the old Lower Road (part of the Boston Post Road, later Route 1) and famous from the mid-nineteenth century on for the blue granite produced in local quarries. To reach downtown Westerly, take exit 1 in Rhode Island on I–95, then proceed south on Route 3, which will eventually bring you to the heart of downtown.

The largest town in South County, Westerly nonetheless retains a small-town feel. Much of the credit is due to beautiful **Wilcox Park** (www.westerly library.org), eighteen acres of gardens, statues, and serene pathways located on High Street in the heart of downtown. Besides being a nice place to walk around or relax under a shady tree, Wilcox Park is home to a free Shakespeare festival on July evenings. Designed by a student of Frederick Law Olmsted, who created New York's Central Park, Wilcox Park features a wide variety of interesting plants and trees, with a unique garden that includes braille descriptions for the visually impaired. The park is open from dawn to 9:00 P.M. daily.

Downtown Westerly features a number of impressive and historic public buildings, including the Westerly Town Hall at the corner of Broad Street and Union Street, the Washington Trust Bank building on Broad Street, Christ Church at Broad and Elm, and the distinctive, yellow-brick Westerly Public Library, also on Broad Street. Next door to the library, fronted by massive columns, is the town post office.

Adding to Westerly's charm are the presence of the Pawcatuck River, which defines the boundary between Westerly and Pawcatuck, Connecticut; a quaint

Victorian train station that marks the passage of the railroad through the heart of downtown; and a fine assortment of well-maintained old homes. Preeminent among the latter is the **Babcock-Smith House** (124 Granite Street, 596–5704; www.babcock-smithhouse.com), a restored circa 1732 Georgian mansion that welcomes visitors by appointment on Saturday (2:00 to 5:00 P.M.) May to October (also Friday in July and August). The house belonged to Dr. Joshua Babcock, a physician who served as a member of the general assembly and Chief Justice of the Rhode Island Supreme Court. Babcock also was a friend of Benjamin Franklin, who often visited Babcock's home. Orlando Smith, who owned the house in the mid-nineteenth century, was the man who discovered the granite deposits that made Westerly world famous.

The Babcock-Smith House is fully furnished and decorated, including authentic eighteenth-century wall and floor treatments and fine antique furniture, with many eighteenth- and nineteenth-century pieces belonging to the Smith family, who lived here until 1972. Admission is $5.00 for adults and $1.00 for children.

Also on Granite Street is the brooding Greek-Revival building that houses the **Granite Theatre** (1 Granite Street, 596–2341; www.granitetheatre.com). This professional theater group presents a full schedule of contemporary musicals, comedies, and dramas. The Granite Theatre's presentation of *A Christmas Carol* has become an annual tradition.

The Granite Theatre's performances are enhanced by the ambience of the setting, Westerly's 150-year-old former First Congregational Church building, which is listed on the National Register. Performance ticket prices are $17 for adults, $14 for seniors, and $10 for students. The season runs from March through December.

Downtown shopping in Westerly includes stores that appeal to all ages, from the chain-link chic of the **Seven Ply Skate Shop** (3 Canal Street, 348–0656; www.7ply.com)—a mecca for Rhode Island and Connecticut skateboarders that sells equipment, clothing, and body jewelry to local flatlanders and street skaters (open Monday to Friday 11:00 A.M. to 7:00 P.M., Saturday 10:00 A.M. to 6:00 P.M., Sunday 11:00 A.M. to 6:00 P.M.)—to the more sublime pleasures of **Stained Glass Designs** (36 High Street; 596–4975; www.glassyladywesterly .com), where artisan Carol Motta's handiwork includes small ornaments and custom-made windows, doors, and cabinets in all shapes and sizes. Open Tuesday to Friday 10:00 A.M. to 5:00 P.M., Saturday 10:00 A.M. to 3:00 P.M.

Documentary film writer Daniel Kamil and wife Emily Steffian tired of the L.A. scene and headed back east, but didn't give up their love of film. Instead, they opened Westerly's **Revival House Cinema and Cafe** (42 High Street, 315–2770; www.revivalhouse.net), a fifty-seat showcase for classic films from

The Shining to *It's a Wonderful Life,* animated features, short subjects, and, of course, documentaries.

Housed in a revitalized storefront that formerly was an antiques store, the cafe opens at noon to allow film lovers to gather early over wine and cheese and fine chocolates. Soups, salad, and panini also are available, and there's outdoor seating in the summer. Two films a week are shown, and Friday and Saturday night shows tend to sell out, so arrive early. Admission is $6.00; shows are at 8:00 P.M., plus a 4:00 P.M. matinee on Wednesday, Saturday, and Sunday.

The funky urban coffeehouse has arrived on the Westerly scene in the form of **Perks and Quirks** (48 High Street, 596–1260; www.perksandquirks.com), a comfortable storefront wine lounge, martini bar, and coffeehouse with scores of wines in stock as well as espresso, cappuccino, chai tea, and lattes. Grab a cup, grab a couch, and chill for a while in this smoke-free cafe. Open Monday and Tuesday 7:00 A.M. to 9:00 P.M., Wednesday and Thursday 7:00 A.M. to 10:00 P.M., Friday and Saturday 7:00 A.M. to 1:00 A.M., and Sunday 8:00 A.M. to 1:00 P.M. (Connoisseurs take note! Breakfast features fresh New York bagels shipped in daily from the Bronx.)

Westerly's dining options include **PizzaPlace Pies & Suds** (43 Broad Street, 348–1803), a spacious restaurant specializing in thin-crust red and white pizzas topped with clams, Thai chicken, pineapple, and bacon, as well as more traditional appointments. PizzaPlace takes the "suds" part seriously, too: There are dozens of varieties of bottled beer to choose from in a large refrigerated case behind the counter. Open Sunday to Thursday 11:30 A.M. to 9:00 P.M., Friday and Saturday 11:30 A.M. to 10:00 P.M.

There's no formal riverwalk in Westerly, but visitors can stroll down a covered walkway behind the line of stores on the west side of Canal Street (accessible from Broad Street) for a look upstream, where the old mill buildings and warehouses lining the river quickly give way to a more pastoral scene.

Straddling the Pawcatuck River on Main Street is the **Upriver Cafe** (37 Main Street, 348–9700; www.theuprivercafe.net). This upscale eatery literally sits over the river: At the time the cotton mill housing the restaurant was built, the Westerly waterfront already was crowded with buildings, so this was the only space left to build on.

Owners Jennifer and Dan King have retained much of the mill's natural beauty, including the wide plank floors and stone walls composed of rocks that once traveled the world as ballast on old sailing ships. Taking advantage of their great location, the Kings also have built a deck onto a small island in the Pawcatuck River for outdoor dining in the summer. The dinner menu features steaks, chops, seafood, and daily vegetarian specials; a more casual bar menu features unique appetizers, "shared plates," and sandwiches. Open 11:30 A.M.

to 3:00 P.M. for lunch and 5:00 to 9:00 P.M. for dinner Monday to Thursday, and 5:00 to 10:00 P.M. Fridays and Saturdays and on summer Sundays. Bar open till 1:00 A.M.

Some might see this as a sign of Westerly's growing sophistication: downtown now has a Mexican restaurant, **Señor Flaco's,** located at 15 Canal Street (315–2626) just across from the train station. The corner location makes this a prominent addition to the local landscape, and inside the restaurant is huge and brightly decorated. Run by the owners of the more upscale Upriver Cafe, Señor Flaco's is a comfortable place to bring the kids (under-twelves eat free on Sundays) or a date for margaritas and enchiladas. Open nightly from 4:00 to 10:00 P.M.

Westerly grew up around the Pawcatuck River, and seeing the town from the water offers an entirely different perspective, with ramshackle docks and walkways falling into decay behind carefully restored storefronts. **Westerly Duck Land Water Tours** provides a nice overview of both sides of Westerly, tootling around downtown with pauses at the Babcock-Smith House, Wilcox Park, and the historic train station before easing into the water for a short cruise downriver, passing the tranquil Riverbend Cemetery along the way.

The tour utilizes a vintage World War II amphibious boat converted to civilian use, and departs from the Westerly-Pawcatuck Chamber of Commerce offices on Post Road (on the north side of the road near the intersection with Route 78; look for the TOURIST INFORMATION sign) daily during July and August and on weekends in September. Tours last about seventy minutes and leave every hour and a half. Tickets are $15.00 for adults and seniors, $10.00 for children ages three to twelve, and $3.75 for children two and under. For information call the chamber at 596–7761 or visit www.ducklandwatertours.com.

One of the roads that intersect in downtown Westerly is Beach Street/Route 1A, which also happens to be your southern passage to Westerly's other major community, **Watch Hill.**

A right turn from Beach Street onto Watch Hill Road brings you onto a winding, hilly road that meanders toward the southwestern corner of Rhode Island. Along the way, you'll pass the **Sun-Up Gallery** (95 Watch Hill Road, 596–3430; www.sunupgallery.com) in the village of Avondale, which has won a strong regional following for its unique American-made clothing, crafts, and jewelry. Open Monday to Saturday 10:00 A.M. to 6:00 P.M.; and Sunday 11:00 A.M. to 5:00 P.M.

Watch Hill's name derives from the fact that it was used during the Revolutionary War as a lookout for British privateers, who made a habit of raiding coastal New England villages. Like Newport and Narragansett, Watch Hill became a fashionable vacation resort in the latter half of the nineteenth century, as evidenced by the many fine homes that sit along the road and up on the hills as you drive into town.

Watch Hill is almost entirely residential with the exception of the length of Bay Street, facing Watch Hill Cove, which is lined with small specialty shops and eateries, most of which are open April through December. Some of the stores run to the T-shirt and snow-globe variety, but most still exude the feel of an upscale New England seaside town.

Nowhere is the atmosphere more traditional than at the **Olympia Tea Room** (74 Bay Street, 348–8211; www.olympiatearoom.com), where black-clad waitresses serve a mix of traditional American dishes and nouvelle cuisine, with an emphasis on seafood. Still going strong after ninety-plus years, the Olympia Tea Room has an art deco look about it, with salmon walls contrasting with dark wood trim on the high-backed booths and large, mirrored bar.

An etching on the bay windows (aptly named, since they offer a great view of the water) eloquently understates "a good dinner served here," although the restaurant is open for breakfast and lunch, too. Try a longtime favorite like a lobster salad roll or the fried local flounder sandwich, or go with the littleneck clams and fresh sausage steamed in marinara sauce—so good that it's still on the ever-changing dinner menu after some twenty-five years. The restaurant is open 11:00 A.M. to 10:00 P.M. daily from April to November; call ahead for off-season hours.

The **St. Clair Annex** (141 Bay Street, 348–8407) has been serving home-made ice cream to summer visitors as long as they have been coming to Watch Hill—the business started in 1880. In a nod to more modern tastes, frozen yogurt has been added to the menu, and a small restaurant serves breakfast and lunch Memorial Day to Labor Day, 7:00 A.M. to 10:00 P.M.

If you needed one reason and one reason only to visit Watch Hill, look no further than the corner of Bay Street and Fort Street. The **Flying Horse Carousel** (348–6007) is the oldest continually operating merry-go-round in the United States. Built in 1867, the open-air carousel doesn't look like much when it is not in operation. The simple structure, which consists of a round, peaked, wooden roof supported by stone pillars and surrounded by a white picket fence, sits right by the roadside on a small lot. But when the old wooden horses are rehung each spring and the joyful sounds of children are added, something magical occurs.

Each one-hundred-year-old, intricately carved horse is made from a single piece of wood and decorated with a mane of real horsehair. Unlike more modern carousels, where the horses are attached by poles to the floor as well as the roof, the horses on the Flying Horse Carousel are attached only at the top, so when the carousel is in motion the horses swing outward and really do "fly." No adults are permitted to ride the carousel, and children must be able to sit without their feet touching the ground. The carousel operates from June 15 to Labor Day, Monday through Friday 1:00 to 8:00 P.M. and Saturday and Sunday 11:00 A.M. to 9:00 P.M. It costs $1.00 to ride.

One of the best things about Watch Hill is the variety of things there are to do in a small area. Striking out from the heart of town, you can explore two areas where history competes with great natural beauty for your attention. From the Flying Horse Carousel, walk down Larkin Road until you reach Lighthouse Road, which you follow to the end. Here stands the *Watch Hill Lighthouse,* a white brick and granite tower built in 1856 to guard the east entrance to Fisher's Island Sound. You can walk around the outside of the lighthouse or simply relax and enjoy the sensation of being surrounded on three sides by ocean. To the southwest you can see Fisher's Island, an isolated outpost of New York State.

Not only does *Napatree Point* offer a panoramic view of the Atlantic Ocean, but if you hike out to the end you can tell your grandchildren that you stood on the westernmost spot in Rhode Island. At the end of Fort Road begins a nature trail that takes you along the privately owned Napatree Beach out to the tip of Napatree Point, about a mile-and-a-half walk. While you're walking, you can reflect on what it must have been like to be living on this narrow strip of land when the hurricane of 1938 struck. Not only were most of the houses on Napatree Point destroyed, but the tip of the point was literally washed away by the storm.

The *Napatree Point Conservation Area* offers some great opportunities for bird-watching, with a nesting area set aside for ospreys and terns. When you reach the end of the point, you are rewarded by the ruins of *Fort Mansfield,* a stone-walled fort built in 1898 to defend the shoreline during the Spanish-American War. Look for the overgrown walls of the fort a few yards inland, up a path that climbs a ridge at the tip of the point.

The *Villa* (190 Shore Road/Route 1A, 596–1054 or 800–722–9240 out of state; www.thevillaatwesterly.com) is not your ordinary bed-and-breakfast. Here, in the land of Victorian- and colonial-era inns and homes, is an Italian villa surrounding a beautiful pool, with market umbrellas shading small tables by the water. Steps away is an outdoor hot tub, and a flight of stairs leads from the patio up to a deck belonging to the inn's La Sala di Verona suite, where Romeo and Juliet would have felt right at home. All eight suites have two-person Jacuzzi tubs, four have fireplaces.

Innkeepers Michael and Barbara Cardiff serve breakfast poolside in the summertime (in-room in the winter) and offer personalized service and friendly dining and touring advice year-round. A new show kitchen allows guests to watch meals being prepared, including dinners on request; it's also used for cooking classes.

This mini-resort occupies a sheltered spot amid flowering gardens, off a gravel drive on Route 1A/Shore Road. In-season rates range from $235 to $305 for the inn's eight suites, each equipped with VCRs and CD players; off-season rates range from $115 to $235.

If you simply must stay by the water, find your way to the **Weekapaug Inn** (25 Spray Rock Road, 322–0301; www.weekapauginn.com), a traditional New England seashore hotel. Simple but elegant, the Weekapaug Inn is a throwback to a time when vacation resorts were expected to provide three meals a day, enough activities to keep you busy for as long as you stayed, and a certain sense of decorum.

All this the Weekapaug does admirably, with fresh local produce and seafood featured prominently in the formal dining room (jacket required for gentlemen) and a weekly Thursday cookout on the lawn. The resort's 2-mile-long private beach is ideal for swimming and sailing, and lawn bowling, tennis, croquet, shuffleboard, and an indoor game room are all available on-site. Join in a game—there are no phones or TVs to distract you.

All rates are Full American Plan and charged per-person; double occupancy is $225 per person, with children's rates set at $150 per day. The Weekapaug Inn is open from mid-June to Labor Day.

Block Island

Block Island is a study in contradiction: Just 12 miles from the coast of Rhode Island, it feels so much farther away; just 11 square miles in area, it feels so much bigger. It has a bustling harbor and village, and its long stretches of road are best navigated by bicycle to take in the full sweep of the island's beauty. With the ocean all around and a pristine sanctuary at its center, it's no wonder that Block Island has been called one of the last great places on earth.

Visitors flock to the island by the thousands in the summer, mostly via the ferries that depart from the State Pier in Galilee. (The Interstate Navigation Company, 783–4613, operates ferries year-round to Block Island.) With so many people on such a small island, it's natural that most of the popular sites—the Southeast Lighthouse; the Mohegan Bluffs; the charming shops, restaurants, and old hotels of the Old Harbor and New Harbor—have been explored pretty thoroughly. Still, Block Island retains hidden places and new experiences for you to discover.

One way to enjoy Block Island is to come during the off-season. Although a good number of the businesses on the island close down after Labor Day, many stay open through September and even year-round. In fact, September is a great time to visit: The summer crowds are gone, but the warm weather and

Bloody Bluffs

The natives of Block Island were called the Manisseans, and they called their home Manisses—the Island of the Little God. So why is the island's most prominent natural feature named after a mainland tribe, the Mohegans?

According to Manissean legend, island natives were preparing for a raid on nearby Long Island when they spied a war party of Mohegans approaching Block Island on a raid of their own. The Manissean warriors quickly turned back to shore and set an ambush for the Mohegans. Taken by surprise, the Mohegan war party was driven to the edge of the cliffs at the southern end of the island, where they threw up an earthen defensive berm in a last-ditch attempt to stave off annihilation.

During the pitched battle that followed, the Mohegans were wiped out. But long after their fortifications faded away and the Manisseans slipped away into history, the battle is remembered in the name of the Mohegan Bluffs.

warm water remain through the end of the month. The annual shopper's stroll is a highlight of the Christmas season. Call the Block Island Chamber of Commerce at (800) 383–BIRI for more information.

A few unusual attractions await you as you step off the ferry. Just a two-minute walk from the ferry dock is the ***Hotel Manisses*** (Spring Street in the Old Harbor, 466–2421; www.blockislandresorts.com), built in 1872 and perhaps the most beautiful of all the Victorian inns on the island. Surprisingly small, the Manisses sits close to Spring Street yet maintains an impeccable, quiet charm and elegance. It's a wonderful place to stay (room rates range from $65 to $330, depending on the season; open April to November), and the restaurant is one of the island's best. For a special treat, take a seat in the Manisses's dessert parlor, located on the main floor of the hotel (upstairs from the restaurant). If you love sweets, this could be the highlight of your trip. Relax in quiet elegance while being served such tantalizing treats as Joan's Delight—delicious sour cream pie filled with blueberries and pineapple in a cracker crust—and the chocolate silk pie with mousse filling and a chocolate cookie crust. Flaming coffees are served tableside, the 151-proof liquor set alight before your eyes. A selection of cinnamon, sugar, whipped cream, and assorted liqueurs is brought on a tray for you to choose from.

In a somewhat jarring contrast to the elegant surroundings, the Hotel Manisses also maintains a small animal farm with exotic creatures sure to delight children and adults alike. Llamas, emus, geese, pygmy goats, camels, black swans, and a Scottish highland steer named Mr. MacDuff are among the beasts roaming the grounds behind the hotel. Recent additions include a zebu, the oldest type of cattle in the Northern Hemisphere, and another type of cattle, a Brahman heifer.

Another sign that relaxed elegance is what Block Island is all about is the farmers' market held at the Manisses each Wednesday morning. Here island farmers and gardeners gather to sell their produce, fresh flowers, herbs, and other homemade products to summer visitors and residents alike. The farmers' market also is held on Saturday at Negus Park on Ocean Avenue.

A short walk farther up the hill on Spring Street in the Old Harbor brings you to the driveway of the *Spring House* (52 Spring Street, 466–5844 or 800–234–9263; www.springhousehotel.com), another of Block Island's grand old Victorians. Set on a fifteen-acre hilltop, this beautiful hotel has a magnificent red-and-white porch running the length of the building and offering unparalleled ocean views. For $225 to $450 (depending on the season), you can rent the honeymoon suite, complete with Jacuzzi, private deck with French

Ghosts of the Palatine

The voyage of the brig *Princess Augusta* began poorly and ended even worse, culminating in a disastrous wreck off the northern tip of Block Island, chronicled in the John Greenleaf Whittier poem, "Wreck of the Palatine."

Carrying more than 300 refugees from the Palatine region of Germany, the *Princess Augusta* set sail from Rotterdam bound for Philadelphia in the fall of 1738. Almost immediately, passengers and crew began getting sick and dying. Contaminated drinking water was eventually determined to be the culprit. But this discovery led to strict rationing of the remaining water supply, which in turn sparked a wave of extortion, mutiny, and murder.

By the time the bedraggled survivors reached the American coastline, they were far north of their destination and three weeks late. Finally, a beacon was spotted, and the ship turned toward land. But just as salvation was apparently within reach, the ship ran hard aground on the Hummocks, a rocky shoal off Block Island.

Whether the light was a ruse used by local salvagers to lure ships onto the rocks was never confirmed; what is known is that the crew of the *Princess Augusta* abandoned the ship along with most of its surviving passengers. Fearing disease, island residents decided to burn the ship, but as they did so, a sound like the screaming of a woman was heard. This led some rescuers to realize—too late—that some passengers might have remained aboard the doomed ship.

In later years, Block Island residents would tell tales of a ghostly brig sailing past the north end of the island, only to burst into flame before vanishing. They say the "Palatine Lights" are still seen from time to time, on nights when wild storms whip the shoreline to offer a furious epithet to the tragic story of the *Princess Augusta*.

Birding on Block Island

Nearly a third of Block Island has been preserved as open space—some in its original, pristine state, some as reclaimed farmers' fields that are slowly returning to nature. Thanks to local conservation efforts and the island's location on a major migratory route, a wide variety of birds make stopovers here, including shorebirds, waterfowl, raptors, and songbirds. Others, like the rare northern harrier, make Block Island their home, patrolling the grassy scrubland prevalent over much of the island in search of food.

Block Island's beaches also provide a sanctuary for nesting birds, although some have been driven out by human activity along the shoreline. The best time to do some serious birding on Block Island is during the fall, when migration is at its peak. For more information contact the Block Island Nature Conservancy at 466–2129.

doors, and another great ocean view. In the summer, schedule your visit to coincide with the Spring House's jazz and rock concerts, held out on the lawn alternating weekends in July and August. Open April through October.

Over in the New Harbor on Ocean Avenue, the 1909 **Narragansett Inn** (466–2626) has a tiny bar (the Sunset Lounge) with an awesome view of the harbor. Most island visitors never find it; you should. Sit at one of the handful of tables inside, or take your drink outside on the deck or onto the lawn to admire the scenery. Of all the island's old hotels, by the way, the Narragansett is the only one to retain its original floor plan. Room rates range from $115 to $160 double occupancy; suites sleeping up to five people cost $225 to $265. Open May 1 to November 1.

Located on Water Street is Block Island's one and only microbrewery, the **Mohegan Cafe & Brewery** (466–5911), located below the Water Street Inn and serving burgers, salads, Tex-Mex entrees, and four varieties of small-batch beer brewed on the premises, including an IPA, English Red, Striper Ale, and a light Summer Citrus. Open daily 11:30 A.M. to 10:00 P.M.

To really get a feel for the "different" side of Block Island, however, you need to get out of town and explore the rest of the island, particularly the north end—accessible only via Corn Neck Road—and the southwestern corner, where many of the sites are reached only by traveling over bumpy dirt roads. If you need to commune alone with the sea, you usually can get your wish at such isolated stretches of sand as **North Light Beach** and **Mansion Beach** on the north end and **Black Rock Beach** (home of the island's unofficial "clothing optional" beach, though local police will ticket nude sunbathers), **Charlestown Beach,** and **Grace's Cove** on the west side. Charlestown Beach and Black Rock Beach lure surfcasters with the promise of biting striped bass—a 75-pound striper was taken from the beaches here in 1984. To get the low-down on local fishing, stop by *Twin Maples* on Beach Avenue (466–5547) and let Jon, the island's fishing guru, bend your ear for a while.

The North Light Beach is located past the eponymous lighthouse. From the end of Corn Neck Road, walk along the shoreline past the lighthouse and around Sandy Point to the beach. While you're here, stop at the *North Light Interpretive Center,* open daily 10:00 A.M. to 4:00 P.M. during the summer and on weekends in the fall; call 466–3200 to check the schedule. Admission is $2.00 and free for children under six.

Mansion Beach is at the end of Mansion Road, a dirt path on the east side of Corn Neck Road just north of the Great Salt Pond. Black Rock Beach is at the end of a very long dirt path off Cooneymus Road. Charlestown Beach is at the end of Coast Guard Road, and Grace's Cove is at the end of Grace's Cove Road; both are off West Side Road.

To explore the island, you first need to choose a mode of transportation. Cars, expensive to bring over on the ferry and useless on many of the island's smaller roads, are a poor choice. Ditto for mopeds, which can be dangerous in the hands of novices and a source of irritation for island residents. The best choice, if you can brave Block Island's many hills, is to ride a bicycle. Either bring your own or rent one on the island from *Block Island Bike and Car Rentals* (Ocean Avenue; 466–2297).

Horseback riding at *Rustic Rides Stables* (West Side Road, 466–5060) is another way to enjoy the western side of Block Island. The expert trail guides will lead your well-mannered mounts through seventy acres of countryside and right down to the shore for a ride on the beach between the cliffs and the sea. The one-hour trail rides are offered every day during the summer between 9:00 A.M. and 6:00 P.M. and off-season from 10:00 A.M. to 4:00 P.M. and cost $45 to $55. There are ponies for the children, too.

Closer to town on West Side Road is the *Island Cemetery,* an interesting place to walk around and a great spot for gravestone etchings. Almost any old New England cemetery holds its fascinations, but Block Island's graveyard is notable for the nautical themes on the markers and the numerous stones with family names like Ball and Dodge—descendants of the sixteen original white settlers who landed on the island in 1661. The oldest headstone, remarkably well preserved despite three centuries of saltwater and wind, is that of Margaret Guthry, who died in 1687.

The *Mohegan Bluffs,* 200-foot-tall cliffs carved out of the island by the relentless Atlantic, arguably make up the most famous spot on Block Island. Nearly everyone who visits the island goes to see the bluffs and the adjacent

Southeast Light, the 1875 lighthouse that is equipped with the East Coast's most powerful beacon. Relatively few, however, climb down the seemingly endless stairs that lead to the narrow beach at the foot of the cliffs. Once you descend, there are more than 3 miles of secluded shore to explore, but keep in mind that those who go down must, of necessity, come back up again. It's a workout, but worth it.

Cleared for farming and other human activities during its long history, Block Island today is possessed of relatively few mature trees. One exception is **Maple Leaf Cottage** (Beacon Hill Road, 466–2065; www.mapleleafbi.com), a shady bed-and-breakfast located in the center of the island, near the state airport. Owner and innkeeper Bill Penn has decorated the two guest rooms in his 1825 Cape Cod farmhouse in a Pottery Barn style and welcomes guests from May to October; room rates range from $90 to $125.

The **Island Home** (Beach Avenue, 466–5944 or 800–261–6118; www.the islandhome.com), by contrast, is a stylish Victorian perched atop a treeless ridge, offering some of the best views on the island. Owners Dina and David Chieffo welcome guests to stay in six rooms in the main house and four in the carriage house; ask for the upstairs room in the carriage house, which has a private deck with sweeping views of Old Harbor and Block Island Sound.

Quiet at night, when guests linger in the common room and porch, the Island Home is nevertheless just a few minutes walk from the daytime bustle of Old Harbor and the beach. After sampling Dina's Texas French Toast and other breakfast specialties, you can spend your day exploring the island or just linger on the tree swing, then return for afternoon hors d'oeuvres and wine. Room rates are $125 to $295.

Southeast Light

The Happy Accident of Block Island

Block Island as we know it today probably wouldn't exist if not for a couple of unfortunate turns of fate that befell this small community.

Like most of New England, big chunks of Block Island were cleared for farming during the eighteenth and nineteenth centuries. And as on the mainland, the local farming industry went into near-terminal decline in the middle of the twentieth century, as big Midwestern farms and modern shipping and preservation techniques undercut the region's produce market. This only added to the problems of an island economy already battered by the decline of the tourist trade after World War I, which had left many of the island's big Victorian-era inns shuttered and empty.

When preservationists and the tourist industry rediscovered Block Island in the 1970s, both found a diamond in the rough. Groups like the Nature Conservancy began working to preserve all of those old farmers' fields that had grown wild again, as well as tracts of land that had never been developed. At the same time, work began on restoring the big hotels—many of which remained intact despite years of neglect, partly because no one could afford to tear them down.

So, whenever you look at Block Island's beautiful man-made and natural wonders, it's appropriate to remember the old adage: When life hands you lemons, make lemonade. They've sure made some sweet stuff here.

We won't say that a stay at the **Sasafrash** bed-and-breakfast (Center Road, 466–5486; www.blockisland.com/cozybandbs) will be a religious experience, but one of the charms of this island B&B is that it's located in a turn-of-the-century church. The building, which also houses an antiques shop, retains many vestiges of its former use, including stained-glass windows, a choir loft, and a raised pulpit. Guests often come away enraptured by the large, clean rooms and the hospitality of innkeeper Shirley Kessler. Each morning is welcomed with an expanded continental breakfast served in the former church sanctuary. The Sasafrash has two guest rooms, and rates range from an off-season low of $95 to $155 during the summer.

The circa 1870 **Woonsocket House,** standing at the corner of Old Town Road and Ocean Avenue, is home to the **Block Island Historical Society** (466–2481), which has a museum that's open to the public. Part of the exhibit depicts the interior of a typical island home of the late nineteenth century, with antique furnishings, dishes, and an old loom. An upstairs gallery is devoted to changing exhibits on different aspects of the island's history and heritage, including fishing and farming. The museum and gift shop are open 10:00 A.M. to 4:00 P.M. from the end of June to Labor Day and on weekends through Columbus Day; call ahead for hours.

There are any number of fishing charter companies going for fluke, striped bass, blues, and other wild fish in the local waters, including Capt. Bill Gould's **G. Willie Makit Charters** (466–5151 or 245–7831), **Linesider Fishing Charters** and *The Rooster* (439–5386) and **Blockhead Charters** for fly and light-tackle fishing (477–6950 or 466–5131). **Block Island Fishworks** (Ocean Avenue, New Harbor, 466–5392) can also put you in touch with a charter captain.

Locals say that one of the best ways to see Block Island is from the water, so if you'd rather sail than fish, Larry and Laura Puckett's **Passion for Sailing Charters** (741–1926; www.rulingpassion.com) offers sunset and wine-and-cheese excursions from New Harbor aboard the 45-foot Trimaran *Ruling Passion*. Sails May to October; excursions range from $40 to $45 for adults, $20 to $45 for children. For an even closer look, rent a kayak for a leisurely paddle around the protected Great Salt Pond; **Pond and Beyond** (742–5460 or 466–5467) offers guided kayak tours, and you can also rent from **Aldo's** at Champlin Marina (466–5811).

For more of a thrill ride, **Block Island Parasail & Watersports** (864–2474; http://blockislandparasail.com) offers solo or tandem parasailing flights along the Block Island coastline; they also rent jet boats (even to novice mariners) by the hour and do half-hour rides for groups of up to ten on a towed banana boat—a little like whitewater rafting on the ocean! Located on the Old Harbor dock across from the ferry landing. Open daily June to October, 9:00 A.M. to sunset.

Finally, don't forget to take the time to explore the **Greenway**, the network of trails that link a series of properties preserved by the Nature Conservancy and other island residents—more than 600 acres in all. There are access points for the Greenway off many of the island's main roads, and paths take you from **Rodman's Hollow**, carved by an ancient glacier and overlooking Black Rock, to the shores of the Great Salt Pond. Across the street from Littlefield's Bee Farm on Corn Neck Road is the entrance to the Nature Conservancy's **Clay Head** nature preserve, which features hiking trails down to a secluded beach edged by clay bluffs. A highlight of any visit to Block Island should be a walk through The Maze, a unique pine forest crisscrossed by trails off the main path at Clay Head.

One of Block Island's newest nature preserves is the **Hodge Family Wildlife Preserve**, established in 2004 and maintained by The Nature Conservancy. Located off Corn Neck Road a quarter-mile north of the Clay Head Preserve entrance, the preserve includes a trail leading to isolated Middle Pond that features views of undeveloped coastline, the North Light, and an observation tower used during World War II to spot German submarines. Bird-lovers should keep a sharp eye out for the American woodcock, which patrols the preserve's meadows, and egrets, herons, and other waterfowl at the pond.

Call the Block Island Conservancy's headquarters (352 High Street, 466–2129; www.nature.org) for more information, or you can get a Greenway map at the group's office. The Nature Conservancy also runs daily guided nature walks in the summer; staff members and volunteers also do a guided winter walk for groups if you call ahead.

Places to Stay in South County—The Ocean Shore and Block Island

(All Area Codes 401)

NARRAGANSETT

The Four Gables
12 South Pier Road
789–6948

The Lighthouse Inn
307 Great Island Road
Galilee
789–9341 or (800) 336–6662

1900 House B&B
59 Kingstown Road
789–7971

The Ocean Rose Inn
113 Ocean Road
783–4704

The Pleasant Cottage B&B
104 Robinson Street
783–6895

The Richards B&B
144 Gibson Avenue
789–7746

The Village Inn
One Beach Street
783–6767 or
(800) THE–PIER

SOUTH KINGSTOWN

The Admiral Dewey Inn
668 Matunuck Beach Road
789–2090 or
(800) 457–2090

Almost Heaven in Snug Harbor B&B
49 West Street
783–9272

The Applewood Greene B&B
841 East Mooresfield Road
789–1937

The King's Rose
1747 Mooresfield Road
783–5222 or
(800) 230–ROSE

The Larchwood Inn
521 Main Street
Wakefield
783–5454

Matunuck Breakers
955 Matunuck Beach Road
789–3801 or 273–9849

CHARLESTOWN

The General Stanton Inn
Route 1A
364–8888 or 364–0100

Hathaway's B&B
4470 Old Post Road
364–6665

The Ocean View Motor Inn
5407B Post Road, Route 1
364–0080

The Willows Motel-Resort
5310 Post Road
364–7727 or
(800) 842–2181

WESTERLY

Grandview B&B
212 Shore Road
596–6384 or (800) 447–6384

The Inn at Watch Hill
118 Bay Street
Watch Hill
596–0665

The Ocean House
2 Bluff Avenue
Watch Hill
348–8161

Pine Lodge Motel
92 Old Post Road
322–0333

Pleasant View Inn
65 Atlantic Avenue
Misquamicut
348–8200 or (800) 782–3224

The Shelter Harbor Inn
10 Wagner Road
322–8883

The Villa
190 Shore Road
596–1054 or
(800) 722–9240

The Watch Hill Inn
38 Bay Street, Watch Hill
348–6300 or
(800) 356–9314

OTHER NOTEWORTHY ATTRACTIONS AND EVENTS IN SOUTH COUNTY—THE OCEAN SHORE AND BLOCK ISLAND

Adventureland
Narragansett

Atlantic Beach Amusement Park
Westerly

Burlingame Management Area
Charlestown

Charlestown Seafood Festival
Charlestown; August

Kimball Wildlife Refuge
Charlestown

Narragansett Art Festival
Narragansett; June

Narragansett Indian Monument
Narragansett

Point Judith Lighthouse
Narragansett

Shakespeare in the Park
Westerly; July

South County Hot Air Balloon Festival
Kingston; July

Swamp Yankee Days
Charlestown; September

Virtu Art Festival
Westerly; May

Water Wizz
Westerly

The Weekapaug Inn
25 Spray Rock Road
Weekapaug
322–0301

The Winnapaug Inn
169 Shore Road
Scenic Route 1A
348–8350 or
(800) 288–9906

Woody Hill B&B
149 South Woody Hill Road
322–0452

BLOCK ISLAND

The Atlantic Inn
High Street
466–5883

Ballard's Inn
Water Street
466–2231

The Blue Dory Inn
Dodge Street
466–5891 or (800) 992–7290

Calico Hill B&B
Old Town Road
466–2136

Champlin's Hotel
West Side Road
466–2641 or (800) 762–4541

The Fagan Cottage B&B
Beacon Hill Road
466–5383

The Gables Inn
Dodge Street
466–2213

The Gothic Inn
440 Dodge Street
466–2918

The Harborside Inn
Water Street
466 5504 or (800) 892 2022

The Hotel Manisses
Spring Street
466–2063 or 466–2421

The Island Manor Resort
Chapel Street
466–5567 or 466–2431

The Narragansett Inn
Ocean Avenue
466–2626

The National Hotel
Water Street
466–2901

The Pondview B&B
Mitchell Lane
466–2937

The Rose Farm Inn
Roslyn Road
466–2034

The Sasafrash B&B
Center Road
466–5486

The Seacrest Inn B&B
High Street
466–2882

The Sheffield House
High Street
466–2494

The 1661 Inn
Spring Street
466–2421 or 466–2063

The Spring House
52 Spring Street
466–5844, 466–2633, or
(800) 234–9263

The Sullivan House
416 Corn Neck Road
466–5020

The Water Street Inn
Water Street
466–2605
or (800) 825–6254

Places to Eat in South County—The Ocean Shore and Block Island

(All Area Codes 401)

NARRAGANSETT

Aunt Carrie's Seafood
Restaurant
1240 Ocean Road
783–7930

Charlie O's Tavern
on the Point
2 Sand Hill Cove Road
782–2002

George's of Galilee
250 Sand Hill Cove Road
783–2306

Spain Restaurant
1144 Ocean Road
783–9770

Terms Restaurant
135 Boon Street
782–4242

Twin Willows
865 Boston Neck Road
789–8153

SOUTH KINGSTOWN

The Italian Village
195 Main Street
783–3777

The Mews Tavern
456 Main Street
783–9370

The Pump House
1464 Kingstown Road
789–4944

HELPFUL WEB SITES ABOUT SOUTH COUNTY—THE OCEAN SHORE AND BLOCK ISLAND

Block Island
www.blockislandchamber.com

Charlestown Home Page
www.charlestownri.com

Narragansett
www.narragansettri.com

South County
www.southcounty.com

South Kingstown
Chamber of Commerce
www.skchamber.com

Town of Westerly
www.townofwesterly.com

Visit Watch Hill
www.visitwatchhill.com

Watch Hill
Westerly
www.watchhill.com

Westerly-Pawcatuck Chamber
of Commerce
www.westerlychamber.org

Westerly Visitor's Guide
www.cshell.com/wcc

SELECTED CHAMBERS OF COMMERCE IN SOUTH COUNTY—THE OCEAN SHORE AND BLOCK ISLAND

Block Island Chamber of Commerce
One Water Street
Block Island 02807
466–2982

Charlestown Chamber of Commerce
P.O. Box 633
Charlestown 02813
364–3878

Narragansett Chamber of Commerce
P.O. Box 742
Narragansett 02882-3612
783–7121

South Kingstown Chamber of Commerce
322 Main Street
Wakefield 02879-7404
783–2801

Westerly–Pawcatuck Chamber of Commerce
One Chamber Way
Westerly 02891-2600
596–7761

CHARLESTOWN

Charlestown Lobster Pot
Route 1
322–7686

Duke's Umbrella Cafe
Fantastic Umbrella Factory
Scenic Route 1A
364–2030

The Nordic Lodge
178 East Pasquiset Trail
783–4515

The Wilcox Tavern
5153 Old Post Road
322–1829

WESTERLY

Mary's Italian Restaurant
Route 1
Haversham Corners
322–0444

Olympia Tea Room
74 Bay Street
348–8211

Rafters
55 Beach Street
596–5709

The Shelter Harbor Inn
10 Wagner Road
322–8883

Three Fish
37 Main Street
348–9700

BLOCK ISLAND

Aldo's Place
130 Chapel Street
466–5871

The Atlantic Inn
High Street
466–5883

Ballard's Inn
Water Street
Old Harbor
466–2231

The Beachhead
Corn Neck Road
466–2249

Bethany's Airport Diner
466–3100

Dead Eye Dick's
Payne's Dock
New Harbor
466–2654

The Hotel Manisses
Spring Street
466–2063 or 466–2421

The Oar
New Harbor
466–8820

Veranda Cafe
The Spring House
Spring Street
466–5844

Winfield's
Corn Neck Road
466–5855

Index

About the Author

A resident of Rhode Island since 1991, author Bob Curley is still finding new things to do and interesting places to visit in the Ocean State—often by accident, since well-marked roads and adequate street signs are not among the state's charms.

When not driving around visiting bed-and-breakfasts, museums, and Del's lemonade stands, Bob works out of his North Kingstown home as a full-time freelance writer and editor, covering such topics as travel, public policy, computers and technology, and health care. Bob shares home/office space with his wife, Christine, an attorney in private practice. The Curleys have two children, Christopher and Shannon, who are wise enough to occasionally drag their parents away from the office and out to play.